Multiculturalism, Identity and Rights

WITHDRAWN

Multiculturalism is a fact of contemporary political life. Yet it is also an issue that threatens to undermine the viability of a modern democratic state, with its ideal of equal citizenship.

This innovative volume brings a selection of leading political theorists to the wide-ranging debate on multiculturalism and political legitimacy. By focusing on the challenge to mainstream liberal theory posed by the resurgence of interest in the cultural identities that inform and legitimize polities, the authors confront issues such as human rights, liberalism, cultural pluralism and power relations.

At issue here is the very idea of a polity as a discursive community. This book will be of interest to students of social and political theory and to anyone concerned with the shape of politics in the modern world.

Bruce Haddock is Professor of Modern European Social and Political Thought at Cardiff University. He is the author of *An Introduction to Historical Thought*, *Vico's Political Thought* and co-editor of *The Politics of Italian National Identity*.

Peter Sutch is Lecturer in Politics in the School of European Studies at Cardiff University. He is also the author of *Ethics, Justice and International Relations*.

Routledge Innovations in Political Theory

Multiculturalism, Identity and Rights

Edited by Bruce Haddock and Peter Sutch

Routledge
Taylor & Francis Group

LONDON AND NEW YORK

First published 2003
by Routledge
2 Park Square, Milton Park, Abingdon, Oxon OX14 4RN

Simultaneously published in the USA and Canada
by Routledge
711 Third Avenue, New York, NY 10017

Routledge is an imprint of the Taylor & Francis Group

© 2003 Bruce Haddock and Peter Sutch for selection and editorial
material; individual contributors for their contributions

First issued in paperback 2013

Typeset in Baskerville by Taylor & Francis Books Ltd

British Library Cataloguing in Publication Data
A catalogue record for this book is available from the British Library

Library of Congress Cataloging in Publication Data
Multiculturalism, identity, and rights/ edited by Bruce Haddock and Peter
Sutch.
p. cm. Includes bibliographical references and index.
1. Multiculturalism. I. Haddock, Bruce, 1948– II. Sutch, Peter, 1971–
HM1271. M843153 2003
305.8–dc21   2002154531

ISBN 978-0-415-31514-2 (hbk)
ISBN 978-0-415-86000-0 (pbk)

Contents

Notes on Contributors

Andrea Baumeister is Senior Lecturer in Politics at the University of Stirling.

David Boucher is Professor of Politics at Cardiff University.

Mark Evans is Lecturer in Politics at University of Wales, Swansea.

Mark Francis is Professor of Politics at the University of Canterbury, New Zealand.

Bruce Haddock is Professor of Modern European Social and Political Thought at Cardiff University.

John Horton is Reader in Politics at Keele University.

Paul Kelly is Senior Lecturer in Politics at the London School of Economics.

Rex Martin is Professor of Philosophy at the University of Kansas.

Margaret Moore is Professor of Politics at Queen's University, Canada.

Peri Roberts is Lecturer in Politics at Cardiff University.

Jonathan Seglow is Lecturer in Politics at Royal Holloway College, University of London.

Peter Sutch is Lecturer in Politics at Cardiff University.

Andrew Vincent is Professor of Politics at the University of Sheffield.

Acknowledgements

We are grateful to colleagues in the School of European Studies at Cardiff University for help and encouragement with this project. Peri Roberts, in particular, has given invaluable assistance to us throughout the past year. David Boucher, Paul Furlong, Karen Owen and Suzi Williams have also been wonderfully supportive.

1 Introduction

Bruce Haddock and Peter Sutch

Political theory has always had an uneasy relationship with the political world. The language of normative theory has been forged in response to political forms varying from small city states to vast empires, yet out of practical necessity we have had to avail ourselves of concepts fashioned in widely different circumstances. This has generated confusions which, as historians of political ideas, we can try to address and resolve. We enjoy no such luxury in our normative theorizing. Contingent situations demand attention. We bring received understandings to bear on problems that resist orthodox treatment. From time to time we despair of our established institutions and theories. Moral and political theory, we are sometimes told, rest on a mistake.[1] Without the support of grounding assumptions that we can no longer take seriously, our normative theorizing might come to resemble a sophisticated species of special pleading. But even in these circumstances, we cannot avoid the necessity of making normative judgements. These may be well or ill considered, but the demands of social co-operation and co-ordination are relentless. The complexity of our circumstances makes normative theorizing difficult; yet as practical agents we are compelled to try to chart a course through a labyrinth of possibilities.

In this book we focus on the challenge to mainstream liberal theory posed by the resurgence of interest in the cultural identities that inform and legitimize polities, particularly since the 1990s. Our concern is primarily theoretical, though we are profoundly aware of the difficult practical issues raised by groups and sub-cultures within states that reject standard liberal means of adjudicating conflict and allocating resources. Claims for special treatment or exemptions from certain burdens necessarily introduce divisions within a citizen body. Liberals have always acknowledged that additional resources may be required to enable disadvantaged groups to contribute effectively to cultural, economic and political life. But the problem becomes much murkier if the fundamental values of particular groups are hostile to the standard tenets of liberal political order. The liberal principle of equal respect may be exploited in order to foster and facilitate projects and attitudes that actually constrain the options of individuals. Faith-based schools may propagate a limiting view of a woman's role; parents may claim an exclusive right to make important life choices for their children; the diversity of a modern society may be treated as a cultural threat. Liberals are torn between endorsing a pluralism that may help to sustain fundamentally illiberal practices and views and insisting that conditions of equal citizenship should prevail. The problem is rendered more acute because the universalist assumptions on which liberalism was built are now widely questioned. Few people now find very plausible the view of society as an aggregation of atomic units. And yet acknowledging the cultural contingency of values makes it difficult to distinguish between reasonable and unreasonable pluralisms. This is a very old argument that goes back to the Romantic critique of the Enlightenment. What is novel in the modern context is that some liberals are themselves deeply sceptical about the individualism and rationalism of the Enlightenment.

Contemporary discussions of these issues have been at the forefront of political philosophy and political theory, with practical implications that are evident and sometimes disturbing. What is especially revealing theoretically is that some proponents of 'identity' politics adopt positions which discount the possibility of resolving disputes discursively. We can all recognize situations in which discursive politics is difficult. It is quite another matter to assume from the outset that it is impossible (a 'clash of civilizations'[2]). In this volume we have brought together scholars who have helped to shape the argument in order to explore the assumptions that underpin contrasting views. The point is not simply to benefit from the clash of ideas but also to see in practice how far theoretical bridges can be built between sharply divergent positions.

Various chapters in the book focus on the scope for a restatement of liberal principles that avoids the charge that ethical and political theory is always (and necessarily) parochial. Communitarians and multiculturalists, exploiting earlier Marxist, poststructuralist and postmodern critiques, have sought to show that liberalism, like any other political doctrine, serves as a vehicle for the articulation of economic and cultural interests. Liberal universalism, in this view, is simply an effective strategy for the projection of dominant interests in the complex game of global political and economic competition.

Criticisms of liberal universalism have been drawn from a variety of positions, some appealing to little more than the fact of cultural diversity. Indeed, it is clear that elaborate ideological positions (beliefs, values, and so on) often look like enclosed worlds of ideas. Practical reason is at its most vulnerable when attempts are made to discriminate between world views taken as a whole. And experience of mutual incomprehension at one level is taken as an illustration of the culturally parochial nature of practical reason as a phenomenon. Bruce Haddock ('Practical Reason and Identity') focuses, instead, on the style of practical reason in everyday situations. We recognize that we face more or less complex choices that often puzzle us. Our thinking, however, does not presuppose fixed terms of reference, even though our rooted situations demarcate areas of concern. It is a mistake to equate how we think with the matter that we customarily think about. Haddock takes seriously the fact that contingent identities frame our thinking, but he denies that this has radically subversive implications for the exercise of practical reason. Indeed, the complexity and changing nature of our identities presupposes a capacity to shape and amend our identities through reflection and engagement. Discourse is primary in identity formation. Questions of identity only arise because our identities are complex. The puzzles that confront us about identity are a reflection of our ability to abstract from the contingent circumstances we actually encounter. This is not to say that 'reason' floats mysteriously above and beyond our interests and identities; rather, discordance between ideas and identities forces us to think. In this sense, finding our way through pluralist cultures is not different in kind from negotiating issues between them. A 'thin' universlism pervades our efforts in both spheres, though how it might best be characterized and defended remains a deeply contentious question.

John Horton ('Liberalism and Multiculturalism: Once More unto the Breach') addresses the debate as it has emerged in recent discussions of minority rights in the context of a hegemonic liberal culture. Kymlicka and Parekh, in particular, have been prominent, arguing that the realization of (at least some) liberal values in a context of deep value pluralism necessarily involves recognition and respect for groups which may be hostile or indifferent to a dominant political culture. Kymlicka has tried to stretch the liberal position such that consensual collective expression will be treated as a core commitment, even when the substance of that expression may be incompatible with standard liberal rights. The point is not that core liberal rights should be devalued, rather that there should be public recognition of the incommensurable values that may be endorsed in pluralist cultures. Parekh, similarly, stresses the need for dialogue between groups if the public culture is not to be authoritarian or exclusive. Brian Barry, by contrast, argues that according a privileged place to substantive values undermines both the impartiality of the liberal state and the commitment to equal citizenship that is its distinguishing feature. Horton explores how far the multicultural position is, in fact, incompatible with a defensible view of individuality and claims that, in the event of conflict, it should not simply be assumed that the minority multicultural position would have to adapt. Everything depends here on whether or not the ground on which the liberal stands can be regarded as foundational. If liberalism needs foundations, and yet the traditional theoretical defences of foundationalism cannot be accepted, then political accommodation between cultures has to be pursued in more cautious ways. A strong commitment to substantive liberal values in a context of acknowledged value pluralism would involve indefensible political intrusion in individual life choices. Horton contends that Barry is both insensitive to the coercive impact of liberal values and naïve in assuming that theory is equipped to resolve tensions in cultural practices in any straightforward sense. In Horton's view, theory is a form of cultural self-understanding. While it should not be limited to a merely expressive role, it must remain sensitive to the cultural forms that sustain it.

Andrew Vincent ('What is so Different about Difference?') accepts the fact of cultural pluralism but queries its adoption as a political criterion. At the very least, when we grant that specific cultural differences are politically relevant, we must be appealing to a criterion that enables us to distinguish between kinds of 'difference'. Access to public goods may need to be facilitated in all sorts of ways; and this may include lowering the cultural threshold for inclusion in various public projects and activities. This involves a recognition of cultural costs that may be borne disproportionately by specific minority groups. But judgements still have to be made about which public goods need to be distributed more broadly. In practical terms, there may be limits to the extent that a particular public good can be stretched before it ceases to be a good of a relevant kind. The argument about the political significance of actual difference (cultural, economic, linguistic, and so on) will have to be cast in terms of a discourse that is more than an articulation of the core values of a particular cultural community. Effective political argument in conditions of deep pluralism is driven towards inclusion rather than exclusion. This may not amount to a commitment to universalism in a strong or abstract sense, but it necessarily involves the construction of principled positions that justify particular commitments from an outsider's perspective.

Mark Evans ('"Authenticity" in the Jargon of Multiculturalism') focuses on a key issue at the heart of multicultural political theory. He distinguishes Charles Taylor as one of the few thinkers broadly sympathetic to a multicultural politics of recognition who has taken seriously the ethical question of distinguishing between different conceptions of the good life. Evans argues that multicultural theory fails sufficiently to *problematize* the ethical. Taylor, by contrast, recognizes that the condition of modernity typically forces us to see our life choices as contingent and revisable. For Taylor, 'authenticity' is the paradigmatic ethical ideal. Taken as a free-standing notion, it has a tendency to slide into capricious subjectivism and narcissism. Taylor argues that these tendencies can be resisted if individuals see themselves as culturally embedded creatures, endorsing in their daily lives attitudes and projects that derive from an external cultural framework. Evans contends, however, that even when we grant (as we must) the Hegelian dialogical account of identity, we should resist Taylor's 'neutering' of identity. Such a profoundly anti-assimilationist ethic actually hampers the principled accommodation that is the primary objective of a multiculturalist political morality. Evans goes back to Lionel Trilling, one of Taylor's authorities, in order to defend 'sincerity' as a more congenial candidate for a multiculturalist ethic. Pinning down multiculturalism to a specific kind of 'politics of difference', Evans argues, allows us to reflect more rigorously on the likely nature of favoured forms of the good life under such a regime. Developing arguments from Trilling, Evans shows that discriminating between multicultural alternatives obliges us to take seriously the relatively difference-insensitive criteria of traditional liberal politics.

Jonathan Seglow ('Theorizing Recognition'), on the other hand, contends that empirical work on the profile of multicultural societies should be reflected in normative theoretical argument. The universalist criteria of traditional liberal theory can be shown to facilitate outcomes that liberals should deplore. Equal citizenship in practice reinforces the positions of dominant groups that are best placed to frame political agendas. The assumption that the liberal state should be culturally neutral must be rejected. Seglow claims that orthodox liberal constitutional designs are shot through with partisan ethnocultural norms. Developing arguments from Kymlicka, Seglow suggests (*pace* Barry) that to continue to aspire to impartiality effectively perpetuates ethnocultural injustice. He argues that if we take liberal goals seriously, then we must necessarily address multicultural issues. Facilitating fair terms of political co-operation in deeply pluralist societies commits us to an endorsement and celebration of cultural difference. On this view, liberal values require a republican theory of multicultural society.

Multicultural politics makes heavy demands on the redistributive capacity of the state. It is a question not simply of aggregate resources here, but of the criteria to be adopted in discriminating between claimants. A politics of recognition involves discretionary judgements. Successful claimants will be exploiting cultural identities as trumps in a game of political brokerage. In this context, marginal cultural groups are likely to remain the most vulnerable. Paul Kelly ('Identity, Equality and Power: Tensions in Parekh's Political Theory of Multiculturalism') highlights the neglect of power relations in multicultural theory, focusing in particular on Parekh's defence of a cross-cultural discursive politics. He argues that effective representation, especially of the most disadvantaged groups, is best facilitated by universal commitments that do not require discretionary endorsement. In this view, the fact that rights claims are culture-blind is actually an advantage, leaving groups to pursue their interests in a public realm that involves all citizens. Kelly claims that marginal interests are best promoted through universal welfare provision. We can argue about the adequacy of established redistributive policies. But to link the receipt of benefits to the effectiveness of minority political advocacy would be a reversal of liberal priorities. Outcomes would be unpredictable and the upshot would be a clientelistic politics that would further divide a fragmented citizenry.

Andrea Baumeister ('The Limits of Universalism') challenges attempts to restate a liberal universalist position. She takes issue precisely with the aspiration expressed in Brian Barry's *Culture and Equality* that 'eventually a common standard of reasonableness will prevail over a certain range of ethical questions, in a way similar to that in which the acknowledgement of the soundness of the physical sciences diffused through the world', defending instead a version of value pluralism associated with Hampshire, Berlin, Bellamy, Gray and Parekh. She contends that, contrary to Barry, liberal value pluralism does not entail a belief that all cultures are of equal value. Thus value pluralism does not imply relativism. Nor is value pluralism insensitive to the fact that human flourishing requires certain values and commitments, such as some form of justice. However, whereas Barry seeks to characterize these norms in an impartial manner, value pluralists believe these norms manifest themselves in a variety of ways, each historically and culturally specific. Finally, while Barry fears that a regard for cultural diversity will give rise to a tendency to ossify cultures and thus hinder the development of a common standard or shared point of view, value pluralism need imply no such commitment. On the contrary, value pluralists such as Parekh expressly stress the importance of dialogue and mutual adaptation. Baumeister concludes that a commitment to value pluralism gives rise to a distinct political conception of liberalism which differs notably from the form of liberal universalism advocated by Barry. Whereas Barry remains firmly wedded to the liberal Enlightenment project, a liberalism informed by value pluralism will not only acknowledge its own historical contingency, but will also accept that it cannot insulate itself from the dynamic entailed in value conflict.

Issues of inclusion and exclusion have been raised in an especially acute form in relation to the rights of indigenous peoples. Ex-colonies based originally on the expropriation of 'First Peoples' confront issues that tax conventional liberal redistributive policies to breaking point. Toleration, integration and assimilation seem to be inadequate responses to the stark economic and cultural reality of domination and marginalization. Canadian political theorists, in particular, have made a concerted effort to reconcile the irreconcilable. Mark Francis ('Canadian Indigenous Peoples and the Transformation of Political Theory into Cultural Identity') traces sustained efforts to address the issue through the language of both rights and participation. He argues that both discourses endorse styles of nation building that fail to reflect the interests and views of indigenous peoples. Cultural identity, which figures so largely in the writings of Will Kymlicka, James Tully and Charles Taylor, lacks effective normative content. The failure of liberal universalism in these difficult cases, however, should not be treated as a pretext for abandoning normative arguments which extend beyond the confines of particular cultures. Yet it remains an open question how these arguments might be grounded.

Peri Roberts ('Identity, Reflection and Justification') explores an assumption at the heart of communitarian and multicultural theory. The strong rejection of different versions of universalism hinges on the claim that there are impenetrable boundaries to intelligibility that undercut the legitimacy or relevance of external criticism of practices and principles. The boundaries of intelligibility here are a consequence of the familiar communitarian assumption that key aspects of the cultural world and the inner world of the self are constitutive, beyond reflection and therefore necessarily antecedent to any choices that an individual might make. It follows (so the argument goes) that identities, both personal and cultural, have fixed elements that make cultures inherently exclusive. Liberal universalists (such as Barry) argue that this amounts to giving up on rational argument across boundaries. The key question here is whether the relevance or intelligibility of arguments is restricted by a frame of cultural reference. Roberts attempts to address this dilemma by developing recent defences of a 'constructivist' liberalism, in particular by exploiting a distinction between primary and secondary constructivism. To grant that in the variety of secondary constructions substantive values are culturally framed does not commit us to denying the intelligibility of defences of values from cross-cultural perspectives. The dynamic of critical cultural reflection provides a basis for comparative evaluation, even if the scope for practical accommodation remains limited. Crucially, however, limits to understanding are contingent rather than conceptual. Further, the process of critical reflection upon cultural understandings that underwrites the possibility of cross-cultural intelligibility may bring resources to bear that allow us, at the primary level, to construct minimal but substantive principles.

Among basic rights that liberals defend, rights to pursue our own life plans and to concern ourselves collectively with matters of public concern figure prominently. Margaret Moore ('Brian Barry's Egalitarian Critique of Multiculturalism: A Liberal Nationalist Defence') argues that this commitment to self-determination (both personal and public) cannot be effectively sustained if cultural constraints on collective engagement are not factored into our presentation of defensible public institutions and practices. A conception of rights that tacitly condoned avoidable obstacles to effective agency would fail to meet declared liberal aspirations. Moore specifically challenges Barry's attempt to marginalize 'culture' as a criterion in the appraisal of appropriate rights. She focuses on the implications for minority nationalists of a theory that champions equal citizenship against cultural particularity. She claims that the expansive concept of 'culture' employed by Barry (embracing ethnicity, national groups, religious groups, and so on) is not helpful when we focus more precisely on the circumstances that prevent minority national groups from assuming collective responsibility for their own public affairs. Moore argues forcefully, drawing on her earlier work, that liberals have to treat self-determination as a core value; and this commits them to endorsing the claims of minority nationalities to self-government in viable circumstances. A liberalism that failed to respect liberal nationalist ambitions would be a contradiction in terms.

Rex Martin ('Rights and Human Rights') explores the compatibility of universalist and particularist justifications of rights. He advances two central claims: (1) that civil rights can be treated as universal within a given society; (2) that they can be justified in distinctive ways. He argues, further, that active civil rights require an agency to formulate, maintain and harmonize them. From where we stand in the modern world, Martin suggests that democratic institutions provide the best political means of both realizing rights and securing a high level of consensus for their support. He treats rights as justified claims; and, in the typical case, they will be justified claims against governments. An effective defence of rights thus depends crucially on political recognition. Effective normative justification of rights within a polity must be coupled with authoritative political endorsement and enforcement. Even in the international arena, the language of rights, if it is not to lose its credibility, must be tied to effective maintenance (through confederations of states or looser international coalitions). Human rights can be projected beyond particular polities and cultures, but they will be rooted in specific communities and practices. The tension between universalist and particularist perspectives is resolved if we insist that universalist positions arise in particular contexts. Specific normative debate creates and extends normative horizons.

David Boucher ('The Transition from Natural Rights to the Culture of Human Rights') focuses on the consolidation of a human rights culture on a global scale after 1945. He shows how early versions of rights arguments in seventeenth-century natural rights and natural law theory depended upon theological assumptions which are no longer invoked. Belief has been effectively 'privatized' within this discourse. Secular versions of the natural rights argument in the Enlightenment were vulnerable to criticism from conservative and reactionary thinkers who defended the entrenched practices and customs of local communities. Local values were championed instead of an unattractive (and easily parodied) cosmpolitanism. The Romantic challenge to the Enlightenment seriously restricted the persuasive appeal of any moral or political theory. Yet cross-cultural judgements of value still had to be made. The response was to portray communities as historically rooted, yet as being integral components of a complex chain of development. Hegel and the idealists, in particular, defended a view of progress that was not tied to a utopian blueprint. The evolution of human culture on a global scale was to be the touchstone for judgements regarding particular communities and practices. In the post-war period the historicism of this position has been endorsed, without the supporting metaphysics. Boucher shows how commitments to human rights have been successively reiterated as states become functioning participants in the international community. Strong commitments to universal rights, however, are dependent upon shifting political accommodations on an international stage, involving (crucially) states strong enough to ensure that legal obligations are fulfilled. This leaves the language of rights seriously exposed to theoretical objections. Yet we do not have an alternative language to defend a politics of basic decency.

Clearly, the normative horizon cannot be restricted to the state. Just as issues surrounding multiculturalism and 'hyphenated' identity frame our understanding of justice in domestic politics, so they shape our understanding of politics in the international sphere. Peter Sutch ('Reiterating Rights: International Society in Transition') addresses these issues through a reiteratively universal political theory. He examines Walzer's claim to have elaborated a functional theory of internationally relevant and morally universal ethics that leaves room for the meaningful expression of separate national identities. Walzer's approach to issues of universality has long been criticized (by liberals) as delivering only a severely limited set of principles that can transcend national boundaries, whilst being welcomed (by communitarians and multiculturalists) for its sensitivity to the diversity of moral and political identity. Sutch, drawing on some of Walzer's most recent writings, argues that the reiterative approach has the theoretical tools to build effective moral and political bridges between the liberal and multiculturalist camps. Indeed, he argues that Walzer, while remaining committed to the view that cultural identities are morally significant, constructs political principles that are globalist (or cosmopolitan) in reach.

In this volume we focus on issues that bring together theoretical and practical perspectives in challenging ways. High mobility (actual and virtual) poses a new range of dilemmas for both policy makers and citizens. We treat these problems in the wider context that has always interested political philosophers. The fact of cultural diversity challenges us to think about what it means to be a member of a polity. The identities that inform modern polities are shifting and contested. What may once have been taken for granted as the necessary starting point for normative theorizing (a bounded territory with an identifiable citizenry) must now be regarded as problematic. States (with their coercive powers) remain a primary focus for political theory; but modes of justification have had to be adapted to changing circumstances. Multicultural theorists have self-consciously questioned the ability of liberal normative theory to respond to radically new conditions. Our contributors, however, with their distinctive points of view, are writing within a tradition of political theory and also extending it.

Notes

1 See H. A. Prichard, 'Does Moral Philosophy Rest on a Mistake?', in his *Moral Obligation*, Oxford: Clarendon Press, 1949, pp. 1–17.
2 Samuel P. Huntington, *The Clash of Civilizations and the Remaking of World Order*, New York: Simon and Schuster, 1996.

2 Practical reason and identity

Bruce Haddock

Most people are sensible most of the time. They make mistakes, of course, miscalculate their interests, antagonize other people unnecessarily, and from time to time (in private moments) may well confess to being inept. But for all that social co-operation can go badly wrong, we would be astonished if the dentist, bank clerk, car mechanic (or even professional colleague) proclaimed that they had theoretical grounds for supposing that consensual co-operation is simply too demanding for ordinary human ingenuity. Only political philosophers are taken seriously when they argue that there are ineradicable cultural or structural obstacles to effective communication and co-operation. Note the stress here on *effective* communication. The point is not that we ever understand one another completely. We are never entirely transparent, even to ourselves. But from the simple observation that we sometimes get our wires crossed, it seems a little precipitate to conclude that we can never (in principle) sort them out.

My ambitions in this chapter (despite the grand ring of the title) are actually modest. I am taking for granted that conceptions of the political world are always contested or contestable. Even in stable and relatively closed cultures, we can never be sure what we owe to each other (in Scanlon's phrase[1]). Children, footballers and the Azande have conceptions of fairness that will be stretched in certain circumstances. We can imagine them (in their different ways) moving from concerns about the fairness of particular decisions to larger worries about the concept of fairness. We must assume that this will not happen very often. But it would be very odd to assume that dilemmas of this order could not (in principle) arise. Put simply, we can say that any co-operative venture involves authoritative procedures for the allocation of benefits and burdens. Given that procedures are conventions, they can be challenged. When that happens we find ourselves doing something like political philosophy, even if our language is very crude. For the moment all I want to insist on is the possibility of certain sorts of problems arising. I don't want to defend a specific set of authoritative procedures, and certainly not a specific conception of practical reason. My point is simply that we cannot preclude the need to justify a practice in any context.

At a basic level I am taking practical judgement as an irreducible datum. I am assuming that we are faced with choices in contexts in which outcomes are uncertain. Even our pursuit of narrow personal interests, as Aristotle argued, involves the exercise of judgement and discretion in a form that may be modelled on a 'practical syllogism'.[2] Looking back on our conduct, we may feel that we acted well or badly. Other people may also have views on the effectiveness of our conduct. In deciding what to do in social contexts, we open ourselves to critical scrutiny even before the impact of our conduct on others comes into question. These possibilities are implicit in the language of practical deliberation. We may tell ourselves not to make the same mistake twice, or deplore the fact that we keep on repeating the same old mistakes. In a deep sense, then, private rumination has a conversational form that necessarily involves normative criteria.

The point about a model of deliberation is that it always involves hypothetical consideration of outcomes in unpredictable circumstances. This is just as true of our pursuit of private satisfactions ('desires') as of more complex situations that involve social co-operation. My claim may be controversial, at least in relation to specialized literature in philosophy of action, but it captures our first-person experience of wondering what to do in uncertain situations. If we are in a fix, ordinarily we might try to think hard about the possibilities that confront us. In this chapter I simply want to focus on the normative implications of our experience of thinking hard.

I am assuming that philosophical accounts of what people can do or should do will be modelled on ordinary experience of deliberating and acting. Yet it is by no means clear what direct experience of 'thinking hard' amounts to. A dominant strand in British philosophy deriving from Hobbes and Hume insists that deciding what to do is little more than endorsing dominant desires. In some versions we may even be portrayed as causally determined to act on dominant desires. I don't want to go into the detail of a complex literature here, but even the most sophisticated treatments of this position generate paradoxes that have to be explained away. Bernard Williams's celebrated paper 'Internal and External Reasons' presupposes that actions will be unintelligible unless we assume that an agent's 'subjective motivational set' provides sufficient incentive to act.[3] There is nothing problematic about this account of agency in simple situations where we know what we want. Our motivational set generates sufficient ('internal') reasons for us to decide on one course or another. But we don't always know what we want even in ordinary circumstances. I may want to watch football and read Wittgenstein right now. As it happens, I decide that I ought to finish this chapter. Williams may claim that what I finally do will indicate the force of a dominant desire. Yet I really don't know how to measure the force of desires. I ask myself what I ought to do, all things considered. And the form of my private rumination would be similar in kind to the advice I might give to a student to read more Wittgenstein and watch less football. I may want the student to make my ('external') reason a part of his motivational set. I certainly don't assume that his motivational set is fixed. And I treat my advice as authoritative, at least as far as the student's future as a philosopher is concerned.

The crux of this issue revolves around the claim that practical reasons (properly understood) must be construed as causes of action. Yet to say (clumsily) that a good reason caused me to act is not to say that necessary and sufficient conditions can be specified that caused me to act. Philosophers arguing from different perspectives have shown convincingly that an appeal to reasons does not have to be couched in terms of the satisfaction of desires. Korsgaard, for example, has contended that instrumental reasoning has necessarily to invoke normative criteria, suggesting that hypothetical imperatives only make sense if we assume the possibility of categorical imperatives.[4] This is a stronger (and more contentious) argument than I need for present purposes. Searle has argued, instead, that all we need to recognize is the commitment to say something in a natural language.[5] Statements make claims that can be assessed. Imperatives exhort us in authoritative terms to behave in certain ways in the face of alternative options. When we listen we construe a speaker's meaning by drawing inferences, more or less accurately and attentively. All these linguistic activities involve appraisal and judgement. We can make mistakes. And, of course, in Searle's account, speaking is a form of acting.[6] However else we portray the exercise of practical reason, it must be compatible with a logic of conversation. Whatever we say may be mistaken or misunderstood. Seeking (even self-)clarification is an exercise in practical reason because we recognize that we are confronting a contingent dilemma. Understanding, in this sense, is something we do, not something that happens to us.

Something we do every day (exercise practical reason) is regarded by many political philosophers as inherently problematic. Explaining how we came to find ourselves in this predicament would require a complex story that cannot be told here. Part of the problem is that political philosophy, in its quest for systematic completeness, has often been driven to over-reach itself. More is promised than can possibly be delivered, especially in the practical domain. And practical disappointment has generated theoretical disillusion. The history of political philosophy can be presented as a series of arguments at cross-purposes that could never possibly be resolved. Yet questions persistently arise and we find ourselves devising arguments that seem to display a series of family resemblances. These family resemblances seem to me to be much more than historical contingencies, though I won't be pursuing that issue here. What many of us have concluded instead is that the spectacle of theoretical failure should chasten us all. If the very best minds have failed to resolve normative questions effectively, it may be that we have been asking the wrong questions all along, or at least demanding inappropriate answers. The holy grail of a conception of practical reason valid for all times and places looks untenable (indeed dangerous) in light of the ineradicable diversity that confronts us in the modern world. The rich literature of the last thirty years dealing with the social construction of identities should serve as a warning to moderate our

normative ambitions. Yet despite being told every generation or so that normative theory is impossible, we still find that we are led irresistibly back to it.
Political philosophy is clearly a kind of original sin. We don't have the theoretical resources to do it properly, yet somehow we can't leave it alone.

At one level, arguments against normative theory look very strong indeed. If
terms of reference change radically, arguments across cultures or historical
periods will simply miss their mark. We may have our own reasons for
constructing an *ideal* conversation (the canon of classic texts) but it would not
be a real argument between protagonists. Nor would it model our actual arguments if we failed to recognize that culturally contingent terms of reference
limit the relevance of arguments. Many liberals (Berlin and his followers[7]) have
accepted that the values we endorse may have no claims for universal applicability. In this view, our political arguments are necessarily parochial. Even
Rawls (at least from 1985) accepted that his political theory was narrowly
addressed to the concerns of modern constitutional democracies.[8] Arguments
across traditions are rendered, if not impossible, at least deeply problematical.
And some liberals have been content to press the point further, arguing that
the intelligibility of arguments depends upon (at least some) shared values.
From this perspective, arguments framed by radically divergent values are
'incommensurable'.[9]

It is never quite clear what precisely is being claimed in these discussions.
Conflicts of value make mutual comprehension difficult. Some commitments
are mutually exclusive. It is difficult to be a soldier and a pacifist at the same
time. Individuals balance their commitments in relation to their values and
recognize the necessary loss in some of the choices they make. They also revise
their choices in the light of experience. Something further is being suggested,
however, when it is claimed that values are 'incommensurable'. From the
simple fact that we cannot understand or accommodate a position now, it
doesn't follow that we might not do much better next week or next year.
Religious and racial differences, for example, though remaining sources of
conflict, may be better understood now and can often be defused if not
resolved. It is also always possible that our efforts to remedy specific problems
will have unforeseen consequences that may be even more intractable than the
original dilemma. Problems arise, demand attention, and may be more or less
successfully resolved. It simply isn't an option to argue that theory has nothing
to contribute in these cases, though it would surely be naïve to assume that
theory alone will ever be sufficient to address our ills. Berlin, in particular, was
obsessed throughout his career by the devastating consequences of misplaced
utopian enthusiasm. Liberal rationalism must thus be tempered by scepticism
about the very possibility of reconciling all positions. Liberal politics (among
other things) is about the accommodation of difference within acceptable
limits. The point is that we cannot rule out in advance that 'acceptable limits'
will be established. We can envisage, adapting Rawls's terminology, a progres-
sion on any particular issue that runs from conflict, through *modus vivendi*, to
'overlapping consensus', even though the precise details of the sequence may

remain vague.[10] We know that discursive politics sometimes breaks down for all number of contingent reasons. It would be quite another matter to claim that at certain points it must everywhere and always break down.

Nor should it trouble us (as political philosophers) that radical conflicts of value appear intractable at a political level. It is absurd to suppose that all the good things in life should somehow be compatible. To take an obvious example, we can all see that a commitment to equal citizenship might appear to undermine the authority of the extended family in certain contexts. The practical and legal dilemmas thrown up by such conflicts of value should concern us. Hard cases of this kind push us to develop our ideas as political philosophers. We are not telling people how to run their lives, but rather exploring anomalies that arise in received moral and political understandings. What agents make of philosophical reflection (if anything) is up to them. The philosophical point is simply that certain conceptions of citizenship (the Aristotelian stress on shared substantive values, say, or a culture-blind commitment to formal equality in a unitary republic) become problematic as circumstances change. High mobility (virtual and actual) together with complex economic, technological and environmental interdependence has transformed the way we live, though not beyond recognition. Old certainties become manifest obstacles to effective co-operation. In this situation we have a number of options, some of which are much more acceptable to relatively ill-informed democratic electorates than others. Appraising options looks like a philosophical task, at least implicitly. As political philosophers we have to ask ourselves whether we have anything to add to the line of least political resistance. We have tried to adopt a rule of normative abstinence in the past (value neutrality), with philosophical consequences that were deeply unsatisfactory. It would be very bad news (especially for minorities) if respect for cultural diversity were to be construed as a justification for suspending normative judgement in the situation we currently find ourselves in.

In this chapter I am taking very seriously Hegel's claim that philosophy is 'its own time comprehended in thoughts'.[11] The agenda for political philosophy is set by a world that is the product of a configuration of factors and forces. I am assuming (with Hegel) that philosophy appears on the scene too late for us to aspire to putting philosophical theory into practice in any straightforward sense. Grasping where we stand, however, is a necessary condition for taking our next few steps, especially if we need to rely on social co-operation of any complexity. Different ways of clarifying where we do stand will generate different possibilities for agents pursuing particular agendas. Whether or not it ever made sense to assume that we share a 'thick' public culture, it clearly won't get us very far today, at least in a political sense. It is surely significant that in multicultural contexts we don't know what we can presuppose about strangers, other than that they will need to seek co-operative arrangements for the effective pursuit of some of their ends. We need to make some initial assumptions if communication is to be possible, but we can't assume that we share anything like a world view. It probably isn't very helpful to try to distinguish categorially between political doctrines and comprehensive doctrines, because comprehensive doctrines will impinge on political positions in all manner of ways. The point is that the cultural prerequisites of effective co-operation should not be set too high. Practical co-operation should not involve the disavowal of our deepest convictions, though we may want to revise our views of what our commitments involve. This is simply to suggest that everyone, everywhere, shares the burdens of judgement, especially in a world that throws us together in unprecedented ways.

The fact that we all have to make practical judgements doesn't tell us anything about the way those judgements are made. Yet if political philosophy is in some sense modelling the way actual judgements are made, it is surely significant that (at least in the political domain) we can't simply agree to differ about everything. Political decisions (unlike aesthetic judgements) involve authoritative allocations that are implicitly (and sometimes explicitly) coercive. Effective coercion is also a form of social co-operation. It would be inappropriate to talk about public justification in such contexts because the relevant 'public' may be exceedingly small. But Augustine made the point long ago that even robber bands have to establish terms of co-operation if they are to prosper.[12] Robbers, we may assume, like citizens, have their own agendas. They may (or may not) have substantive interests in common beyond their predilection for stealing. The point to stress here is that we can envisage social co-operation even in such unlikely circumstances, without invoking a shared conception of the good or cultural affinity. Kant argued explicitly in *Perpetual Peace* that even 'a nation of devils' should be assumed to have sufficient intellectual resources to establish co-operative means for the pursuit of mutual advantage.[13] No doubt we can co-operate more readily if we share substantive values in common; but it would be misleading to insist on shared values as a necessary condition for social co-operation.

In what follows I want to focus attention specifically on the normative problems that arise for reflective citizens in multicultural contexts. Whether or not it was ever desirable to conceive of citizenship in terms of cultural solidarity, it looks unhelpful now. A Sandel-style celebration of the things we share in common would simply leave too many groups disenfranchised at the margins of our societies.[14] If we have set ourselves the theoretical task of establishing consensual terms of social co-operation, then a preoccupation with the core values of a dominant culture looks to be counter-productive. We can't say that it won't work for some political purposes. We know that dominant groups can manufacture cultural hegemony. The point is that the cost to marginal groups of subscribing to a cultural consensus may be excessive, indeed disabling. Universalist liberals have often been accused of being insensitive to the costs incurred by traditional cultures in subscribing to a rights agenda. The Kantian model, even in its modern versions, makes very few concessions to the idea that conceptions of rights (and practical reason more broadly) may be products of cultural identities variously reiterated in contingent circumstances. Indeed, some modern liberals (Brian Barry would be prominent here[15]) have argued that commitments to equal citizenship have necessarily to be insensitive to cultural identities. Citizens have claims upon one another not because they share substantive values but because they share a public space. No doubt there are problems with Barry's categorical reassertion of this position, some of which are rehearsed in this volume.[16] But Barry has effectively focused our minds on the consequences of maintaining the priority of the good over the right. It is not simply that we can't resolve complex normative issues; we can barely get into conversation.

Everything hinges in these discussions on the way cultural identities are characterized. A stock objection to some versions of communitarianism has been that the conception of culture doing the work is a theoretical abstraction, reflecting a yearning for cultural and moral coherence that (so it is claimed) has been lost in the modern world.[17] The claim may be that human flourishing depends upon feeling at home in the world (in the Hegelian or Aristotelian sense), and that certain ways of characterizing social co-operation underplay the significance of the cultural preconditions for the initiation of co-operative projects in the first place. In essence this is a conceptual reworking of certain standard objections to social contract theory (typically, but misleadingly, attributed to Hegel).[18]

But suppose we focus instead on the way cultures are constituted. Cultures, like traditions, are the product of bewilderingly complex (and necessarily open-ended) interactions. Sociologists and anthropologists argue fiercely among themselves about the process of culture formation. Yet political philosophers sometimes seem inclined to invoke a conception of culture as if it were uncontentious. Some of the most influential figures (Charles Taylor, for example[19]) adopt an expressivist view of culture, stemming originally from Herder, that would be rejected out of hand as a piece of romantic nonsense by most modern sociologists. I am not suggesting that this conception necessarily is nonsense, only that it would need elaborate defence before being employed in contemporary normative argument. And, of course, political philosophers are seldom sufficiently interested in the detail to do the job effectively them-selves. Yet, from work I have done in other contexts, I am confident that assumptions we make about cohesive cultural units are seriously flawed. Students of Italian unification would not be advised to take Mazzini's view of Italian cultural identity at face value. This was one (very powerful) view among others, rhetorically effective but based on historical assumptions that are simply wrong.[20] It is interesting to trace the way different rhetorical strategies enable groups to create a constituency for certain views rather than others. It matters hugely that theoretical positions should be plausible, not that they should be right. In these polemical contexts, conceptions of the nation are treated as political trumps, but they are always open to challenge.[21] To go on to use conceptions of culture that ground these polemical debates in other contexts really is confusion confounded.

Theoretical mistakes about the character of nineteenth-century nationalism are hardly alarming. In contemporary Europe, however, especially in the wake of the implosion of the Soviet empire, we can see positions staked out on a nationalist spectrum, with liberal reformists being effectively marginalized as programmes of structural institutional and economic reform encounter problems. I don't want to dwell on these maters in any detail here.[22] The point to stress is that liberal nationalist positions (Kymlicka and Tamir have been prominent, with Berlin's massive authority lurking in the background[23]) have allowed dominant groups to treat essentialist conceptions of culture as if they are compatible with (at least some versions of) liberalism. The language issue has been especially explosive. To identify a shared language as a key component in cultural membership, as Kymlicka often does, makes it extremely difficult to treat minority language users as full citizens if the legitimacy of the state is identified in ethno-cultural terms.[24] Kymlicka's use of the term 'ethnocultural justice' is especially worrying, despite the concessions he makes to minority cultures.[25] Hungarian speakers in Romania, for example, can readily be treated as a threat to the legitimacy of the unitary Romanian state if they demand the right to educate their children in their native language. And, of course, this issue resonates powerfully in some western European polities, not least in Wales.

A fine line needs to be drawn here between responding sympathetically to the many viable ways of viewing the world and highlighting the moral and political implications of particular views peoples may form of themselves. It is surely significant that the rejection of some forms of essentialism, focused specifically on the rationalism that is sometimes seen as a distinguishing feature of mainstream western theory, should create the conceptual space for the endorsement of particular identities that remain critically unexamined. Our traditions are no doubt very comforting to us in troubled times. But they have never been fixed and finished. As Oakeshott put the point, traditions may be blind but (like bats) they have the resources to negotiate uncharted territory. Oakeshott's celebrated depiction of rooted agents pursuing 'intimations' within traditions actually diverts attention away from the theoretical issues that arise in the business of organizing priorities in contested contexts.[26] We know why he objected to certain forms of rationalism. Yet he was also profoundly aware of the need to maintain a form of association that enables agents pursuing very different life projects to resolve difficulties when interests clash. We probably can't specify in advance an ideal theoretical form for a discursive politics along these lines. But it would be extraordinary if (as theorists) we could say nothing about the minimal conditions that had to be observed.

Oakeshott himself never satisfactorily resolved the vexed question of the relation between theory and practice in his own writings. His categorial insistence on 'practical experience' as a distinct and autonomous mode of understanding in *Experience and its Modes* appeared to render normative political philosophy an irredeemable species of conceptual confusion.[27] And yet in polemical essays throughout his career, most notably in *Rationalism in Politics* but also in *On Human Conduct*, he treated conceptual clarification of the idea of a practice or mode of conduct as a matter that could (at least) warn us of the practical consequences of the worst sort of theoretical folly.[28] If we understand what a practice is (necessarily), we would be unlikely to insist that all peoples, everywhere, should organize their political institutions in the same fashion. And we only have to state the distinction between 'civil association' and 'enterprise association' to realize that it has implications for our understanding of an appropriate role for the modern state.[29] These are controversial questions. My simple point here is that reflection at this level cannot be regarded as categorially irrelevant to the practical judgements we make.

We also have to pay careful attention to the way political identities are constructed. We don't have to become experts on the detail of identity construction, though I have to say that my own forays in that direction have helped me to focus my mind on difficult problems in received normative positions. In a seminal paper, Clifford Geertz has invited liberal theorists in particular to take seriously the complexity of the world they are trying to generalize about.[30] His starting point is the basic Hegelian position that I highlighted at the outset of this chapter, though he doesn't put it that way. Theoretical questions are driven by problems that arise in changing contexts. Our language, however, has a tendency to get fixed. We are no longer silly enough to treat the state, obligation, duties, rights, justice, and so on, in uppercase terms. But, despite our best efforts, we still sound impossibly grand and abstract. We can repeat the mantra that 'linguistic contexts' are decisive and still entitle books *The Foundations of Modern Political Thought*.[31] The title of Geertz's paper is revealing. He talks about 'the world in pieces', focusing on the complex engagements that shape perceptions and identities in given circumstances. Self-understandings are vital here, though they cannot be treated as decisive in every case. We can hardly deny, as either citizens or theorists, that political folly sometimes has appalling consequences. What has changed is that we now recognize the radical contingency of the positions from which we make judgements.[32] If we don't make disciplined judgements, we will still make judgements of some kinds. Unlike the literary critic, we can't simply suspend disbelief. Something has to be done. Indeed, it may be the case that some forms of popular politics encourage us to behave badly. It would be mildly disturbing if we endorsed forms of political theory that were similarly negligent.

The constructivist position takes complex identities seriously. It treats identities as outcomes of politics rather than straightforward bases for political positioning. Where we come from colours what we say but can't be treated as a fixed point. It may serve our political purposes to talk up certain positions. Identity politics has very effectively mobilized constituencies in the pursuit of specific objectives. Unlike Brian Barry, I have no problem with that.[33] It is disturbing, however, if the contingency of our identities is treated as an insuperable obstacle to mutual comprehension and agreement, at least in limited spheres. We can highlight the abuse of particular conceptions of practical reason that are tied to discrete identities. The values of specific hegemonic groups may be paraded as the embodiment of universal reasonableness. In our society, white middle-class, middle-aged men obviously have a lot to answer for. But it doesn't follow from the fact that we sometimes get things wrong, that we can never (in principle) get them right. Constructivist literature suggests, from where we stand today, that we are always likely to be dealing with fragmentary situations. We also know that things are likely to change in unpredictable ways. In this situation we can throw up our arms in horror ('clash of civilizations' talk[34]) or think hard. We shouldn't expect too much from theory. It won't tell us how to live. But it may furnish rudimentary principles for the establishment of reasonable terms of co-operation in deeply divided circumstances.

In conditions of deep pluralism, we are faced with stark choices. Political power will be exercised somehow or other. We may recognize that our principal theories reflect a situation that no longer prevails. One response might be to give up on normative theory altogether. In recent work, John Gray has sought to draw a line under a tradition of normative reflection, most notably in *Endgames*.[35] The thought seems to be that the world is too complicated for our meagre theoretical resources. All we have to fall back on is raw politics, a kind of stand-off between positions that cannot sustain common ground. We are left with *modus vivendi* rather than *overlapping consensus*, with scarcely any normative constraint on the way a *modus vivendi* may be attained. To be sure, this may be the best we can do when things go badly wrong. Gray treats it as the kernel of truth in Hobbes's *Leviathan*. But it stops well short of *Leviathan* in normative terms. Hobbes offered a normative defence of stability that could be accepted by reasonable people, given the situation they found themselves in. The argument serves as a justification for coercion, but not on any terms for any purposes. Gray drops the argument. What we are left with is a balance of power that will shift in relation to changing circumstances. It may not be the worst thing we might have to endure. But it doesn't provide stability and it isn't predictable, precisely the conditions that Hobbes valued most highly.

It would be a mistake, in this context, to make too much of the distinctions that Rawls has fashioned for us. In *Political Liberalism* Rawls is not very clear about the path from *modus vivendi* to *overlapping consensus*. Gray's objection is that the stakes are too high to make an overlapping consensus feasible. We are simply not in a position to insist on stability for the right reasons. Stability of any kind will give us massive advantages for the ordinary conduct of our affairs. The point I want to insist on here is that 'thin' principles are at work when we accept a stand-off between contending parties. At the very least, it involves recognition of someone else's place in a public space. Supporting arguments will not usually be spelt out but may nevertheless be theoretically significant. Non-interference can be construed as a minimal form of co-operation. It will also often involve tacit acknowledgement of rights to some public goods. Space, after all, is a public good. And, of course, co-operative agreements get thicker as the benefits of means to manage mutual interdependence in relation to security, resource management, and so on, become evident. I'm not talking about elaborate agreements here. Tribes (so we are told) need to establish reciprocal relations in order to guarantee their survival.[36] Modern technology transfers are a sophisticated version of a very old practice. At some level, we can all do it. A *modus vivendi* is precisely a 'thin' principled agreement. It is a simple corollary of the fact of interdependence.

How can we respond to someone who refuses to take interdependence seriously? Very old arguments are to hand, not least Hobbes's celebrated dismissal of the 'fool' in *Leviathan*.[37] We all know that cheating in a one-shot game is unlikely to prove disastrous, which may explain why we sometimes behave so badly on our holidays. Effective co-operation over the long term, however, requires trust, and no one trusts cheats. If we stay with the argument from Hobbes, normative theory gives us instrumental reasons for doing what we ought to do anyway. His concern is to challenge us to reflect on the practical implications of our preferences and values. He takes for granted that we are unlikely to agree about basic values. We start thinking politically precisely where our values generate conflict.

For the purposes of this chapter, it really doesn't matter what we think about the detail of Hobbes's argument. What I want to stress is the form of a philosophical response to a manifest conflict of values. Hobbes insists that such conflicts won't go away. He accepts value incommensurability but tries to develop a philosophical response. And we can, of course, imagine many other philosophical responses. Accepting value incommensurability at face value, however, is a bit like refusing to consider hard cases. Yet it is precisely hard cases that oblige us to think philosophically. The fact that we have often claimed too much for philosophy should not justify a refusal to claim anything at all.

Where does this leave us as we confront political problems on a global scale, yet within value systems that are fragmented both within and between states? To some citizens and commentators the challenges seem too daunting for constructive thought. Parekh, for example, claims that 'multicultural societies throw up problems that have no parallel in history'.[38] Yet there is nothing new about striving to reconcile 'the legitimate demands of unity and diversity'.[39] Long-standing empires have done it effectively, though not without incurring political costs that we are no longer prepared to pay. The nineteenth-century ideal of a homogeneous culture underpinning a state has made the task more difficult. But it can hardly be claimed that we are in uncharted territory. Parekh himself gives a nuanced account of the resources of the various theoretical traditions we can draw upon. He is right to suggest that 'no political doctrine or ideology can represent the full truth of human life'.[40] No system of ideas, of whatever kind, could embrace everything that mattered to us. Certainly political ideologies are poor creatures. Parekh insists that we cannot work exclusively within liberal (or any other specific) terms of reference. Yet the arguments he deploys come largely out of liberal theory sensitized to cultural diversity. What he is trying to do is political philosophy of a rather traditional kind. It really doesn't matter whether we call it liberal, post-liberal or whatever. The point is that he cannot avoid the normative arguments that modern liberal theorists typically address.

Note, for example, Parekh's frank acknowledgement that a multicultural society must maintain certain normative standards if it is to flourish. 'No multicultural society can be stable and vibrant unless it ensures that its constituent communities receive both just recognition and a just share of economic and political power.'[41] The point could have come straight out of Rawls. What 'just recognition' might amount to is not specified, though it would presumably not be misleading to think in terms of the social bases of self-respect. Similarly a claim to 'a just share of economic and political power' could invoke the 'difference principle' or something like it. My concern here is not to defend any particular conception of justice in these cases, but rather to insist that a conception of justice must be assumed if we are to make any sense of the ordinary business of co-operating in complex situations. We cannot defend pluralism on any terms. The good sense that is filtered through political cultures will be sufficient for most purposes. But 'good sense' is a product of practical reason exercised on myriad occasions by countless individuals. Sometimes, with the best will in the world, we are unsure how we should respond, what we should do next. On these occasions, as agents, we have to think harder. As philosophers we may be encouraged to model what is going on when difficult choices are made. We don't put philosophy into practice; yet practical life throws up the dilemmas that oblige us to think philosophically.

Multicultural politics shifts our focus of attention, but we are not doing anything qualitatively different. Parekh stresses the need for a dialogue between cultures. We can deepen our personal experience by taking seriously other possible ways of living. All this is unexceptionable. Yet dialogue would only be constructive if it were conducted on reasonable terms. We can hold conversations behind the barrel of a gun. We can also charmingly allow people to give vent to their feelings and then blithely carry on doing what we were minded to do anyway. Dialogue can be loaded, token, dishonest or serious. How we approach dialogue tells us a great deal about the way we regard others. It may be seen as an indicator of what we suppose we owe them. And, indeed, sometimes we will not be sure precisely what we do in fact owe them. Dialogue is a charged term. We need to think about its appropriate limits. How these should be specified, whether in terms of categorical rules or ideal situations, is much less important for my present purpose than simple ackowledgement that normative criteria apply.

One of the most intriguing developments of recent years is that critics of deontological liberalism have granted the need to invoke a 'thin' universalism, without commenting in any detail on the justificatory grounds for defending that universalism. Walzer, for example, combines a commitment to immanent critique within traditions with a recognition of a wider solidarity that manifests itself at times of crisis across cultures. In *Thick and Thin* he salutes the end of the Soviet empire as an event that evoked reactions on a global scale, yet he still insists that the bases for those responses should be sought within the various conceptual worlds in which we habitually operate.[42] Other theorists (Rorty is prominent[43]) meanwhile celebrate the *de facto* extension of a human rights culture globally, without supplying the arguments that might justify that enthusiasm.

From the other side of the argument, Rawls retreated from (what was seen as) the abstract universalism of *A Theory of Justice* to a weaker universalism dependent on self-understandings within democratic political cultures. This theoretical convergence has not been universally welcomed. Barry tells us that he would not want to defend anything that Rawls wrote after 1975.[44] Barry's concern is that too much is being made of the fact that we belong to specific cultures. Wherever we stand, we have to make judgements. If these judgements are seen *merely* as rationalizations of interests and identities, then prospects for a discursive politics look poor.

My claim here, however, is that Barry's worries are misplaced. Divisions in modern polities may be deeper than arguments, but the need to co-operate in complex situations obliges us to moderate our claims. Effective political argument needs to embrace a variety of positions. Indeed, argument ceases to be effective if it is seen simply as a statement of sectional preference, though there is no need to assume that 'practical reason' is somehow free-floating above interests, adjudicating between competing claims. Intelligibility in any context depends upon a 'thin' universalism. In this respect, what goes on within cultures is similar in kind to what goes on between them.

What I have sought to highlight in this chapter is that formal discussion of practical reason (in any context) has implications for any defensible conception of society as a scheme of social co-operation. To be sure, considerations at this level will not typically be focused on the competing preferences of agents pursuing objectives in everyday circumstances. Philosophical reflection on practical reason will not tell us what to do, any more than a universal grammar will enable us to speak. But it may nonetheless help us to frame the ordinary business of practical decision in ways that reflect our experience of thinking hard in difficult circumstances. Theorists who contrast a politics of recognition (Taylor, Walzer, Parekh) with a politics of impartial adjudication (Dworkin, Rawls, Barry) are thus missing the common ground that makes argument work. Discursive politics has to defend its own universal ground.

Notes

1   See T. M. Scanlon, *What We Owe to Each Other*, Cambridge, Mass.: Harvard University Press, 1998.
2   See Aristotle, *Nicomachean Ethics*, ed. Roger Crisp, Cambridge: Cambridge University Press, 2000, pp. 116–17.
3   Bernard Williams, 'Internal and External Reasons', in his *Moral Luck*, Cambridge: Cambridge University Press, 1981, p. 102.
4   See Christine M. Korsgaard, 'The Normativity of Instrumental Reason', in Garrett Cullity and Berys Gaut, eds, *Ethics and Practical Reason*, Oxford: Clarendon Press, 1997, pp. 215–54; and Christine M. Korsgaard, *The Sources of Normativity*, Cambridge: Cambridge University Press, 1996.
5   See John R. Searle, *Rationality in Action*, Cambridge, Mass.: MIT Press, 2001, especially pp. 97–134.

6   See John R. Searle, *Speech Acts: An Essay in the Philosophy of Language*, Cambridge: Cambridge University Press, 1969.

7   See Isaiah Berlin, 'Two Concepts of Liberty', in his *Four Essays on Liberty*, London: Oxford University Press, 1969, pp. 118–72; John Gray, *Berlin*, London: Fontana, 1995; and William A. Galston, *Liberal Pluralism: The Implications of Value Pluralism for Political Theory and Practice*, Cambridge: Cambridge University Press, 2002.

8   See John Rawls, 'Justice as Fairness: Political not Metaphysical', in his *Collected Papers*, ed. Samuel Freeman, Cambridge, Mass.: Harvard University Press, 1999, pp. 388–414.

9   See Joseph Raz, *The Morality of Freedom*, Oxford: Clarendon Press, 1986, pp. 321–66; W. B. Gallie, 'Essentially Contested Concepts', *Proceedings of the Aristotelian Society*, LXVI, 1955–6, pp. 167–98; and John Gray, 'Political Power, Social Theory and Essential Contestability', in D. Miller and L. Siedentop, eds, *The Nature of Political Theory*, Oxford: Oxford University Press, 1983, pp. 75–101.

10 See John Rawls, *Political Liberalism*, New York: Columbia University Press, 1993, pp. 133–72.

11 G. W. F. Hegel, *Elements of the Philosophy of Right*, ed. Allen W. Wood, Cambridge: Cambridge University Press, 1991, p. 21.

12 See St Augustine, *Concerning the City of God against the Pagans*, trans. Henry Bettenson, Harmondsworth: Penguin Books, 1972, p. 139: 'A gang is a group of men under the command of a leader, bound by a compact of association, in which the plunder is divided according to an agreed convention.'

13 'Perpetual Peace: A Philosophical Sketch', in Hans Reiss, ed., *Kant's Political Writings*, Cambridge: Cambridge University Press, 1970, p. 112.

14 See Michael J. Sandel, *Liberalism and the Limits of Justice*, Cambridge: Cambridge University Press, 1982.

15 See Brian Barry, *Culture and Equality: An Egalitarrian Critique of Multiculturalism*, Cambridge: Polity, 2001.

16 See, in particular, chapters by John Horton, Margaret Moore and Andrea Baumeister.

17 The tendency is evident, for example, in Charles Taylor, *Sources of the Self: The Making of Modern Identity*, Cambridge: Cambridge University Press, 1989; and Alasdair MacIntyre, *After Virtue: A Study in Moral Theory*, 2nd edn, London: Duckworth, 1985.

18 See Bruce Haddock, 'Hegel's Critique of the Theory of Social Contract', in David Boucher and Paul Kelly, eds, *The Social Contract from Hobbes to Rawls*, London, Routledge, 1994, pp. 147–63.

19 See Charles Taylor, *Hegel*, Cambridge: Cambridge University Press, 1975, pp. 3–50.

20 See Bruce Haddock, 'State and Nation in Mazzini's Political Thought', *History of Political Thought*, 20, 1999, pp. 313–36.

21 See Bruce Haddock, 'State, Nation and Risorgimento', in Gino Bedani and Bruce Haddock, eds, *The Politics of Italian National Identity: A Multidisciplinary Perspective*, Cardiff: University of Wales Press, 2000, pp. 11–49.

22 But see Bruce Haddock and Ovidiu Caraiani, 'Nationalism and Civil Society in Romania', *Political Studies*, XLVII, 1999, pp. 258–74; and Bruce Haddock and Ovidiu Caraiani, 'Legitimacy, National Identity and Civil Association', in Lucian Boia, ed., *Nation and National Ideology: Past, Present and Prospects*, Bucharest: New Europe College, 2002, pp. 377–89.

23 See Will Kymlicka, *Politics in the Vernacular: Nationalism, Multiculturalism, and Citizenship*, Oxford: Oxford University Press, 2001; and Yael Tamir, *Liberal Nationalism*, Princeton: Princeton University Press, 1993. See also the reservations expressed in Andrew Vincent, 'Liberal Nationalism: An Irresponsible Compound?', *Political Studies*, XLV, 1997, pp. 275–95.

24 See Will Kymlicka, 'Western Political Theory and Ethnic Relations in Eastern Europe', in Will Kymlicka and Magda Opalski, eds, *Can Liberal Pluralism be Exported? Western Political Theory and Ethnic Relations in Eastern Europe*, Oxford: Oxford University Press, 2001, pp. 13–105.
25 Ibid., p. 48.
26 See Michael Oakeshott, 'Political Education', in his *Rationalism in Politics and Other Essays*, London: Methuen, 1962, pp. 111–36, especially pp. 133–6.
27 See Michael Oakeshott, *Experience and Its Modes*, Cambridge: Cambridge University Press, 1933, pp. 247–321.
28 See Michael Oakeshott, *On Human Conduct*, Oxford: Clarendon Press, 1975; and for further development of this point, see Bruce Haddock, 'Michael Oakeshott: *Rationalism in Politics*', in Murray Forsyth and Maurice Keens-Soper, eds, *The Political Classics: Green to Dworkin*, Oxford: Oxford University Press, 1996, pp. 100–20.
29 See Oakeshott, *On Human Conduct*, pp. 108–84.
30 Clifford Geertz, 'The World in Pieces: Culture and Politics at the End of the Century', in his *Available Light: Anthropological Reflections on Philosophical Topics*, Princeton: Princeton University Press, 2000, pp. 218–63.
31 See Quentin Skinner, *The Foundations of Modern Political Thought*, Cambridge: Cambridge University Press, 1978.
32 See Bruce Haddock, 'Liberalism and Contingency', in Mark Evans, ed., *The Edinburgh Companion to Contemporary Liberalism*, Edinburgh: Edinburgh University Press, 2001, pp. 162–71.
33 See Bernard Yack, 'Multiculturalism and the Political Theorists', *European Journal of Political Theory*, 1, 2002, pp. 107–19.
34 See Samuel P. Huntington, *The Clash of Civilizations and the Remaking of World Order*, New York: Simon and Schuster, 1996.
35 See John Gray, *Endgames: Questions in Late Modern Political Thought*, Cambridge: Polity, 1997, especially pp. 51–4.
36 See E. E. Evans-Pritchard, *Kinship and Marriage among the Nuer*, Oxford: Clarendon Press, 1951.
37 See Thomas Hobbes, *Leviathan*, ed. Richard Tuck, Cambridge: Cambridge University Press, 1991, pp. 101–3. For discussion see Jean Hampton, *Hobbes and the Social Contract Tradition*, Cambridge: Cambridge University Press, 1986, pp. 58–79.
38 Bhikhu Parekh, *Rethinking Multiculturalism: Cultural Diversity and Political Theory*, Basingstoke: Macmillan, 2000, p. 343.
39 Ibid.
40 Ibid., p. 338.
41 Ibid., p. 343.
42 See Michael Walzer, *Thick and Thin: Moral Arguments at Home and Abroad*, Notre Dame, Ind.: University of Notre Dame Press, 1994.
43 See Richard Rorty, *Contingency, Irony and Solidarity*, Cambridge: Cambridge University Press, 1989.
44 See Barry, *Culture and Equality*, p. 331, fn. 27.

3 Liberalism and multiculturalism

Once more unto the breach

John Horton

The relationship between 'liberalism' and 'multiculturalism' is both immensely complex and fiercely contested and, as a result, the geography of the various positions in this intellectual terrain is not easily mapped. For instance, most liberal theorists believe that the legitimate claims of multiculturalism can be met by an adequate liberal political theory. But, of course, this does not mean that liberals agree with each other. Thus, multicultural liberals, themselves as different as Jacob Levy, Joseph Raz and Will Kymlicka, seek to go much further in incorporating multicultural concerns than a universalist, egalitarian liberal like Brian Barry.[1] While Barry too endorses the view that liberalism can accommodate the *legitimate* concerns of multiculturalism, this is largely because he thinks most such concerns are *illegitimate*. Barry, therefore, is a remorseless critic of multicultural liberals, arguing that their commitment to multiculturalism involves a fundamental betrayal of their liberalism. Moreover, to complicate matters further, some writers who see themselves as critical of liberalism, for instance Bhikhu Parekh, are regarded by many multicultural liberals, although not by universalist, egalitarian liberals, as very much closer to liberalism than they believe themselves to be.[2]

Any attempt at a comprehensive discussion of the relationship between liberalism and multiculturalism, therefore, would be an overly ambitious aspiration for a single chapter. There are too many liberalisms, too many multiculturalisms and too many issues and arguments. Instead, the inquiry undertaken here is much more narrowly focused. What I want to do is examine in the context of one particularly robust version of liberalism – the universalist, egalitarian liberalism of Brian Barry[3] – how far, and in what ways, some of the challenges and problems to which the existence within a society of significant cultural differences can give rise are effaced or distorted within such a liberalism. However, although I shall certainly be vigorously criticizing Barry's treatment of this issue, I do so primarily (and here I differ from most theorists who have written about these issues) with the aim neither of vindicating or refuting liberalism or multiculturalism, nor of advocating any particular policies or institutional structures. I shall not even be defending any set of political principles. My purpose is essentially threefold. First, it is intended that the discussion of these issues should shed some light on the limitations of one prominent and influential strand of liberal thinking. Second, it is to try to get a better understanding of what is involved in some of the issues of multiculturalism as they arise in western liberal democratic societies, and how framing them within the style of the liberal theorizing I examine fails adequately to address what it is that matters to those who are drawn to the multiculturalist agenda. Finally, if only briefly and sketchily, I want to raise some larger questions about the limits of contemporary liberal political theorizing more generally.

The argument is advanced principally through an examination of three broad areas of concern as they are presented in Barry's *Culture and Equality*. These are: impartiality and inequality of impact; the meaning and value of culture; and the legitimate legal enforcement of local social norms. I shall explain more fully what each of these means as I discuss them. I should, though, make it clear from the beginning that, although what follows is strongly critical of Barry's views, there is much in his book that is persuasive. There is no doubt that Barry often effectively debunks some weak or specious arguments that have been advanced in favour of multicultural principles and policies. Multiculturalism has become a fashionable issue in political theory and, as with most fashions, this has resulted in some nonsense. Unfortunately, and this is my quarrel with Barry, he seems to see nothing but nonsense; and in the proverbial sorting of the wheat from the chaff, it turns out on his view that there is only chaff. I also share some of his misgivings – an understatement in Barry's case – about many multicultural policy proposals. However, in doing so, I do not share his confident belief that this is because the complaints that justify those policies are simply without any legitimate basis. I shall say a little more about this in the concluding section.

One final preliminary point may also be appropriate. I use 'multiculturalism' and associated terms rather loosely, although not I hope damagingly so. Generally, I use the term 'multiculturalists' as a label for those theorists who believe that the presence of deep cultural diversity within modern liberal democratic states poses some sort of significant challenge to traditional liberalism, without distinguishing those who think liberalism can be adapted to accommodate that challenge from those who do not. 'Multiculturalism' itself is used mostly as a generic term for the co-existence of a significant plurality of diverse cultural groups with sometimes conflicting values or ways of life within a single polity. The argument here, it should be noted, does not address groups that seek political independence or secession, only those seeking accommodation within a society. The cultural groups I principally have in mind are religious or ethnic groups, or indigenous peoples: Muslims, Sikhs, Jews, Gypsies, Inuit and Aboriginals are all examples of such groups. Women, however, are not a cultural group in this sense, although this is not to deny that some of the arguments deployed may not also apply to them to some degree. Moreover, culture is not of course only a property of minority groups: it is an ever-present feature of social life. Basically, I endorse Bhikhu Parekh's conception of a culture as 'a historically created system of meaning and significance, or what comes to the same thing, a system of beliefs and practices in terms of which a group of human beings understand, regulate and structure their individual and collective lives'.[4] Broad and indeterminate though this conception is, it is narrower than a notion such as 'difference'. In thinking of culture in this way it is important not to essentialize or reify it. The 'system' of beliefs and practices has to be understood as interrelated in complex, diverse and changing ways – some elements will be more central than others, some more easily modified or abandoned, and so on. Furthermore, 'cultures' as such do not *do* anything: it is people who make claims or feel marginalized, and so on; and people will often disagree, sometimes quite fundamentally, about how their culture should be interpreted or understood. Finally, especially in modern societies, cultures cannot always be sharply distinguished one from another. However, while the pervasiveness of hybridity often complicates matters considerably, it does not negate the idea of systematic cultural differences.

Impartiality and inequality of impact

I begin with impartiality and 'inequality of impact'. This takes off from a simple and familiar point. The claim that liberalism is neutral or impartial – I shall not differentiate between these ideas here – is sometimes objected to by pointing to the unequal impact of liberal laws on some groups rather than others. This unequal impact may take the form of making illegal some activity associated with a particular culture or simply making the performance of the activity more burdensome, either more difficult or more costly or both. An example of the former would be a law prohibiting the carrying of 'knives and other sharply pointed objects' in public, which impacts on Sikhs (through preventing the carrying of *kirpans*) in a way that it does not impact on Christians (who at most are expected to carry with them only the metaphorical sword of God). An example of the latter might be where Sikhs, though legally exempted from the requirement of wearing crash helmets when riding motorcycles or hard hats when working on building sites, are required to bear the costs of any resulting injury to themselves, whereas those whose beliefs do not prohibit them from wearing designated protective headgear will be eligible for compensation through safety legislation.

Barry's response to this objection is characteristically dismissive, if in an irrelevant way also incontrovertible. The principal point he makes is as familiar as the objection: any law will have an unequal impact on some people. Restrictions on smoking restrict smokers, speed limits restrict those who want to drive fast, and so on. As Barry puts it: 'The notion that inequality of impact is a sign of unfairness is not an insight derived from a more sophisticated conception of justice than that previously found in political philosophy. It is simply a mistake.'[5] Of course Barry is right if one takes *any* inequality of impact to be necessarily unjust – such a position is obviously incoherent, being incompatible with almost any legislation. However, he is attacking the proverbial 'straw man' here, as the obvious absurdity of this view rightly suggests that it is not one that is seriously advanced by multiculturalists. Moreover, Barry himself, immediately after the quote above, concedes that 'the unequal impact of a law may in some cases be an indication of its unfairness'.[6] So, appearances to the contrary notwithstanding, Barry's response settles nothing that anybody (perhaps I should be more cautious and say almost anybody) has disputed. The issue, as all parties agree, concerns the circumstances under which the unequal impact of a law may be unfair.

One of the striking features of the way in which Barry discusses this question (and indeed much else) is the supreme confidence he shows in his own judgement when dealing with particular examples. The two examples he discusses most fully in this context are ritual animal slaughter (not always an apt characterization of the practices he has in mind) and whether Sikhs should be exempted from the legal requirement to wear a crash helmet when riding a motorcycle. In both cases he sees little merit in what he calls the 'rule-and-exemption' approach. This is the view that while legislation on these matters is generally justified, there may also be a strong case for particular exemptions from it on the grounds that the law will unfairly impact on some cultural, often religious, group. My concern here is not so much with the answers he gives as with the way in which he discusses the examples. In particular, I want to draw attention to a number of features of that discussion. The first concerns the equal or impartial application of a rule or law. For Barry, it seems entirely unproblematic what will count as the equal application of a rule: hence his presentation of the issue in terms of the model of rule and exemption. But it is not clear that what counts as the equal application of a rule is as straightforward as Barry assumes. This is because the actions that are supposed to fall under the rule may have different meanings. As Jacob Levy observes:

> in most cases in which an exemption is demanded or granted, a practice which has a distinctive status and meaning in a minority culture is banned, regulated, or compelled because of a very different meaning it has for the majority culture. The exemption is justified as recognition of that difference, as an attempt not to unduly burden the minority culture or religion *en route* to the law's legitimate goals.[7]

In short, there may be more than one reasonable (for example, not wilfully perverse) view about how the law should be interpreted. For instance, even such an apparently simple question as how to apply the law penalizing those who carry 'knives and other sharply pointed objects' in public is fraught with difficulties. If, as Barry recommends, the Sikh ceremonial dagger should not (as in English law it is) be exempted from this law, why does he not also recommend the prosecution of all those darts players who carry their darts to the pub? And there are many other sharply pointed objects that can cause serious harm but which nobody seriously thinks people should be prosecuted for carrying. No doubt something that Barry would call 'common sense' is at work here. Common sense, however, is not culturally innocent: Sikhs may plausibly think it is common sense to distinguish *kirpans* from other knives.

These kinds of issue, however, are still more problematic when examining another of Barry's examples, ritual animal slaughter. It is deeply contentious to suggest that the ritual sacrifice of an animal is the same type of action as the torture of that animal by a group of sadists. To insist that it is is to impose one meaning on an action when that meaning is not only contestable but also vehemently rejected by those on whom it is being imposed. What is being prohibited is, under some appropriate description, not the same type of action. Moreover, it would be quite wrong to suggest that even liberals like Barry are unwilling to allow 'exemptions' from such a law. For example, it is very common (although not of course uncontroversial) for the imposition of suffering on animals to be allowed for purposes of medical research. This is not an exemption on strictly cultural grounds, although it clearly has to do with the high value that is attached to medical research in our society. Once we have granted that there can be 'exceptions', though, why must we exclude culture as being one possible reasonable ground for such exemptions?

Barry's arguments against exemptions on cultural grounds are unimpressive. We do not, for instance, need to spend long on his jocular observation that it will not matter to the animal what the reason is that someone is making it suffer.[8] This simply presupposes that the animal's interests must be paramount. But this need not be so, even though the reason for the law restricting the imposition of suffering on animals is the interests of the animals, as can plainly be seen from the medical research case. Somewhat more interesting is Barry's apparent denial of the relevance of the distinction between beliefs and preferences.[9] To be fair, I am not sure that he does deny that there is *any* relevant distinction here, but the only context in which he offers a sustained discussion of beliefs and preferences is in rejecting the view that the latter are any more changeable by an act of will than are the former. Barry is right that the contrast between beliefs and preferences can be overdrawn, if preferences are taken to be always subject to the will, while beliefs are always independent of it. But this does not mean that there can be no significant and relevant differences between some kinds of belief and many preferences. In particular, to treat people's moral and religious beliefs in the same way as, say, their preference for Indian cuisine rather than Chinese, or for football over cricket, as all falling equally within something called 'a conception of the good', is a radical misunderstanding of what is at stake, notwithstanding its ubiquity within a certain style of liberal theorizing. Of course, liberals *can* choose to ignore the status that people's fundamental ethical and religious convictions have for them. But that is precisely one of the major complaints that multiculturalists typically level against such a liberalism. This significance is to be understood not primarily in terms of relative intensity – some straightforward preferences can be felt with great intensity – but in the way in which such beliefs connect with conceptions of right and wrong, or piety and sinfulness or with our sense of shame and self-respect. To treat these beliefs as if they are just another preference is to be wilfully oblivious of their significance for those who hold them. To say the least, therefore, to argue that a law prohibiting certain forms of animal slaughter is

appropriately impartial precisely because it does *not* distinguish between a religious ritual on the one hand, and somebody's desire to have a bit of sadistic fun
by torturing animals on the other, seems to miss the point rather spectacularly.
This is not, I emphasize, to suggest that invoking such beliefs is decisive, but it is
to show that the whole issue of what is to count as the equal application of a
rule or a law is much more deeply problematic than Barry's discussion allows.

Barry does not entirely reject the possibility that the rule-and-exception
approach may occasionally be justified, but he is clearly very hostile towards it,
making two further points in defence of his position. First, he thinks that the
circumstances under which both a law and an exemption can be justified will be
very rare.[10] Roughly, his view is that if there is a good case for a law, then there
is unlikely to be a good argument for exemptions to it; while if there is a good
case for an exemption, it is probably better that there not be a law. We have
already seen with the medical research exemption from laws prohibiting the
infliction of suffering on animals, that Barry's view may be rather blinkered.
Numerous other examples of this strategy could be given, even, for instance,
regarding laws as uncontroversial as those prohibiting the intentional infliction
of physical harm on other human beings. In English law, the consent of the
'victim' does not normally nullify a charge of assault. There are good reasons
for this to do with avoiding victims being cowed into claiming they consented
when they did not. Yet the sport of boxing, which might be thought of as an
institutionalization of physical assault, is unproblematically (if controversially)
exempted from this law. Does Barry think, too, that either we should abolish
speed limits on roads or require the emergency services always to observe them?
His argument seems to reflect a surprisingly naïve view of the law: law is typically replete with qualifications, special cases, exceptions, stipulative definitions,
excusing conditions, assumptions about what is reasonable, implicit *ceteris paribus*
clauses, and so on. One good reason for law having these features is that laws
usually need to cover a vast range and complexity of differing and sometimes
unanticipated situations. Taking account of significant cultural differences can
be understood as one such complexity.

Barry's second point about the rule-and-exemption approach appears to be
that it is open to abuse by any group claiming that something illegal is contrary
to their culture. Again, however, he makes heavy weather of something that is
entirely familiar. Judgements regularly have to be made in relation to laws as to,
for instance, what counts as a religion (for example, in determining charitable
status) or conscientious conviction (for example, pacifists in time of war), and
more generally in relation to the intention or motive of a person or group.
These are often difficult judgements, and they are indeed open to attempts to
cynically exploit them, but there is no reason to think that exemptions to laws
on religious or cultural grounds are necessarily more (or less) difficult or open to
abuse than many others.

In the case of exemptions for Sikhs from the law requiring motorcyclists to
wear crash helmets, Barry maintains that:

it is hard to steer a path between the conclusion that wearing a crash helmet is so important that all motorcyclists should have to do it and the alternative of saying that this is a matter that people should be left to decide for themselves.[11]

But it is not hard at all; and it is perhaps symptomatic of how far his theory has led him astray that Barry should have so lost his bearings. There is no 'hard path' to be steered in holding that everyone riding motorcycles should wear crash helmets unless he or she has a higher interest in not doing so. A religious conviction might reasonably count as a higher interest, whereas liking the wind in one's hair might not.[12] This is not to deny that judgements about what is a higher interest are contestable, or to say that the rule-and-exemption approach is the best policy for dealing with this issue. Rather, it is simply to defend it as one reasonable and plausible way of treating the issue that acknowledges the unequal impact of legislation on different cultural groups, and the concern that this creates among those most seriously disadvantaged as a result. Judgements about how different cultural understandings are to be acknowledged and nego-tiated cannot be avoided, even by the most neutral liberal, simply because a refusal to do so is itself to make such a judgement.

The meaning and value of culture

As we have already seen, one will only consider the rule-and-exemption approach if one accepts that the unequal impact of legislation or regulation is something about which those who are disadvantaged have some sort of legiti-mate complaint, and this will not always be the case. In the preceding discussion, the examples concerned religious practices, and it will be widely agreed, including by most liberals if not by Barry, that legislation which disad-vantages people because of their religion is a serious matter. However, it is important to see that the issue goes beyond religion. So the second area of concern I want to look at is the meaning and value of culture more generally, and the kind of harm that systematically disadvantaging cultural groups can cause. This is a huge topic and one about which my remarks are inevitably selective and sketchy, but it obviously lies at the heart of questions about the relationship between liberalism and multiculturalism.

Earlier, I endorsed a brief characterization of culture offered by Bhikhu Parekh, but it is now necessary to pursue a little further the question of culture, in particular why and how it matters. Barry is not alone in showing consider-able impatience with references to people's culture, and there is no doubt that it is a concept that is loosely used and sometimes abused. But neither the fact that it does not admit of precise definition, nor that its vagueness leaves it open to abuse, is sufficient to show that there is nothing real and important which lies at the heart of the idea of culture. One false move at this point that should be resisted is the easy claim that because cultures may include practices that are widely regarded, not least by liberals, as wrong, the appeal to culture can have no independent value. There are two observations worth making here. First, even where a culture does contain practices that harm some of its members, it does not *necessarily* follow that even those who are so harmed do not derive overall benefit and value from that culture. Second, we must avoid the tendency, not uncommon in liberal theorizing and a frequent rhetorical device employed by Barry, of counter-posing an idealized liberal society to a warts-and-all presentation of particular cultural groups.[13] It is true that cultural groups often fail to live up to their ideals and values, and that in doing so particular practices become corrupted and degraded. However, this is not a process to which liberal societies are immune. One only has to reflect for a moment on the way in which the high ideal of freedom of speech is manifest in the levels of prurience, scurrilous abuse and mind-numbing vulgarity and trivia which characterize societies like our own. Moreover, if we are to be 'knowing' and 'realistic' about, say, the abuse of women within 'Muslim culture', we should be equally so about sexual exploitation, domestic violence, the material inequality of women and so on, in liberal societies. None of this is to deny that particular cultural groups may indeed embrace practices as an authentic part of that culture that liberals, and many non-liberals too, will find repugnant, and sometimes simply unacceptable. It is, though, to remind us that in reality the alternative will not be the idealized and sanitized society of liberal theory.

Prior to the 1970s, and the emergence of multiculturalism as a serious political project, what we might call 'enlightened opinion' largely favoured the assimilation of different religious and ethnic groups (and, where they existed, of indigenous peoples too) within the host or dominant culture. This, of course, is the *bête noire* of modern multiculturalists; and contemporary advocates of integration are usually careful to distinguish it from assimilation. Assimilation, at least when pursued through policies which effectively disadvantage minority cultures, is seen as a kind of cultural imperialism. This may be so, but I believe proponents of assimilation, however misguided we may have come to view them, recognized something important. This is that social and political institutions and practices are embedded in particular cultural forms, and that they function, to varying degrees, in more or less specific cultural contexts. Assimilation, therefore, from the point of view of the dominant culture and if it could be brought about without too much dislocation and antipathy, was, in a sense, rightly recognized as the most 'effective' means of integrating different ethnic and religious groups within a single society. In saying that assimilation, if achievable, is the most 'effective' means of integration for the dominant culture, I am not, it should be clear, endorsing or approving it. Rather, I want simply to point to the fact, and I take it to be a fact, that the more a culture is shared, the easier it is to presuppose that culture is the unspoken and often invisible background to the way in which social institutions and practices operate.

Culture is a medium through which we live our lives, a dimension of our subjectivity as social agents. It shapes and forms the myriad details of our beliefs, attitudes, expectations and behaviour; it is embedded in social practices, our sense of history, the conventions that regulate public life – in what we take to be 'normal'. To give a small local example: if we are organizing a social function for graduates' parents it is routine to provide ample non-alcoholic beverages. But how often is it even considered that some students' parents may have beliefs that prevent them from being present where alcohol is being consumed?[14] This is a fairly trivial example but, when multiplied many times and across a range of situations over a long period of time, it may assume larger dimensions. It also nicely illustrates how such exclusions or marginalizations can be so mundane as to be invisible to their perpetrators: there is no deliberate intention to exclude these people, but we are literally 'thoughtless' towards them. Such examples draw our attention to how substantive assumptions about what is normal, natural, standard, reasonable, ordinary, proper, decent, courteous, appropriate, civil and so on, constitute the context of our lives. That there is some such context of assumptions is, in my view, unavoidable; but of course this does not mean that they must have the *particular* content that they do or that, once brought to our attention, they cannot (at least to some extent) be renegotiated.

I want to draw attention to the mundane aspect of culture both as a corrective to an exclusive concern with a narrow range of 'big' questions about, for instance, particular 'controversial' religious practices, and as part of a contextual explanation of why an issue sometimes comes to assume a significance out of all proportion to what might seem to be its real importance. For instance, I believe it to be part of the explanation of why *The Satanic Verses* became such a source of grievance and of the celebrated Islamic headscarf affair in France. With respect to this latter case, thousands of Islamic schoolgirls had attended state schools in France without the issue being pressed (and it should be added that in the small number of cases where it had been, schools had generally turned a blind eye to it). But, eventually, the ongoing and pervasive pressure to conform to cultural norms that are not one's own, especially when combined with an officious enforcement of them by some authority, is likely at some point to generate an 'issue'. The occasion of the issue may as a result seem disproportionate to the ensuing controversy, but this is because the occasion is usually only a small part of the real cause. I shall have more to say about another aspect of this in the final part of the chapter when I consider the legitimacy of the legal enforcement of local norms. Here, however, I want to focus on culture as the medium through which we live our lives, as an essential strand in the fabric of our experience and an expression of our situatedness as social beings, which locates us and helps us feel 'at home' in the world. In so far as our culture receives no public recognition, rendering us either invisible or abnormal, and cultural differences disadvantage us, so we are made to feel marginal and alienated; we are perceived as 'difficult' or 'a problem' within the dominant culture.

It is largely this feature of culture that has led some liberals to try to adapt liberalism to take account of multicultural concerns, though in rather limited ways, such as Kymlicka's conception of culture as a context of choice or Galeotti's conception of 'toleration as recognition'.[15] Barry says surprisingly little about this directly, although he is unswervingly hostile to most of the modifications to or departures from his universal, egalitarian liberalism that Kymlicka and others of his kind permit in their desire to effect such an accommodation.[16] For what it's worth, I share some of Barry's reservations about some of the particular policy recommendations of thinkers like Kymlicka. This, though, is not my concern here. What I share with multiculturalists, on the other hand, is the sense that there is a serious issue here, a problem, something deep and difficult that merits serious thought and careful attention. My complaint about Barry is that he does not. The existence of more or less different minority cultures within a dominant culture does not, for him, seem to give rise to any concerns about marginalization, disadvantage or social exclusion that cannot be overcome through a brisk dose of universal, egalitarian liberalism. Why is it that Barry's brand of liberalism seems to blind him to the problems that so many see, even if they differ dramatically in how they think such problems should be addressed?

No doubt there is more than one reason why this is so. For instance, it may have something to do with the inherent individualism of liberalism, but this is not the reason that I want to take up. What I want to focus on is the difficulty that Barry and, to some degree, most liberals have in adequately incorporating features of human life that are to a significant extent non-voluntary, of which much of culture is a conspicuous instance. Moreover, this difficulty runs deep as it is partly because culture has this non-voluntary quality that it plays the role in our lives that it does. As Bhikhu Parekh expresses it:

> A cultural community performs a role in human life that a voluntary association cannot. It gives its members a sense of rootedness, existential stability, the feeling of belonging to an ongoing community of ancient and misty origins. And does all this *only because* it is not a conscious human creation and one's membership of it is neither a matter of choice nor can be easily terminated by oneself or others.[17]

Barry flatly rejects the idea that such non-voluntary commitments present any problems. Liberals, he says,

> have no problems in recognizing that human beings are born into a number of communities – ethnic, cultural, religious, linguistic, and so on – as well as into families. Colin Bird rightly refers to those who harp on 'the unchosen nature of our social identity' as purveyors of 'platitudes'.[18]

Platitudes they may be; but the issue in question is how liberalism deals with these truths, however platitudinous.

Certainly, Barry is right that liberals need not deny that these attachments are *originally* unchosen. They would be rather silly if they did; but then so too would anyone who thought liberals must deny this. All of which rather suggests that *origins* are not to the point. What I want to suggest is to the point is that Barry does seem to think that these originally unchosen attachments only *continue* to have any value if people voluntarily choose to endorse them; and what makes for voluntariness here is ease of exit or detachment. Any group from which exit is difficult or costly is an object of liberal suspicion, and the aim of liberal policy should be, in Barry's words, 'to ensure as far as possible that members of associations have real exit options available to them'.[19] Throughout *Culture and Equality* the importance of the voluntariness of groups and of free association is repeated *ad nauseam*. The difficulty is, as the quote from Parekh makes clear, that the value of culture seems to depend, in part at least, on its being non-voluntary, and detachment or exit being difficult and probably costly. 'Rootedness' is almost axiomatically a quality that implies a difficulty of detachment, and a sense of loss when one is so sundered. To have roots which are easily and cheaply cast off is not to have especially good roots; rather it is to be rootless, to be deracinated. It is not that having roots, or at least the particular roots one has, is always and necessarily a good thing, or of course that cultural change is impossible or undesirable, but that in so far as an important part of the value of culture to people lies in this sense of rootedness, it is not easily amenable to any attempt to make it more voluntary without its losing that value. Cultural identity is normally difficult to change dramatically, and it typically takes quite a long time, even when embraced wholeheartedly, for someone to feel comfortable with such a change. Of course culture is not all of a piece, and we are faced not with a simple contrast between 'freely chosen' and 'unalterable', but with a continuum, or continua, with varying degrees of choice and changeability. The general point, however, is that the value of some things may depend upon their being difficult to cast off or escape, and their value may only be diminished or destroyed by attempts to make them more voluntary. This is not a point that liberals find easy to accommodate, and it is at least one of the reasons why culture *does* present a problem for the liberal emphasis on voluntary membership and free association.

This also explains why Barry's distinction between different kinds of 'exit costs' is largely irrelevant. The distinction between 'intrinsic costs', that is, costs that are ineliminably associated with loss of group membership; 'associative costs', those costs that are not necessary but may legitimately be imposed by members on those who leave; and 'external costs', which are contingently and illegitimately imposed on those who leave, works rather well when dealing with voluntary associations. The point about culture, however, is that for the most part a cultural group is *not* a voluntary association. Barry's pretence that it is probably results from his desire to avoid the consequences in terms of his own theory of admitting it is not. For if a person's cultural identity is not something for which he or she can be held fully responsible, then those who belong to cultural groups that are socially disadvantaged may, on Barry's own theory, be entitled to some compensation: it would be an inequality that was not the result simply of their own choices. Cultural disadvantage may function in a similar way to economic disadvantage in making access to many 'goods' more difficult. Naturally, this is not a road along which Barry wants to travel. He avoids it, however, only by treating cultural membership as a matter of choice, on a par with membership of a voluntary association. Of course, in saying this, I am not suggesting that disadvantaged cultures are inherently disadvantageous; only that, in a social context where life is made systematically more difficult for their members because their culture is disadvantaged within the dominant culture, marginalization and a sense of exclusion are the likely result.

Cultures are never entirely homogeneous or uncontentious; and, even where cultural diversity is less marked, problems of cultural conflict are still an ever-present possibility, although likely to be manifest only in ways that have limited political salience. Where, however, a relatively distinctive cultural community is significantly less favourably situated than some other cultural group, the scope for political conflict is altogether more substantial and deep. Where a cultural group finds its norms, standards and assumptions markedly at variance with those of the dominant culture through which social inclusion is articulated, problems of marginalization or exclusion are likely to be serious. This is what multiculturalists recognize and seek to address. Barry's version of universal, egalitarian liberalism does not address it, because it does not acknowledge that there is anything of substance to address.[20] Indeed, arguably, Barry only exacerbates the problem in his treatment of another issue, that of the legitimacy of the legal enforcement of local norms, which is the third and final of the broad areas I want to examine.

The legal enforcement of local norms

Barry begins his chapter entitled 'The Abuse of Culture' with a resoundingly rhetorical question: 'How could anybody seriously imagine that citing the mere fact of a tradition or custom could *ever* function as a self-contained justificatory move?'[21] One might anticipate on this basis that Barry is rather boldly proposing a radical rejection of the legal enforcement of any cultural norms. However, this is not the case, and a few pages later he is even insisting that '[n]obody has *any* doubts about the adequacy in *many* circumstances of "This is the way we do things here" as a justification for the legal imposition of some norm'.[22] Indeed, he goes on, '[o]nly a misunderstanding of the nature of liberal principles could lead anyone to imagine that they cannot countenance the legal enforcement of conventional norms'.[23] While agreeing with Barry in general terms, not least because it seems to me impossible to entirely avoid legislating some cultural norms, there are still important questions to be asked in this connection. In particular, how does it get decided which and whose norms can be legitimately legally enforced, and where does that leave those who do not share those norms that are 'legitimately' enforced, and whose own norms will be at best disregarded and at worst made illegitimate?

There are some types of conventional norms that Barry mentions that are largely uncontroversial – which side of the road to drive on being the hackneyed example. Another type of example that I do not wish to consider here is the provision of public goods, such as clean water. Altogether more revealing are two other examples that Barry discusses: public order and decency. Barry writes of them that

> [e]xcluding as illegitimate any conceptions of public order or decency that are not universally applicable would mean that there could be virtually no permissible regulations framed in terms of those values. The whole point of concepts such as 'public order' and 'decency' is that they are simply place-holders waiting to be fleshed out by giving them a content derived from local norms.[24]

In these passages there is a recognition both that such values need to be given specific content if they are to be more than empty concepts, and that the content can legitimately vary across different societies. What is disappointing, however, especially in a book the very *raison d'être* of which is multiculturalism, is that Barry has almost nothing to say about these values as sites of cultural contestation within a society. The uncharacteristically bland reference to 'local norms' simply tends to erase such contestation.

Barry is certainly right that standards of public decency have to come from somewhere since they cannot be derived from the concept of public decency itself. In fact, he says very little about these standards, but it can scarcely be doubted that in a country like Britain these derive mostly from its Christian heritage, combined with an increasing secularization that is almost continuously eating away at the remnants of that heritage. But what of other groups whose culture may give them a different understanding of public decency? What if the 'local' norms are not their norms? Is it straightforwardly unproblematic and legitimate that 'through the democratic process' the majority impose their norms of public decency on minorities entirely without regard to their sensibilities? Nothing Barry says seems to suggest otherwise. While elsewhere he refers to the harm principle as some sort of limit, it is hard to see how that would have any application to public decency, as that does not typically involve any 'harm', at least not as he understands it. If, though, we are concerned with the sense of exclusion often felt within minority cultures, then this kind of imposition of local norms is likely to be part of the problem. Again, what I want to stress here is not the rightness or wrongness of a particular policy, but only that there is something here that deserves attention – a complaint that is neither absurd nor unreasonable – which ought to concern even liberals of Barry's stripe.

Barry's second example relates to public order. He considers the decision of an Australian court to uphold the appeal by an Aboriginal woman on grounds of indirect racial discrimination against the decision of her local housing authority to evict her. The eviction was the outcome of numerous complaints by her white neighbours about the unruliness of the large number of children and grandchildren who lived with her in a small cottage. Barry thinks that the court was wrong, and that the local housing authority was entirely within its rights to evict her on the grounds that the family was causing a disturbance as defined by local norms. He appears to think that it is of *no* relevance that these were not the standards of the Aboriginal culture to which the woman belonged. Barry interprets the court as taking 'the line that, if it was an Aboriginal custom to gather together all one's children and grandchildren, this had to be upheld *regardless of the consequences* for others living in the vicinity'.[1] Whether or not this is a correct gloss on the decision, there is another reading of it that is much more defensible. For all that needs to be claimed is that it is a legitimate consideration, with some independent deliberative weight, that the way of life complained of conformed to Aboriginal norms. In this case, it was deemed sufficient for the court to uphold the appeal, but there need be no implication that this would always be so. It is, however, just this recognition that such behaviour is part of a particular way of life that Barry seems to object to, even though of course the norms of what is accepted as a disturbance have no other basis than their roots in a different way of life. One set of local norms is enforced through the law, in a manner that may seriously threaten the social structure of the minority culture, on the grounds of the nuisance it causes to those who subscribe to those norms, while the norms of the minority culture can find expression only through a political process in which they may be doomed always to be defeated.

In short, therefore, Barry's discussion of local norms tends to ignore or erase their contested character; and he entirely neglects the possibility that some groups may be able to get their norms accepted as *the* local norms across almost all areas in which they can be legitimately enforced, thereby comprehensively and systematically disadvantaging other groups. One way in which he does this is by naïvely assuming that culture and geography coincide. Hence, he is quite willing to say that in Aboriginal communities their local norms would prevail (subject always to the overarching constraints of liberal principles). Similarly with 'gypsy encampments'. However, the world is not neatly divided in this way, as Barry well knows. Many issues of multiculturalism would simply not arise if it were not for the existence of a variety of 'local' norms jostling for recognition within the same geographical and political space. Moreover, Barry's apparent willingness to give the majority *carte blanche* over these matters is perhaps indicative of how unimportant he really thinks culture is. Otherwise he would surely be more sensitive to the less than liberal character of what he proposes.

Reflections on 'theory'

Very briefly, I need now to try to draw these comments towards a conclusion; although to speak of 'a conclusion' is perhaps rather misleading. For I have not attempted to argue directly for or against any specific policies or particular principles in relation to multiculturalism. I must stress this, because some readers may think it disingenuous, believing me to be at least implicitly defending a robust agenda of multicultural policies. What I have been arguing, however, is something rather different and more limited, but still important: this is that the kind of universalist, egalitarian liberal theory espoused by Barry fails adequately to do justice to, or in some cases even to acknowledge, the deepest concerns that are expressed through the agenda of multiculturalism. But this is *not* to say that once those concerns are acknowledged and properly understood, some form of multiculturalist policy *must* result. Indeed, it may sometimes even be thought that the 'cultural reform' of some group is the only acceptable policy in order to eliminate practices which are regarded as intolerable within a liberal society.[26] More commonly, it may be that the remedies advocated by multiculturalists give rise to insuperable practical problems or involve too high a price in compromising other values. I also take very seriously worries about social cohesion, and the fear that at least some multiculturalist policies risk a damaging fragmentation of the polity and the weakening of a sense of common citizenship. It is quite proper for Barry, and indeed anyone, to be concerned about such matters. Certainly nothing I have argued is supposed to suggest otherwise.

There are, though, two points I want to press. The first is to insist on the inadequacy of Barry's treatment of what is at stake in debates over multiculturalism. This is partly, as I have argued, a matter of the procrustean character of his theory, but it also, I suggest, has to do with the level of abstraction at which this kind of theory operates. We need a much more contextualized and nuanced approach that is sensitive and attentive to the particularity and specificity of the immensely diverse range of circumstances in which 'multicultural questions' arise.[27] One of the most discouraging features of *Culture and Equality* is the tin ear it displays when it comes to *listening* to different views. Indeed, it is evident from the very first page of the preface that Barry is largely contemptuous of cultural practices that do not conform to his prejudices about what is acceptable and of those political theorists who have tried, whether or not one agrees with them, to take seriously the consequences of multiculturalism.

The second point also concerns the limitations of political theory and, in particular, the frequent failure of liberal political theorists especially to accept that political problems may not admit of 'solutions', even in theory. For instance, it is important to acknowledge the real possibility, even when we reject for what we believe to be good reasons the public or institutional accommodation of a particular claim by a cultural group, that their motivating sense of grievance may still have legitimacy. That for whatever reasons we genuinely believe that we cannot incorporate a particular claim for differential treatment, or cannot do so adequately, does not necessarily mean that we *must* reject the validity of the complaint. Of course we may do; but there is no contradiction in not doing so. A sense of unfairness, or being hard done by, may legitimately persist in the minority, and can be accepted as justified by the rest of us, notwithstanding that we believe that we should not do all that might be necessary to eliminate the cause of that complaint. The point here is that political problems are not like puzzles that must have an answer; and certainly they are not *guaranteed* to have a solution that all parties, even if they are 'reasonable', *must* accept as fair.[28] It is a possibility all too often neglected by political theorists that we may face situations in which there are a variety of legitimate concerns that cannot be reconciled, either in theory or practice, in a way that is fair to all.

Where this is the case, the responsibility of political theorists is to acknowledge that this is so, and not to see ourselves as some sort of ersatz politicians conjuring a 'solution' through some theoretical sleight of hand;[29] real politicians, of course, may quite properly be governed by different imperatives.

The principal contention of this chapter has been that there is a depth and complexity to the concerns that underlie and inform the agenda of multiculturalism that register only fitfully and inadequately within the framework of Barry's universalist, egalitarian liberalism. Complaints are illegitimately dismissed because they have not been heard as anything more than the special pleading for favourable treatment by sectional interests. I have supported this claim through a discussion of three issues that arise in the context of Barry's own argument. In doing so I have not aimed to defend any particular theory or to recommend any set of institutions or policies. But in the closing remarks I have also tried to indicate how there is more at stake than the merits or otherwise of specific arguments in *Culture and Equality*. One of those issues at stake is what our responsibilities are when we do political theory.

Notes

I am very grateful for comments on earlier drafts of this chapter to the participants in the 'Identity, Legitimacy and Rights Conference' held at Cardiff University; to my colleagues in the 'Political and International Theory Group' at Keele; and in particular to Andrea Baumeister, Eve Garrard, Bruce Haddock and Hidemi Suganami.

1 J. Levy, *The Multiculturalism of Fear*, Oxford: Oxford University Press, 2000; J. Raz, *Ethics in the Public Domain: Essays in the Morality of Law and Politics*, Oxford: Oxford University Press, 1994, ch. 7; W. Kymlicka, *Multicultural Citizenship: A Liberal Theory of Minority Rights*, Oxford: Oxford University Press, 1995; W. Kymlicka, *Politics in the Vernacular: Nationalism, Multiculturalism, and Citizenship*, Oxford: Oxford University Press, 2001; B. Barry, *Culture and Equality: An Egalitarian Critique of Multiculturalism*, Cambridge: Polity, 2001.

2 B. Parekh, *Rethinking Multiculturalism: Cultural Diversity and Political Theory*, Basingstoke: Macmillan, 2000.

3 My comments are directed towards Barry's arguments in *Culture and Equality*. For a fuller statement of the theory that informs his discussion of multiculturalism, see B. Barry, *Justice as Impartiality*, Oxford: Oxford University Press, 1995.

4 B. Parekh, *Rethinking Multiculturalism*, p. 143.

5 Barry, *Culture and Equality*, p. 34.

6 Ibid.

7 Levy, *The Multiculturalism of Fear*, p. 131.

8 Barry, *Culture and Equality*, p. 43.

9 Ibid., pp. 35–7.

10 Ibid., p. 39.

11 Ibid., p. 46.

12 Barry does consider 'religious freedom' as a possible ground for an exemption, but argues that, as the law does not explicitly state that Sikhs are prohibited from riding motorcycles, and anyway we can choose not to ride a motorcycle, a law without an exemption is not discriminatory (ibid., p. 45). But (a) a law without an exemption does *effectively* say that Sikhs while acting in accordance with their religious beliefs cannot ride a motorcycle, and (b) we can avoid most discriminatory legislation by choosing not to do what it prohibits.

13 I cannot resist recalling one of Barry's more extraordinary claims about British society, of which he writes: 'waving union jacks and singing jingoistic songs is an activity now largely relegated to the increasingly postmodern Last Night of the Proms' (ibid., p. 83). To which the only possible response is that he really does need to get out a bit more.

14 It is sometimes suggested that in this kind of example, as in many other multicultural disputes, the issue is best framed in terms of the question: who should bear the burden of belief (for example, P. Jones, 'Bearing the Consequences of Belief', *Journal of Political Philosophy*, 2, 1994, pp.24–43)? However, it seems to me that this is already to weight matters in a particular direction. After all, is not the view that there is nothing wrong with being present when alcohol is consumed also a belief?

15 W. Kymlicka, *Liberalism, Community and Culture*, Oxford: Oxford University Press, 1989; A. E. Galeotti, *Toleration as Recognition*, Cambridge: Cambridge University Press, 2002.

16 See, for example, Barry, *Culture and Equality*, pp. 310–17.

17 Parekh, *Rethinking Multiculturalism*, p. 162.

18 Barry, *Culture and Equality*, pp. 148–9.

19 Ibid., p. 149.

20 Another reason why this may be so is because of the sharp demarcation of questions of justice in Barry's theory. But whether or not many of the disadvantages arising from cultural differences should be conceived as questions of justice (according to some controversial philosophical theory), they are certainly political concerns.

21 Barry, *Culture and Equality*, p. 253, my emphasis.

22 Ibid., p. 279, my emphasis.

23 Ibid., p. 287.

24 Ibid., p. 288.

25 Ibid., p. 290, my emphasis.

26 See A. Kernohan, *Liberalism, Equality and Cultural Oppression*, Cambridge: Cambridge University Press, 1998.

27 See J. H. Carens, *Culture, Citizenship and Community: A Contextual Exploration of Justice as Evenhandedness*, Oxford: Oxford University Press, 2000.

28 I have argued this more fully elsewhere with respect to John Rawls's account of public reason in J. Horton, 'Rawls, Public Reason and the Limits of Liberal Justification', *Contemporary Political Theory*, 2, 2003, pp. 5–23.

29 For an example of what I mean, see S. O'Neill, 'Liberty, Equality and the Rights of Cultures: The Marching Controversy at Drumcree', *The British Journal of Politics and International Relations*, 2, 2000, pp. 26–45.

4 What is so different about difference?

Andrew Vincent

One feature of recent political theory has been a gradual but marked drift away from universalist forms of argument towards favouring communities, cultures and groups. Such groups or cultures are often seen to be the ground-work for human identity. It is no surprise in this context that the notion of universal characteristics to human nature, universal human needs, values or rights, has been viewed with increasing scepticism from certain quarters. In this scenario, the idea that the task of political theory is to seek out universal grounds or foundations for social and political judgements is temporarily in abeyance. For the moment, at least, for many theorists, the only good universal is a dead one. This chapter focuses on one facet of this broader critical move-ment, namely difference theory. The theorists I have in mind here are those such as Iris Marion Young, Anne Phillips, Bonnie Honig, William Connolly, Judith Butler and, to some extent, Chantal Mouffe and James Tully. The chapter briefly contextualizes the debate over difference, provides a quick sketch of the philosophical components of difference arguments, and then turns to four major criticisms of difference arguments. It concludes that differ-ence theory is a flawed form of thought committed to an overly 'ideal' notion of justice and that most of its preoccupations are already adequately accounted for within existing institutional arrangements.

The context of difference

Difference theory has only arisen as a self-conscious idea within the last few decades. Socially and politically it has often appeared under the rubric of multicultural and identitarian debate. However, its relation with multicultur-alism still remains unclear. Some have seen it as a radical option within multiculturalism; for others it is simply a synonym for multiculturalism; others, again, use it as a synonym for the more capacious concept of pluralism. In my own reading, the roots of difference are more directly related (than multicul-turalism) to movements in social and political theory. In other words, 'difference' has a more immediate theoretical or philosophical patina than multiculturalism. Multiculturalism, on the other hand, has had a more direct relation to political practice and policy making.[1]

However, all the public debates about difference, pluralism and multiculturalism are comparatively recent. The idea of multiculturalism has made increasing inroads over the last three decades. It made its first hesitant appearance in Australia, New Zealand and Canada during the 1970s, particularly with changes in immigration laws. It is not surprising in this context that much of the initial theorizing about the idea arose particularly from Canadian and Australian academics.[2] It then appeared in the early 1980s as a significant and often tense oppositional issue within United States politics. Although often discussed in the context of North American liberalism and communitarianism, it has also figured as a critical component within feminist, ethnic, postmodern and postcolonial political theories. Nathan Glazer, for example, thinks that multiculturalism is, characteristically, a North American concept (linked to a strong rights-based tradition with deep immigrant and racial divisions in society) and consequently has no real connection with European politics.[3] Multiculturalism did, however, begin to make a critical appearance in European debate after 1989, though whether this is the same idea as appears in North America or Australia is a contentious point. Nevertheless, some still see the lifetime of *effectual* multicultural politics as comparatively short. For Glazer, it is a product (largely in educational circles) of the last twenty years. For Kymlicka, it has only been effectively present since the 1990s.[4] Debate over difference arguments have largely followed in the wake of multiculturalism.

Why the interest in multiculturalism and difference? Briefly, the 1990s particularly saw the end of the cold war, the opening up of markets and societies, considerable growth of international population movement, acceleration of trade, communication and capital flows across the globe, coupled with the rediscovery of older idiosyncratic nationality, ethnic and religious affiliations. The fortuitous combination of globalizing forces and the mixing of populations, together with the renewed interest in ethnicity and culture, has underpinned a more general, if diffuse, interest in culture, identity and the like. Yet, one important point to mention here is that it is far from clear that multiculturalism and difference are consistent or coherent phenomena. Whether the recent European experience has anything to learn from or to teach North American, New Zealand or Australian forms remains unclear and unresolved. In each case, multiculturalism and difference appear to be contextual responses to events.[5] As Homi Bhabha remarked on multiculturalism (and the same could apply to difference), it is a 'portmanteau term for anything from minority discourse to postcolonial critique'.[6]

One problem is that each term – difference, polyethnicity, multicultural, and the like – has become a rallying point for heated debate. Usually, more heat than light is generated by such debate, since there is little clarity as to the precise reference or meaning of the terms involved. It is important, in this context, to get some handle on this internal conceptual complexity of difference-based claims.

A sketch of difference

First, as indicated, the idea of difference has cognate links with other concepts, for example pluralism and multiculturalism. One common way to navigate these disparate categories is to limit pluralism to forms of liberalism, and focus difference on radical multiculturalism. However, this misses the point that pluralism is a much richer and more varied concept in twentieth-century thought. There is *no* necessary conceptual link between pluralism and liberalism, any more than there are necessary conceptual ties between pluralism and relativism, or difference and multiculturalism. In my own usage, pluralism is taken as the key background, if multi-dimensional, concept. In this sense, there can be liberal pluralism, multicultural pluralism and difference-based pluralism.

However, an additional difficulty here is that each of these concepts carries its own idiosyncratic baggage. In the case of pluralism, for example, when mentioned in political settings, this still prima facie conjures up visions of mass ranks of bright-eyed and bushy-tailed, usually North American, political scientists ready to do battle over pressure or interest groups – just before they lurch into bed with rational choice in the late 1980s. If one mentioned pluralism to most political theorists before the 1990s, they would probably have looked slightly blank, or mentioned, tentatively, Isaiah Berlin, or sophisticated US pluralists such as Robert Dahl or, if they were longer in the tooth, English pluralists such as John Neville Figgis. To philosophers of ethics and epistemology, pluralism conjures up debates over moral or conceptual relativism, or again, if they were longer in the tooth, it would raise the spectre of philosophical pragmatism, *qua* John Dewey or William James.

This present discussion distinguishes, briefly, metaphysical, socio-cultural, political and ethical dimensions of pluralism. In the final analysis, there are overlaps between all of these categories. Thus, the distinctions drawn here are simply pedagogical devices to focus discussion. Metaphysical pluralism refers to long-standing philosophical traditions concerned with multiple worlds, realities and truths.[7] This implies that both our 'being in the world' and our 'knowledge of it' are irremediably fragmented. In my reading, this implicitly or explicitly underpins most serious pluralist arguments, of any form. Socio-cultural pluralism implies that humans are subject to diverse social and cultural conditions and that there are many types and forms of such conditions. This thesis raises the spectre of differentiated and fragmented human identities. Political pluralism focuses on the institutional recognition, accommodation or representation of social or cultural differences. This political recognition moves along a broad spectrum from 'political indifference' to 'positive representation and cultivation'. Ethical pluralism is concerned with a diversity of ethical codes, rules, goals and ends. It embodies the thesis that there are many different (often incommensurable) goods required for human flourishing. Moral values are therefore both plural and internally complex. Difference theory, in my reading, figures within this broad pluralist structure. It can range, in fact, across the whole spectrum.[8] However, in the literature, difference is commonly associated with more radical or extreme variants of pluralism.

The discussion turns now to a quick sketch of (what I take to be) the theoretical structures underpinning the difference concept. Part of the problem of getting a handle on the difference idea is its excessively messy genealogy. First, a number of current difference theorists come from both a transformed feminist difference background and a disillusioned Marxist diaspora, originating in the 1970s.[9] Second, postmodern and poststructural arguments have also had a profound effect on difference arguments, often blending in writers, such as Judith Butler or Iris Marion Young, with the earlier feminist difference argument. In the context of postmodern theory, Nietzsche's 'perspectivism', Derrida's critique of the 'metaphysics of presence', Michel Foucault's exploration of the genealogy of the self, and Jean-François Lyotard's analysis of the *differend* are all of considerable background importance for understanding the play of much recent difference argument. Thus, characteristically, theoretical reduction to any unity of substance is seen to *repress* difference.[10] Third, democratic theory has been given close attention in difference theory, particularly in theorists such as Iris Marion Young, William Connolly, Anne Phillips and Chantal Mouffe.[11] Democracy – usually more recent deliberative and communicative forms – is seen to both disclose and accommodate difference more easily than any other type of political regime. Fourth, post-Wittgensteinian linguistic philosophy, which stresses the multiplicity of 'language games' and 'forms of life', is also manifest in some difference arguments, particularly in the writings of Lyotard, Rorty and Tully.[12] Fifth, older movements, such as expressivist romantic nationalism – where authenticity and uniqueness are tied to diverse cultures – also forms an underlying valorization for different cultures. It should be emphasized, however, that one should not expect much coherence amongst these perspectives.[13] Current difference theory is the outcome of a random, fortuitous and contingent combination of theories.

In order to gain some purchase on the difference standpoint, it is important to identify its underlying assumptions. First, difference is clearly not about eccentricity or individuality (unless one adopted a catholic view of individuality). There is an underlying philosophical thesis here. This can initially be expressed negatively, namely the philosophical figure to which difference is opposed is an aggregate composed of universalism, impartiality, neutrality, cosmopolitanism, foundationalism, logocentrism and monism. To keep matters simpler, the core negative figure (for difference argument) is taken to be 'monism'. Monism implies, very roughly, the belief that there is one foundational, objective and exclusive truth which explains or accounts for the diversity of human experiences and existence. There have been many such 'one things': God, nature, reason, natural science or the philosophical absolute. Each provides the world with unifying thematic identity. Ultimately, in the final analysis, monism contends that there are not many separate things in the world; rather, there is one thing which is explanatory of all the separate things. Difference theory, at root, objects to this monistic perspective.

The reason for this objection – which is the second key theme of difference – is that there are no transcendental, objective truths, sanctions, rules or norms in the world, which could incorporate all the separate things. Separate things remain separate. The multiplicity remains multiple. It follows, therefore, thirdly, that there are no neutral or impartial ways of thinking about the world. Every piece of thinking or valuing is done from within a perspective, or from within one of those separate things. There is no interpretation which stands outside the world. Human activity is always tied to a particular position or perspective and reflects the substance of that perspective. There are therefore multiple possible realities and multiple possible group identities for human beings.

Fourth, moving outside metaphysics and epistemology, recent difference accounts locate the actual multiple things and perspectives with groups, not human individuals. There are ambiguities on this point, since difference is a form of pluralism and liberal pluralism has, characteristically, focused on human individuals. However, recent difference theory does not converge on human individuality; conversely, it focuses on groups (marginalized or otherwise). In fact, paradoxically, liberal individuality is frequently theorized by difference accounts as yet another underlying manifestation of monism. Therefore, the 'publics' of most societies – and most difference accounts focus on urban, (post-)industrialized publics – are considered heterogeneous in *group* terms.[14] Groups are thus the key 'particles' from which the multiple knowledges and values emanate. Homogeneity, in this reading, becomes an epistemological and ontological horror for difference accounts. All forms of unifying identity are considered as philosophically suspect. Groups also have no essence or identity (this point is important and will be returned to). Essentialism of any type is vilified. Finally, it follows from the above that unifying monistic notions – such as the common good, general interest, equal legal citizenship and rights, impartial or neutral reason, universal justice – are all, by definition, suspect conceptual entities for difference theory.

Criticism of difference

Having briefly identified the concept and outlined the key philosophical assumptions of difference, the discussion now turns to four critical arguments. The first argument contends that difference theory is not actually different to long-standing metaphysical issues in philosophy concerned with the 'one and many'. The second argument addresses an ambiguity concerned with (what I call) the 'particles of difference', suggesting, in effect, that there are many such particles which do not cohere within the overall difference perspective. The third argument concerns whether difference does actually exist in practice, in the manner that it is deployed in recent difference-based argument.[15] The final argument focuses on an oddity in the logic of difference claims, which has unexpected political implications. In sum, these arguments try to show that difference is not really very different at all to what we are already quite familiar with, and that difference, in itself, gives a very one-sided 'idealized' picture of politics.

Philosophical difference

There is a suggestion within difference theory that difference itself is something that has become a significant problem since the late twentieth century, particularly with the rise of cultural politics, multicultural polities, and the like. However, philosophically pluralistic difference is not a new phenomenon at all. In fact, it is an aspect of a very old problem.

My suggestion would be that all the arguments on difference rest on certain spoken or unspoken philosophical assumptions. Difference has already been taken as objecting, at a fundamental philosophical level, to monism. The monistic 'one' may be taken as a metaphysical premise or a necessary transcendental condition of thinking about the world. Whichever way monism is presented, it has been objected to by certain schools of philosophy. Difference, at root, is yet another manifestation of a much older debate about the 'one and the many' which goes back to Parmenides' invocation of the indivisible Oneness of Being, as against, say, the atomism of Empedocles or Democratus. There are many examples of this; however, if one also looks at, say, Leibniz's monadology – which was notably contrasted to Spinoza's metaphysical monism – a basically very familiar logic appears.

The monad for Leibniz is a 'simple substance … that is to say, without parts.' These monads 'have no windows through which anything can enter or depart.' Leibniz continues: 'It is necessary … that each monad be different from every other. For there are never in nature two beings which are exactly alike and in which it is not possible to find an internal difference.'[16] Monads therefore only relate to each other externally within a plenum of different monads. Leibniz, of course, could not accept the full fragmentation implicit in this approach. In effect, the monads are conceived as souls which, through sufficient reason and God's good will, are all linked together in a monadic hierarchy. However, if you extract God and sufficient reason from the argument, and envisage monads as 'cultural groups', then the argument becomes recognizably more modern. It would not, in this sense, be too far-fetched to say that difference theory is our modern monadology – without God, but with cultures. The 'bridging' role of God and sufficient reason can potentially be covered by communicative or deliberative democracy.

An early twentieth-century example of roughly the same debate would be the conflict between pragmatism and idealism (which directly parallels debates about political pluralism and state-based monism in the same period).[17] As William James put it, in 1909, with his usual waspish turn of phrase,

> philosophers [such as Hegel or Bosanquet] have always aimed at cleaning up the litter with which the world is apparently filled. … As compared with all these rationalizing pictures, the pluralistic empiricism which I

profess offers but a sorry appearance. It is a turbid, muddled, gothic sort of affair, without a sweeping outline and with little pictorial nobility.[18]

Other examples of the same anti-monistic thrust would be Nietzschean 'perspectivism', Nelson Goodman's 'world-making' thesis, Wittgenstein's language games or Richard Rorty's anti-representationalism. Characteristically, the later expression of this argument is often (though not always) connected with a rejection of, or scepticism about, the monistic potential of Enlightenment reason – although this is frequently a cardboard cut-out Enlightenment.[19] This old debate of 'the one and many' could be illustrated more richly; however, suffice it to say that in epistemological terms, difference largely accepts the thesis of disaggregated pluralism and perspectivism, and it should be obvious, in this context, that philosophically there is nothing novel about it. It is the rearticulation of a very old philosophical problem.

One can, of course, detect newer strands to modern difference, namely poststructuralism and postmodernism. There is indeed a very close correlation between postmodernism and certain difference accounts – although one should not immediately jump to the conclusion that all difference is postmodern difference. Yet it would also be true that postmodern theory chimes harmoniously – a nice metaphor for difference and postmodernism – with the theory of multiple realities and heterogeneous publics. For William Connolly, for example, a postmodern position embraces strong difference which, he argues, we should celebrate.[20] Where contemporary liberals try to shield society from strong differences, Connolly wants a future society to embrace them. Where communitarians offer a harmony of communal pre-understandings, he wants real differences exposed to the full. For Connolly, any 'rhetoric of harmonization must be ambiguated and coarsened by those who have not had its faith breathed into their souls, particularly those moved by nontheistic reverence for the rich ambiguity of existence'.[21] Again, it should be noted that this is not a terribly novel idea. In this case, it is yet another Nietzschean statement within a much older metaphysical debate.[22]

Before moving on from this point, let me try to give the difference perspective a slightly more secure (if contentious) philosophical home. Difference equates with a philosophical permutation which sees shifting particulars as the only real things in the world. Universals have no reality or existence, beyond possibly linguistic predicates or simple mental conveniences.[23] This does not mean that over time, through careful induction from many examples of particulars, one cannot make some rough approximations as to what appears to be more general about properties or objects in the world. Yet, it would still only be an approximation which would always be subject to revision. Particulars are the basis of reality. The most forceful statement of this position has been associated with various forms of nominalist philosophy. In this context, only singular or particular objects or properties exist, universals are fictions. Universals may exist at one level, minimally, and somewhat mysteriously, in the human mind. But they must be regarded as psychological props. No universal, as such, has any substantive reality. No one object or property is alike. Each particular is literally unique, unrepeatable, idiosyncratic, individual and therefore different.

Thus, if a philosophical name were to be associated with difference theory, then it would be an implicit form of philosophical nominalism. This nominalism implies that the particular is always contrasted to the universal – the universal denoting ubiquitous, pervasive, common, applying to all cases or comprehensive. Difference-based theory therefore focuses on the particular, as distinct from the universal. Further, when the particular is emphasized, it not only refers to a single thing but also implies, by default, one amongst multiple things. Since there are no adequate universals, therefore, there must be a plethora of different particulars. Thus, particularity, of necessity, implies an untidy or messy plurality of differing particulars.

In summary, from this nominalist perspective, difference denotes a nominalist multiplicity of particular things and a denial of universals. Each constituent of the multiple is one amongst many particulars, each is something wholly different, and is potentially more real, immediate and familiar. From this philosophical nominalist perspective, therefore, difference implies that the reality of both morality and politics can *only* be found within the diversity of group particulars. Universals, such as abstract reason, universal justice, cosmopolitan ethics or human rights, do not really exist, except as mental props and fictions for the weak-minded. The universal is, in fact, envisaged as a distortion or imaginary unity imposed upon the complex difference of the world. The emphasis consequently falls upon a series of terms which express this difference – alterity, dissonance, *différance* or *le différend*. However, again, it is worth underscoring the point that this is a rearticulation of a very old philosophical point.

Particles of difference

The second argument on difference can be stated fairly simply. In present difference theory there is *no* settled sense of exactly *what* particle is to be taken as different. In fact, there is often deep conflict between these particles, within difference-based arguments. For example, race, gender, beliefs, language, language games, culture, age, race, class, nation and ethnicity have all been singled out as key 'particles of difference'. Consequently, the concept of what is different is internally incoherent.

Widening the net of plurality and difference, consider human individuals. Prima facie, each human individual is quite different and unique. Individuality – practically and etymologically – implies uniqueness and difference. In fact, this is one key reading of a liberal sense of difference. As Berlin stated,

> if, as I believe, the ends of [individual] men are many, and not all of them are in principle compatible with each other, then the possibility of conflict

– and of tragedy – can never wholly be eliminated from human life, either personal or social.[24]

Society is punctuated by numerous opposing values which cannot be amicably combined in an individual life or society. There are therefore no uniquely right solutions. As Berlin put it, 'forms of life differ. Ends, moral principles, are many.'[25] No ultimate commensurability is possible. This conception of liberal value pluralism thus emphasizes the tragic difference and contingency of values and beliefs. The *particles* of difference are thus individuals and their incommensurable value beliefs.

However, the above 'differences' do not appear 'real' to some more radical difference theorists. A typical example of this contention is the argument that reducing the plurality of moral subjects to one notion of human individuality is an invocation of sameness.[26] Thus, reduction to human individuality is seen to repress difference. William Connolly, for example, argues that individualism actually crushes real difference. He contends that liberal individualism 'insinuates a dense set of standards, conventions, and expectations into the identity of the self'. Liberal individualism, in effect, evades real difference.[27] Connolly suggests that such individualism is 'not merely a benign perspective that does not go far enough. It is an anachronism.' A 'mere *ethic* of individuality evades an encounter with the Foucauldian world of discipline and normalization'.[28] Writers such as Iris Marion Young, Judith Butler and Connolly thus suggest that emancipation can only take place through recognition and respect for real difference. What is really different here remains slightly more obscure; however, it appears to be linked to some notion of group and/or cultural difference.

Bonnie Honig adds another dimension to the above perspective. She emphasizes the point that difference exists within all identity. Each human being thus becomes a psychological multiplicity. She rather awkwardly calls this 'agentic fragmentation'. Difference, in this sense, is much deeper than even many difference proponents suggest. Young and James Tully, for example, do not appear to take this step. Honig, however, is insistent that difference is not just another word for normative or political pluralism. Difference is not an adjective of identity; it is about the *substance* of all identity. For Honig, making difference an adjective makes it safe. She is thus deeply critical of the liberal pluralism of Berlin, Stuart Hampshire and Bernard Williams which, she argues, does not take real difference with full seriousness. She complains, for example, that Bernard Williams tries to 'relocate' the dilemma of difference 'from the inside of subjectivity to its outside'.[29] From Young's, Connolly's, Honig's or even Tully's perspectives, the liberal perspective (including individual right claims) denies real difference and, in consequence, is oppressive and 'difference-blind'.

In meeting the claim to acknowledge real difference, some theorists (although *not* Connolly, Honig, Tully or Young) who consider that the really different particles are groups or cultures have therefore moved to issues of groups rights. However, individual rights exponents have responded, with equal justification, that granting groups or cultures rights can be as oppressive to the 'real' idiosyncratic differences of human individuals. Difference theory (*qua* groups and cultures) can therefore also be accused (from a liberal difference standpoint) of being equally 'difference-blind' from the perspective of different individuals. For example, gay, gendered, ethnic or aboriginal groups can all be deeply oppressive in not recognizing the genuine real differences between human individuals.

If we widened the theoretical net further, then 'real difference' for communitarians and nationalists is distinct again.[30] Difference can work, for example, at the level of both national cultures and cultural communities. However, nationalists and communitarians often take a very dim view of other (often more radical) difference-based views. For David Miller, for example, Iris Marion Young presents an 'unacceptable' face of difference, although she is clearly not offering the most radical version of difference.[31] Primarily, for Miller, the stronger difference thesis relies upon a false contrast between the 'allegedly authentic group identities' and an 'artificially imposed common national identity'.[32] Miller also points out that group identities of any type can be wholly artificial. Micro-group identity (*qua*, say, multiculturalism) is not necessarily more real than anything else. Second, for Miller, stronger difference-based accounts fail to recognize that secure national identity is the foundation to all micro-identity. Micro-groups are therefore vulnerable without the nation. In addition, many of the significant injustices suffered by individuals take place *within* the confines of the group. This is the same argument that Will Kymlicka directs at radical difference theory. Thus, although strong difference theories focus on injustices against groups, they do not show how these are to be resolved without some core national unity and communal sense of what justice and fairness requires in the whole society. For Miller, there is a need for some overarching (if still particular) unity. In sum, for nationalism, the really significantly different 'particle' is the nation. Nations are significantly different, but *not* cultures within nations.

It is worth briefly noting here that Miller also contrasts the importance of real national difference to Kymlicka's milder group-based difference account, which allots differential rights to groups (for the sake of individual autonomy). Miller considers that group difference is important, but only to a certain degree, since the prior national difference is the *key* particle, not the micro-group. Consequently, Miller advocates freedoms and opportunities being allotted to minorities by the nation-state, rather than Kymlicka's idea of recognized special rights. For Miller, the demand for group rights is really, in essence, a demand for equal treatment and equal citizenship within the nation. Nationality, *per se*, tends to favour equal citizenship, rather than group fragmentation. Nationality, for Miller, in the final analysis, should not be imposed on groups, but neither should it evaporate into groups.[33]

However, Kymlicka, in response, sees Miller's critique as yet another version of J. S. Mill's position. He comments,

Just as Mill thought that 'united public opinion' necessary for the working of liberal institutions is impossible without a common language and national identity, so Miller thinks that the 'common purpose' necessary for socialist institutions is only possible in a nation state.

Miller therefore assumes that assimilation is viable and possible for a nation state. Kymlicka, however, is not clear that this will work: 'If peoples' bonds to their own language and culture are sufficiently deep, then attempting to suppress the cultural identity and self-government of national minorities may simply aggravate the level of alienation and division.'[34] Kymlicka's own 'particle of difference' refers to a limited range of sub-national immigrant and indigenous groups – largely territorially rooted minorities, each with an 'essential culture'.

The nub of the above discussion is therefore that the 'particles of difference' are heterogeneous. Real difference could refer to individuals, beliefs, values, gender, sexual orientation, ethnicity, class, group identification, group culture, community or nationality. All of these difference particles have been claimed as 'real differences' (and indeed all can be further subdivided). All engage in mutual vilification of the others as false, unreal or insignificant differences. Thus, feminist difference claims that gender is the key difference, often accusing other theories of being 'blind to real sexual difference'. Equally, certain black writers have accused white feminists (amongst many others) of being 'blind to real racial difference'. Postmodern writers see the bulk of normative theory as being blind to real differences built into all identity. Liberal writers have accused postmodernist and some multiculturalists of being blind to the real differences of individuals and the oppressive nature of cultures and groups.

Thus, there is *no* agreement on the actual significant 'particle of difference'. It is clear, therefore, that 'difference' is used in quite different ways and with different understandings of what actually is different. One consequence of this is that what appears to be different to one will often appear as stultifying sameness to another. My own reading is that this is, again, a replay of a very old political problem. The problem of fragmentation and diversity has been a perennial political issue from the time of the Greek *polis* or Roman empire. It is part of the very *meaning of politics*. Differences between religions, nations, ethnicities, groups, cultures, individuals or associations could hardly be said to be anything new. These have always been the bread and butter of states, empires and federations, of many and various types. The concepts of the state and sovereignty, in fact, arose from this very problem of how to deal with difference. Possibly, we might now be marginally more aware of difference, simply due to increases in information and the intensification of population movements. But the problem is as old as the self-consciousness of politics.

Anti-essentialism and difference

A third critical argument is more damaging for difference theory, and this focuses on the problem of the 'nature of difference'. It is often assumed that for much recent difference theory, groups (and group cultures) are the significantly different particles, and that what makes them significant is that they embody substantive identities which need to be recognized. This is a position that has been an important aspect of group-based argument and is certainly present in writers such as Kymlicka and Joseph Raz.[35]

However, the central problem of this argument is a point that has already been touched upon in theorists such as Young, Honig and Connolly, namely that difference theory is *not* always necessarily premised on a substantive identity. No group culture is separate and wholly discrete. Although often criticized for identitarian assumptions, Young, for example, is very insistent that group difference should not be essentialized. Her most recent book, *Inclusion and Democracy* (2002), thus completely dissociates the 'politics of difference' from 'identity politics'. In fairness, unlike Kymlicka, Young has never committed herself to substantive ethnic or national ideas. Difference theory, as she argues in an earlier book,

> does not posit a social group as having an essential nature composed of a set of attributes defining only that group. Rather, a social group exists and is defined as a specific group only in social and interactive relation to others.[36]

Young's own version is what she calls 'relational difference'. This is concerned with 'intersecting voices'. It repudiates the idea that difference has to be concerned with otherness or essentialism. Relational difference indicates that people can be 'together in difference'. Young indeed posits her own version of democracy – communicative democracy – to deal with this phenomenon. Difference therefore embraces both heterogeneity and interdependence. Young contrasts this perspective with visions of either assimilation or separation. She associates assimilation with both liberalism and communism and separation with communitarianism and nationalism, which freeze separate identities. Tully has similar views to Young here. He also criticizes Kymlicka, for example, as tending to falsely essentialize cultures. For Tully there are, characteristically, no 'internally homogeneous' cultures. Each culture is continually 'contested, imagined and re-imagined, transformed and negotiated. ... The identity, and so the meaning, of any culture is thus aspectival.'[37] He therefore suggests that societies should be considered as *intercultural* rather than *multicultural*.

Yet there is a major problem with this form of argument. Primarily, Young's group argument is premised on a background distinction between what she calls voluntary and involuntary groups. Voluntary groups exist where agents come together intentionally for a purpose. These are of no interest to her. It is involuntary 'affinity' groups which are crucial. What constitutes involuntary 'groupness' is a 'social process of interaction' whereby people come to have an affinity for one another. Affinity means sharing assumptions and possessing an affective sense of bonding. Membership is not about satisfying some objective criteria or purpose, but rather a subjective affirmation of affinity. For Young, the involuntary group therefore implies a 'particular sense of history', 'an understanding of social relations' and a common sense of oppression. An involuntary group, however, has the character of what Young calls 'thrownness'. One finds oneself in such a group.[38]

There is something odd here in Young's anti-essentialism and relational overlapping emphasis, particularly when combined with her idea of involuntary 'thrownness'. It does sound very much like a veiled essentialism and identity thesis, namely claiming all the advantages of groups, without their disadvantages. However, even if one acknowledged, at an ontological level, that groups are not essentialized or linked to identity politics, nonetheless, at the political level (in practice) such groups usually are essentialized. This is what '*makes the policy case*' in any political forum.[39] Thus, practice rather than theory determines essences. In addition, if something is relational (or intercultural, as Tully puts it), how would one *know* cognitively what a group or culture is or was, or what was worth maintaining or jettisoning? Further, how would one differentiate between cultures or relational groups in the first place? The indigenous or aboriginal would overflow and overlap with all other cultural or group forms. Cultures and groups would become one amorphous indistinguishable lump.

There is one important response to this critique within difference theory which is worth noting, partly because it creates even more problems. In responding to the above type of criticism, Young makes an interesting argumentative move. She argues that her view of relational groups and difference is not 'her theory', which needs a philosophical justification (which, she suggests, is how many of her critics represent her work). She continues, 'For me, politics does not "flow from" the philosopher's pen.' Politics is rather 'given, and the philosopher can use her blunt tools to try to contribute to a more just outcome of its movements and conflicts'. Theory therefore reflects 'from within the political debates on a particular socio-historical context'.[40] She thus uses a critical theory and hermeneutic perspective to side-step the essentialist and identity-based critique. Her critics are accused of not acknowledging a distinction 'between the point of view of experience and the point of view of theory'. She contends that

> [i]ndividual people come into a world where social groups are a given, and people treat one another partly on the basis of imputed group membership. Because so much about political conflict and social inequality turns on these relational group experiences, I have argued that political theory and public policy must take account of and respond to such experiences rather than try to ignore, level, suppress, or transcend them. For political

theory to do that, however, it cannot take groups as ontologically given but rather requires a social theory of their nature and constitution.[41]

This argument parallels a similar distinction made in the work of Anne Phillips, who, although equally critical of essentialism and identity in groups, also draws a distinction between 'presence' and 'ideational abstraction'. She notes 'that difference has been perceived in an overly cerebral fashion as difference in opinions and beliefs'. She continues that

> what I will call the politics of ideas has proved inadequate to the problems of political exclusion. The diversity most liberals have in mind is a diversity of beliefs ... all of which may stem from a variety of experience, but are considered as in principle detachable from this.

Even the notion of 'interest' has a semi-detached character. Issues of intellectual diversity are distinct from 'political presence'. Presence appears to refer to actual real-world experiences, not ideational abstractions. She notes that 'when the politics of ideas is taken in isolation from ... the politics of presence, it does not deal adequately with the experiences of those social groups who by virtue of their race or ethnicity or religion or gender have felt themselves excluded'.[42] I interpret Phillips's 'presence' claim as parallel to Young's 'point of view of experience' claim (outlined above).

The difficulty here is that, first, the simple acknowledgement of a difference, on a descriptive, anthropological or sociological level (*qua* 'presence' or the 'point of view of experience'), contains *no* necessary normative implications. Something else – a value component – does have to enter the descriptive argument for us to show why observed differences are significant. Second, there is something deceptive in the move which slips out of a tight argumentative corner – namely trying to give a coherent account of non-essential relational groups without essentializing them – by suggesting that what one is really talking about is what *actually* exists (*qua* 'presence' or 'point of view of experience'), *not* some body of ideas or abstract theory which needs to be justified. This deceptive move is surely a classic logical problem, namely *petitio principi*, that is, assuming as true those first principles that one is going about to actually prove. Thus, 'presence' is assumed to be true in order to show the existence of 'presence'. Further, there is surely also a reflexive conundrum here: is the distinction between 'ideas' and 'presence', or 'abstract justificatory theory' and 'the point of view of experience', an ideational abstract distinction or a 'real presence' that is just part of everyday experience?

In summary, the debate about essentialism and the identity of groups within difference theory remains completely unresolved. It would appear that both aspects – identity and non-identity, essentialism and non-essentialism, identity and difference – are required to make the case. Thus, the formulation of difference argument, in writers such as Young, rests on a basic contradiction.

Logically different

Moving now to the last critical argument on difference theory: there may be a case for reconciling identity and difference. However, the question arises: does such a possible reconciliation underpin a difference position?

Much of the case that is made for (or against) difference theory is reliant upon an underlying distinction between identity and difference. Thus, to advocate difference is to deny the claims of a unifying identity or consensus. However, there is a possible dialectical resolution to this argument, which relies upon a distinction between two types of contradiction – *analytical* and *process*. An *analytical* contradiction acknowledges the centrality of the law of the excluded middle, that is, either identity or difference. It implies that the two concepts have different properties. On the other hand, a *process* contradiction acknowledges that there may be an *analytical* contradiction (and this implies that it is false for identity and difference to both be true), but it also implies that both are true. It all depends upon particular frames of reference or conceptual schemata. Thus, whereas analytical contradiction focuses on prima facie external differences, process contradiction allows us to see the internal movement of a concept through various frames of reference or conceptual schemata. Where 'analytical understanding' thrives on fixed contradictions and treats them as absolute questions of truth and falsity, 'process understanding' acknowledges contradictions, but sees them as characterizing different frames of reference, or different modes of experience. Process contradiction therefore suggests that whatever concept exists concretely necessarily contains its opposite. Concepts contain both the unity of identity and difference and the difference of identity and difference.[43] Both are neither completely true, nor completely false; rather they are incomplete. As Habermas states quite neatly, 'Repulsion towards the One and veneration of difference and the Other obscures the dialectical connection between them.'[44] In other words, in my reading, identity and difference are the moving principles of thought.[45] Thought *is* the process that moves via differentiation and then reintegration.

In one sense, some of the difference theorists – under the rubric of 'relational difference' – have tried to cash out something like this dialectical logic. Young's 'together in difference' thesis (outlined earlier) is an example. A resonant line of argument can also be seen in Honig's discussion of identity. Thus, with regard to the identity/difference conundrum, it is 'both and'; in short, every identity contains difference. However, a question arises here: does this dialectical resolution necessarily support a difference perspective?

In my reading, what really hampers the difference perspective is, in fact, its over-emphasis on difference, at the expense of identity. Difference suggests that one must arrange that for every difference (whatever that contested 'difference particle' may be) which seriously affects any person's or groups' function or well-being, there ought therefore to be a different external set of arrangements, or rules, such as to listen to, accommodate or respond to that difference. However, if any state really felt impelled to respond to every differ-ence, theoretically and practically, there would literally be no end in sight. It would be a *reductio ad absurdum* of difference. Full difference logic (in the way it has been deployed) has *no* internal way of constraining difference, since differ-ence is its *modus operandi*. This is another way of expressing the logical dilemma of nominalism which, I have contended, is at the heart of much contemporary difference theory. Thus, a new rule or set of arrangements will have to exist for every difference in individuals, groups or cultures. The social, political and legal structures proposed here would entail an unwieldy conglomeration of reservations and distinctions, such that the character of any general rule would vanish into an infinity of particular differences.

In summary, difference theory, in suggesting that each function, culture, group or valued particular should be registered and accommodated, is committed to as ridiculous a logic as some liberal universalist arguments, which try to accommodate every particular to one conception of the universal. Neither doctrine exists really for humanity in practice. Consequently, either one acknowledges full difference, which creates an unwieldy and ridiculous conception of a polity, which undermines, in turn, primary justice and rights, or one denies difference by emphasizing the universality of some rule or perspective which, in effect, destroys any case for difference.

A resolution to this problem is to suggest that we actually live with the solu-tion already, but possibly we need a gentle reminder. On a very rough-and-ready level, the idea of the state is and always has been an identity in difference (in more or much less effective forms). With changes in the char-acter of difference and perceptions of identity, what we see, over time, is the *process* of the concrete character of the state – which raises many surficial external analytical contradictions. However, the state identity is (and always has been) an internally complex structure of difference. The 'process of the state concept' here would be a form of internally structured, but continuous, 'operative criticism'. Operative criticism of institutions allows apparent differ-ences to flourish.[46]

Conclusion

In conclusion, some may consider this as an 'idealized' view of the state and politics. On the contrary, the view propounded here is quite ordinary and mundane. The motto – characterizing this view of the state as the concrete manifestation of identity in difference – would be 'sufficient unto the day is the means thereof'. It suggests a rough-and-ready conception of justice and polit-ical life which embodies a grasp of the historical changeableness, impermanence, group difference, imperfection and internal complexity of human existence, but coupled with the realization that basic rules are needed for any human life to flourish and mature. Rules, through operative criticism, are continuously reviewed and amended for the sake of this basic justice and ethical development. There is, though, nothing immutable about such rules.

However, to abandon an identity-in-difference conception of the state and to try to address every difference or plural belief, or to suggest, alternatively, that there is one timeless ahistorical universal rule or moral belief which is appropriate for all human existence, that is something wholly different again. Both the latter claims invoke an 'ideal justice' (as distinct from a basic rough-and-ready justice) which is maybe only for god(s) to use. It is an ideal justice which difference theorists (and many of their liberal critics) broach and that requires an omniscience and infinite patience which we all know that neither faction actually possesses.

Notes

1   Multiculturalism is fairly well-established term in public debate in many countries; however, the idea of difference theory would make little sense outside of certain academic circles. For a fuller discussion of multiculturalism and cognate concepts, see A. Vincent, *Nationalism and Particularity*, Cambridge: Cambridge University Press, 2002.

2   Nathan Glazer noticed, in researching his book *We Are All Multiculturalists Now* (Cambridge, Mass.: Harvard University Press, 1997) that in Harvard University Library every item containing the word 'multiculturalism' in the 1970s and 1980s originated either in either Australia or Canada. See also D. Bennett's introduction to his edited collection, *Multicultural State: Rethinking Difference and Identity*, London: Routledge, 1998, pp. 1ff.

3   N. Glazer, 'What Can Europe Learn from North America?', in C. Joppke and S. Lukes, eds, *Multicultural Questions*, Oxford: Oxford University Press, 1999, pp. 183–4.

4   He does, however, see certain specific waves of argument affecting the debates. See W. Kymlicka, 'Liberal Justifications for Group Rights', in Joppke and Lukes, eds, *Multicultural Questions*, pp. 112–13.

5   Glazer concludes that North America has very little to teach or learn from the European experience of multiculturalism. See Glazer, 'What Can Europe Learn from North America?', p. 192. The editors of this latter volume (Lukes and Joppke), in their introduction, broadly agree with Glazer's assessment. They conclude that there is no multiculturalism *tout court*. See introduction to Joppke and Lukes, eds, *Multicultural Questions*, p. 17. Multiculturalism is seen to be wholly context-dependent.

6   H. Bhabha, 'Cultures in Between', in Bennett, ed., *Multicultural State*, p. 31.

7   One could also add here methodological pluralism. In the context of recent lip service within the United Kingdom Economic and Social Research Council, pluralism implies the necessity for multiple research methods and programmes in the social sciences. In fact, in reality, unadorned and unashamed positivism is hegemonic in the ESRC.

8   Even quite mild-mannered liberals such as Berlin have been described in the literature as 'difference theorists'. Andrea Baumeister, for example, in her book *Liberalism and 'the Politics of Difference'* (Edinburgh University Press, 2000), uses difference in this more catholic or inclusive manner.

9   Contemporary feminist difference, however, tends to regard the earlier feminist difference arguments as mistakenly essentializing woman's difference. See A. Vincent, *Modern Political Ideologies*, 2nd edn, Oxford, Blackwell, 1995, pp. 200–1.

10   Such a unifying reduction (for postmoderns) is redolent of both humanism and classical metaphysics. This latter theme also blends in with the earlier critical theory of Max Horkheimer and Theodor Adorno's attack on the 'logic of identity' in

Enlightenment thought. See M. Horkheimer and T. W. Adorno, *Dialectic of Enlightenment*, trans. J. Cumming, London and New York: Verso, 1992.
11 It is, though, a very particular reading of democracy.
12 Lyotard's *The Postmodern Condition: A Report on Knowledge* (trans. G. Bennington and B. Massumi, Manchester: Manchester University Press, 1991) explicitly employs Wittgenstein's idea on language games to articulate the postmodern notion of difference. Tully also uses Wittgenstein in comparative ways. See J. Tully, *Strange Multiplicity: Constitutionalism in a Age of Diversity*, Cambridge: Cambridge University Press, 1995; also R. Rorty, *Contingency, Irony and Solidarity*, Cambridge: Cambridge University Press, 1989.
13 However, genealogy, *qua* Nietzsche, should already have predisposed us to this conclusion.
14 In fact, Young even speaks of the 'erotic' nature of the urban group-based metropolis.
15 A core problem is that for the argument to proceed, some significance has to be accorded to the recognized difference (in fact it has to be recognized as a difference), yet the difference claim tends to deny the character of identity.
16 G. W. F. von Leibniz, 'The Monadology' (1714), in *Leibniz: Selections*, ed. P. Wiener, New York: Charles Scribner and Sons, 1951, pp. 533–4.
17 See, for example, debates about political pluralism in the earlier part of the century. A. Vincent, *Theories of the State*, Oxford: Blackwell, 1987, ch. 6.
18 W. James, *A Pluralistic Universe*, Cambridge, Mass.: Harvard University Press, 1909, p. 45.
19 It might be suggested, for example, that this form of pluralist critique is as much a consequence of the Enlightenment. But I leave that to one side.
20 W. E. Connolly, *Identity/Difference: Democratic Negotiations of Political Paradox*, Ithaca, NY: Cornell University Press, 1991, p. 29.
21 Ibid., p. 90.
22 It is worth noting that one of Martin Heidegger's key criticisms of Nietzsche is that he was a surreptitious metaphysician of subjectivity.
23 Thus, for example, there is nothing actually equivalent to a property such as 'redness', or an object such as 'mountain', in the world that we know. We can only know particular different cases of what we loosely call 'red' or 'mountain'.
24 I. Berlin, *The Proper Study of Mankind*, ed. H. Hardy and R. Hausheer, London: Chatto and Windus, 1997, p. 239.
25 Berlin quoted in M. Ignatieff, *Isaiah Berlin: A Life*, London and New York: Metropolitan Books, 1998, p. 285.
26 See I. M. Young, *Justice and the Politics of Difference*, Princeton: Princeton University Press, 1990, pp. 100ff.
27 Connolly, *Identity/Difference*, p. 74.
28 Liberal individualism treats 'an ethic of individuality as if it were a political theory of identity/difference'. Ibid., pp. 85–7.
29 B. Honig, 'Difference, Dilemmas, and the Politics of Difference', in S. Benhabib, ed., *Democracy and Difference*, Princeton: Princeton University Press, 1996, pp. 260 and 270–1.
30 Communitarians, such as Walzer, have also been classified in the literature as 'difference theorists'. Indeed, Walzer has spoken of himself in this manner. For example, see M. Walzer, 'The Politics of Difference', in R. McKim and J. McMahan, eds, *The Morality of Nationalism*, Oxford: Oxford University Press, 1997, pp. 245–57.
31 Lyotard would probably be a better example.
32 D. Miller, *On Nationality*, Oxford: Clarendon Press, 1995, p. 133.
33 Ibid., pp. 147 and 154.

34 W. Kymlicka, *Multicultural Citizenship: A Liberal Theory of Minority Rights*, Oxford: Clarendon Press, 1995, p. 73.

35 It certainly allows the group-based proponent to make a case for, for example, differentiated group rights.

36 Young, *Justice and the Politics of Difference*, p. 161.

37 Tully, *Strange Multiplicity*, p. 11.

38 Thus, 'a person's identity is defined in relation to how others identify him or her'. I. M. Young, 'Polity and Group Difference: A Critique of the Ideal of Universal Citizenship', in R. Beiner, ed., *Theorizing Citizenship*, New York State: University of New York Press, 1995, pp. 186ff. The term 'thrownness' is actually Heidegger's.

39 Imagine a group trying to make a case for resources from the state whilst denying that there was any coherent essence to their group.

40 I. M. Young, 'Reply', *Political Theory* 30, April 2002, p. 282

41 Ibid, p. 285.

42 A. Phillips, 'Dealing with Difference: A Politics of Ideas, or a Politics of Presence', in Benhabib, ed., *Democracy and Difference*, pp. 140–1.

43 For example, for process contradiction, identity in its simplest form is just empty. It would be equivalent to an analytical proposition, that is, $A = A$, or, the sea = the sea. Yet there is no such thing as 'the sea'. Each sea is different. Yet where every sea is seen as different, there can be no identity, which is the opposite to pure identity. Contradiction (*qua* process) suggests that this cannot be the end of the matter.

44 J. Habermas, 'The Unity of Reason in the Diversity of Voices', in J. Schmidt, ed., *What Is Enlightenment? Eighteenth-century Answers and Twentieth-century Questions*, Berkeley and London: University of California Press, 1996, p. 418.

45 What we see here is the vitality and self-movement of a concept, containing an apparent contradiction between what a concept is and what it might be. This is another way (in my reading) of talking about thought itself.

46 Further, the human individual *per se* does not just exist in any one group or one set of institutions. The individual is also a concrete process – an identity in difference. Individuals stand in a 'mindful' relations to multiple institutions. Each person is a living interstice.

5 'Authenticity' in the jargon of multiculturalism

Mark Evans

The idiom of anti-perfectionism, often used in the wake of John Rawls's *A Theory of Justice* to characterize certain brands of 'impartialist' liberalism, has significantly reconfigured many of the debates in the modern Anglo-American tradition of political theory – and not always helpfully so. One of its consequences is a tendency to obscure the crucial point that political theories, which tell us how we might best organize the exercise of power in society's fundamental institutions, cannot ultimately avoid making some very fundamental *ethical* assumptions: ideas about how it might be good for people to live their lives. Attempts to draw an operational distinction between politically enforceable morality, the 'principles of justice' upon which the impartial state could be based, and the 'conceptions of the good' with respect to which that impartiality is to be attempted (the terms may vary but some such distinction is the basis of anti-perfectionism), misleadingly encourage the idea that it is possible to think politically without squarely broaching questions about the nature of the good life. This is not to say that anti-perfectionisms always explicitly make this mistake. Rawls's 'thin theory of the good' and his 'Aristotelian principle', for example, clearly ground the famous two principles of justice in a distinctive ethical outlook.[1] But his *Theory of Justice* can hardly be described as an 'ethical' treatise in the more genuinely Aristotelian sense I mean to invoke by the term. The ethical claims which ground his theory of justice are supposed to be largely formal or modal and are hence not designed to be the object of much theoretical contestation. They are simply posited, as if their establishment was indeed something that could be safely taken for granted, largely incidental to the actual construction of the main theory.

It is a staple of 'Rawls critique' that his assumptions are far from being purely formal: they inevitably privilege certain ways of life over others (and, of course, his 'political liberalism' might be interpreted as an acknowledgement that he had inappropriately universalized them). The kind of political attitude which inspires, and is inspired by, impartialist liberalism cannot help but find this privileging something of an embarrassment. Even when it admits that some such assumptions cannot be fully avoided in positing any model of politics, impartialist liberalism will try as far as possible to avoid overtly taking ethical sides. But given the ultimate futility of this aspiration, it is hardly evident that the suppres-

sion of debate over ethical questions in political theory encouraged by this
'tendency to neutrality' is desirable. If politics and ethics are significantly inter-
twined, then the attempt to insulate political theory from ethical concerns would
seem to be seriously misconceived.

I am not suggesting that political theory should have the opposite temerity to
offer complete and rigid blueprints for how life should be led, a prospect that
would be terrifyingly sinister were it not ultimately so ridiculous. We are not
faced with a choice between the two crudely polarized extremes of thorough-
going ethical abstinence versus totalitarian ethical straitjacketing. A liberalism
which embraces rather than misguidedly attempts to spurn the ethical, for
example, need do so only with modest caution and humility, seeking to balance
its prescriptions against both the positive recognition of value pluralism and the
wariness over political paternalism that are definitive parts of liberalism's character.[2] As Joseph Raz has noted in his own case against it, one cannot deny that
anti-perfectionism is motivated by some sound (for liberals, at least) intuitions
about human autonomy and diversity.[3] Yet instead of sundering the ethical from
the political – which can never be a clean cut – liberals and others who are sensitive to them should not only see that these intuitions themselves bear a definite
ethical content that warrants scrutiny, but they should also be alert to other
ethical possibilities residing within the boundaries established by their fundamental principles.

I suggest, then, that a significant part of the interest of Charles Taylor's work
lies in its conjunction of ethical and political concerns. In numerous writings, he
has strongly attacked the sharp distinction between the right and the good in
moral and political philosophy, and has consequently accused impartialist liberalism of blindness towards its own dependence upon particular conceptions of
the good. By affirming a realist meta-ethical position, he maintains that it is
possible to argue philosophically, in reason and objectively, over better and worse
ways of living and hence over better and worse forms of politics. In *The Ethics of
Authenticity* and 'The Politics of Recognition' he proposes that 'authenticity' is the
quintessentially modern ethical ideal.[4] But it needs to be rescued from certain
individualistic, indeed egoistic and narcissistic, forms whose prominence in our
culture is due in no small part to certain social and political practices and institutions.[5] Hence, for Taylor, ethical critique entails political critique and vice versa.

In this chapter I seek to demonstrate how Taylor's rescue of authenticity
dovetails with his preparedness to support in some instances that version of the
'politics of recognition' which mandates policies that positively affirm the value
(and hence accommodate the specific needs) of certain minority identities in a
multicultural society whose 'difference' would otherwise deliberately go unno-
ticed in the impartialist-liberal state. His argument suggests that such a politics
can facilitate one of the richest forms of authentic living that he fervently hopes
will become culturally dominant.

However, I want to challenge this claim. Taylor says that he is following the
conception of authenticity laid out in Lionel Trilling's *Sincerity and Authenticity*.[6] I
contend that Trilling's conception of *sincerity* may well be a better candidate for

his purpose. This is no mere verbal nicety. True, both are forms of what I call 'ethics of the inner self'. However, 'authenticity' and 'sincerity' denote potentially highly distinctive forms by which to lead a good life, yet Taylor's argument obscures this. There are potential political ramifications here, for it is hardly clear that a politics which could facilitate ethical projects of sincerity – as I will interpret it in the context of debates about multiculturalism in particular – would be equally hospitable to authentic lives. Perhaps perversely, given my stance on ethics in political theory, this debate suggests that an ethics of the inner self may not be the right kind of ethics for political thinking. This implies no reversion to any attempted impartiality, though. My aim is merely to ensure that ethical reflection in political theorizing does not set off on the wrong foot.

Conflicting conceptions of authenticity

This chapter's title refers to 'authenticity' as 'jargon' because in the debates about multiculturalism it is a term that supposedly denotes a particular normative quality and yet is apt to be used in rather vague and conflicting ways.[7] Before Taylor's contributions, 'authenticity' in this context would be more familiarly applied to cultures. 'Cultural authenticity' typically seems to refer to the ideal of a culture which is able to manifest its unique, definitive characteristics and traditions in its practices and artefacts. In other words, it can 'live' according to the forms and norms which have evolved indigenously. The ideal of cultural authenticity can therefore be cited in opposition to developments which try to stifle, subjugate or infiltrate such a culture, perhaps by attempting to supplant it with alien phenomena ('McDonaldization', say) or to commodify it in a way that somehow violates its integrity and essence (for example, the reduction of its manifestations to theme parks and tourist souvenirs).

The confusion over 'authenticity' really gathers pace when we realize that cultures are not its only subjects. It has been famously employed to characterize an *individual's* mode of being, especially by existentialist philosophers,[8] but there is less agreement as to what this mode should be thought of as entailing. As I wish to argue that confusion over Trilling's categories of authenticity and sincerity reflects this disagreement, I can briefly illustrate this general claim with one such example of it. Jean-Jacques Rousseau's ethical thought has been characterized under both headings. Trilling himself talks of Rousseau's central concern with authentic living.[9] Marshall Berman's *The Politics of Authenticity* features Rousseau as its main protagonist.[10] Conversely, in full knowledge of Trilling's distinction, Arthur M. Melzer depicts him instead as an exemplar of sincerity.[11]

Now it may be the case that these conflicting conceptualizations reflect divergent currents in Rousseau's ethical thought and that both are to some degree warranted.[12] But it also reflects some unclarity in the meaning of the two concepts. As we shall shortly gather, some proponents of authenticity in particular resist moves to give it much generic content on the grounds that this would compromise its own spirit. Yet concepts cannot be content-less and hence criterion-less in their application if one wishes their invocation to be anything more than vacuous wordplay.

Charles Taylor's conception of authenticity does not commit the error of vacuity; indeed, it is given sufficient teeth to have significant bite in ethical critique. The next section lays out this conception and develops the argument that links it to multiculturalist discourse.

Taylor on authenticity

Taylor argues that the notion of authenticity develops out of an inward turn in the conceptualization of morality in western philosophy that can be dated back to the eighteenth century. Instead of treating morality as an externally posited datum (of divine source, say) and considering the business of being moral as a matter of calculating the consequences of one's behaviour with reference to this external source (such as the pursuit of divine rewards over the receipt of divinely inflicted punishments), morality was now seen as an 'inner voice', an intuitive feeling of right and wrong.[13] In other words, 'being in touch with morality' comes to mean 'being in touch with one's (inner) self'. The ideal of an authentic existence emerges with the 'displacement of the moral accent' in this subjective turn.[14] The inner depths of the self come to be seen as original, unique to oneself, and this uniqueness acquires central ethical significance of its own.

> There is a certain way of being human that is *my* way. I am called upon to live my life in this way, and not in imitation of anyone else's. .... [T]his gives a new importance to being true to myself. If I am not, I miss the point of my life, I miss what being human is for *me*.[15]

So: 'being true to myself' means being true to my own originality, and that is something only I can articulate and discover. In articulating it, I am also defining myself.'[16] As an ethical project, authenticity demands an environment in which contact with this inner self can be made without distortion, and the mode of life towards which it points can be allowed to flourish. Crucially, however, despite its individualistic veneer, Taylor stresses that the authentic life cannot be conceptualized outside of a social context:

> We become full human agents, capable of understanding ourselves, and hence of defining an identity, through our acquisition of rich human languages of expression ... not only the words we speak but also other modes of expression whereby we define ourselves, including the 'languages' of art, of gesture, of love, and the like. ... [W]e are inducted into these in exchange with others. No one acquires the languages needed for self-definition on their own. We are introduced to them through exchanges with others who matter to us – what George Herbert Mead called 'significant

others'. The genesis of the human self is not 'monological', not something each accomplishes on his or her own, but dialogical.[17]

The dialogical character of human life is not simply a feature of the self's genesis, however; for Taylor, our interchange with significant others continues throughout life. Even solitary artists work to address a future audience, he says; dialogicality is inescapable even for those who seek isolation from the world (whom, after all, was even the Rousseau of the *Reveries of the Solitary Walker* addressing?).

At this point we make contact with multiculturalist theoretical concerns, for the ideal of authenticity links in with the value of difference-oriented *recognition*: the importance to the formation of one's identity of one's recognition (or not) by others, and whether this is distorted. In modern democratic culture, it has become crucial that individuals relate to each other as equals, for that is what it means to be a member of a democratic society: each needs to be recognized as an equal citizen. But this social recognition by others is not automatically granted in the way it was in pre-modern epochs, where people's social standing had been differentially recognized according to the publicly acknowledged class and status hierarchies (one was recognized as a serf, or a freeman, or a nobleman according to these social categories). As Tocqueville recognized, democratic society is characterized by the destruction of these divisions.[18] And now that identity is no longer given through occupation of a culturally instantiated social role but derived inwardly, recognition of it in whatever concrete form it takes in any instance is no longer necessarily bestowed through social custom. It has to be 'won' in dialogical relationships with others, and its achievement cannot be taken for granted.[19]

Not only is it a definitive prerequisite of a healthy democratic society that individuals recognize each other as equals, it is also necessary for the ideal of authenticity:

> We can see how much an original identity needs and is vulnerable to the recognition given or withheld by significant others. ... [Equal recognition's] refusal can inflict damage on those who are denied it ... . The projecting of an inferior or demeaning image on another can actually distort and oppress, to the extent that it is interiorized.[20]

Here are themes very familiar to multiculturalist theorists: the claims that the denial of equal recognition to groups such as ethnic, religious and sexual minorities (a) marginalizes their voices and interests in democratic society, thus contributing to their oppression; and (b) damages their members' potential for flourishing because of the way their identities are formed and expressed in cultural contexts that denigrate them.

There is one further move to make to link authenticity and multicultural concerns, bridging the apparent gap between individual and culture. Taylor argues that, in attempting to cut themselves off from (or stand in opposition to) their social contexts, narcissistic, solipsistically conceived forms of authentic life are self-undermining, not only because they suppress their inevitably dialogical character but also because they fail to see how the value they seek in life is dependent upon a determinate background social context. As we dialogically work out our identities, we seek a sense of value in what we are and what we do: that our lives have significance. But this significance is not something that individuals can legislate for themselves purely through their own choices, as the so-called 'soft relativists' believe ('something has value by dint of my having chosen it'). Instead, '[t]hings take on significance against a background of intelligibility': a *horizon of significance*.[21] Trying to live authentically and fulfillingly in opposition to all such external horizons must lead, Taylor thinks, to a shallow, trivialized form of life – precisely because such individuals do not appreciate how authenticity is possible:

> I can define my identity only against the background of things that matter. But to bracket out history, nature, society, the demands of solidarity, everything but what I find in myself would be to eliminate all candidates for what matters. Only if I exist in a world in which history, or the demands of nature, or the needs of my fellow human beings, or the duties of citizenship, or the call of God, or something else of this order *matters* crucially, can I define an identity for myself that is not trivial. Authenticity is not the enemy of demands that emanate from beyond the self; it supposes such demands.[22]

The relevant implication here is plain: living according to a particular cultural form, following its traditions, identifying oneself with its history and heritage, its ways and its wisdom, and so forth, in the way multiculturalism celebrates, is entirely compatible with the modern ethic of authenticity. If one is genuinely being true to one's self in such an identification, one is not only living authentically but is doing so in a way that avoids shallowness or 'flatness' in that the meaning and value of that life's content is not one's own purely subjective creation. The culture in question provides one's horizon of significance. Further, what might have seemed to be an individualistic ethical ideal can in fact become part of the case for a politics of difference, which seeks proactively to recognize and accommodate the particularistic identities of various cultural identities as the appropriate way in which the equal dignity of individuals and groups can be respected. Indeed, the ethic of authenticity provides a better normative basis for the politics of difference than does the traditional liberal principle of autonomy. Taylor believes that the latter has tended to support difference-blind impartialist liberalism which, in effectively promoting cultural assimilation, actually fails to show equal respect to those cultural forms which are consequently marginalized.[23] Because the ethic of authenticity explicitly values the concrete particularity of the self's true identity, it is much better able to sanction a politics of difference.[24] A difference-sensitive politics can therefore enhance the possibility of authentic living for the people in question.

This sketch does not exhaust Taylor's theory of the relationship between politics and the ethics of the self. From him, in a multicultural society in particular, social and political fragmentation can be overcome and the health of the polity strengthened through a positive identification by citizens with their political community.[25] There are obvious questions to be asked about the possible tensions that might arise between civic-republican and more culturally specific facets of identity, particularly if they are said to be both sustainable in an authentic way of life. We shall leave these aside for now, though, in order to explore the relationship between authenticity and the kind of lifestyle suggested by a politics of difference.

Trilling on sincerity and authenticity

The relationship in Taylor's thought between autonomy and impartialist liberalism, authenticity and a politics of difference, and the conflicts between them, has been the subject of close philosophical scrutiny.[26] I shall add to the doubts raised by this work to consider whether Taylor has rendered 'authenticity' in a fully satisfactory manner. To do so we should turn to Trilling's analysis, which Taylor cites as his inspiration.

For Trilling, authenticity is actually a successor ethic to 'sincerity' which, for him, seems to have considerable claim to be the first definitively 'modern' ethic. It, too, relies upon the idea of an 'inner self', placing central ethical value on the expression of that self and the retention of its integrity in the course of life. In basic form it denotes 'a congruence between avowal and actual feeling' in the way individuals live their lives, between one's own innermost or 'true' convictions and commitments and how one manifests them outwardly. The insincere person is unwilling or incapable of achieving this congruence, finding him- or herself living schizophrenically and without true integrity (lacking 'unity' in his or her mode of living). The ethic also has an important political counterpart in characterizing the relationship between the principles avowed by a society and its actual conduct.[27] Its potential as the basis of social and political critique is also realized when a society merits condemnation for fostering insincerity in the lives of its citizens (a theme which is of course at the heart of Rousseau's political theory). Trilling makes it clear that strenuous efforts may be demanded by the ethic of sincerity to live by it. Should the inner self never be capable of being held securely as some kind of coherent whole, then such efforts would surely seem to be in vain.

One important difference between 'authenticity' and 'sincerity' might appear to be that the former necessarily presupposes *autonomy* whereas the latter need not. Sincerity's inner self might not have to be one that is consciously chosen and 'worked out'; it could be unconsciously received and still be the object of a concern for congruence. However, this is not how Trilling wishes to conceptualize it. He regards it as nonsensical to ask of pre-modern figures such as Achilles, Abraham or Beowulf as to whether they are sincere, because they are only 'characters'. They lack the interiority of self that sincerity presumes, for they are in essence only how they are publicly manifested. So Trilling's conception posits a self with outer layers and inner depths, with a potential to strive to bring these dimensions into congruence that must presume some form of autonomous agency. Thus we might nuance the concept a little by saying that sincerity is concerned to promote a congruence between that with which the autonomous self most inwardly essentially identifies, and that which the self manifests outwardly in the life that is led and the social context in which it is led.

So what is the actual difference, for Trilling, between authenticity and sincerity? The key lies in the depiction of the inner self's nature. For sincerity, the self, although autonomously affirmed, is fixed: a 'given' against which the surface manifestations of selfhood can be measured. That is not to say that there is no conceptual room for the possibilities of change and self-development, but the notion of congruence or 'adherence to the true self' must presuppose that this self can be 'held fast' as a determinate, concrete and substantive identity and set of identifications at any one time. This fixity in congruence is sincerity's differentiating feature.

Now *cultural* authenticity, as we have seen, refers to a society whose traditions, customs, beliefs, artefacts, are of its own manufacture and embody its own unique history and identity. As an ideal, we might propose that there is a significant similarity between this and sincerity: a demand for congruence between the true self-fashioned identity of the culture and its various manifestations. But when we talk of *individual* authenticity, Trilling's sense of authenticity essentially rejects the idea of congruence; to this extent, it comes much closer than does Taylor to its famed existentialist characterization. Here, the authentic individual is one who does *not* live life according to any standard to which one attempts to conform, even if – as with modern sincerity – that standard is a fixed identity which one autonomously affirms. It emphasizes a constant concern to live wholly 'by one's own lights', a responsibility which it would deem to be abnegated by congruence with any given standard. To that extent, the authentic life in Trilling's sense is not appropriately thought of as a pre-set project or goal in the way that sincerity is (in that it requires one to set oneself the aim of living true to the determinate self that one is). Authenticity is a mode of living that resists *a priori* definition.[28] Both Trilling and Taylor note the connection between authenticity and modern art; Trilling uses the latter to exemplify the former:

> The work of art is … authentic by reason of its entire self-definition: it is understood to exist wholly by the laws of its own being, which include the right to embody painful, ignoble or socially inacceptable [*sic*] subject-matters. Similarly the artist seeks his personal authenticity in his entire autonomousness – his goal is to be as self-defining as the art-object he creates.[29]

Perhaps frustratingly, the implications of authenticity thus characterized for how we might live are meant to resist precise formulation. Yet this much is clear: crucially, authenticity entails an essentially oppositional attitude to the *prevailing social ethos*. And although it may be every bit as strenuous an ethic as sincerity could be for some, it also encourages an *ironic* attitude to whatever form one's self presently takes: it is in this that the rejection of congruence essentially lies. Detaching oneself by irony from that present form facilitates the ceaselessly self-creationist freedom of the authentic individual.[30] By taking no forms and no limits seriously, the self is liberated from the bounds which may constrain it.[31]

Multiculturalism and sincerity

So my basic claim against Taylor's use of 'authenticity' in the context of multi-culturalist ethics and politics is this: the politics of difference is centrally concerned with cultural authenticity. Cultures do not survive unless their beliefs, values and practices are 'lived' in the lives of the individuals who bear them. But this is something that individuals are *not* disposed to do if they seek to live authentically in the sense defined above. In other words, the project of preserving cultural authenticity is better thought of as requiring individuals to live according to an ethic of sincerity in that:

(a) they should embrace the identity framed by their culture as their own;
(b) they should seek to live in accordance with the precepts and traditions of that cultural identity.

Consider just how apt 'sincerity' is for a multiculturalist ethic. Imagine that you identify strongly with the cultural traditions of your social group and believe that difference-sensitive perspectives and policies with respect to that identity are needed in order for you to gain proper recognition. To be sure, you 'create' your own life in that you have choices to make in the unique specificities of your life. But the overall orientation of that life you lead is directed towards living within and, where possible, according to the traditions of your group. 'What does it mean to me, and for me, to live as a Muslim, a Catholic [whatever]?' is the key question you ask yourself. Self-definition here is very clearly a process of self-discovery, of orientation within that tradition. It provides the more-or-less fixed standard that is your 'true' identity, and you rail (or should rail[32]) against circum-stances that prevent you living according to and in full acknowledgement of it. This is *the* familiar ethical dilemma which has fuelled the politics of difference – and it is clearly one that is best explicated using the concept of sincerity.

The case for preferring 'sincerity' over 'authenticity' in this context may be won rather too easily if we interpret authenticity too literally in its existentialist sense. It is tempting to read into its 'anti-assimilationism' the belief that it is possible to shape a life in some sort of hermetic isolation from all external (that is, social) influences. Such a view foolishly neglects the essential truth behind Taylor's dialogical account of the sources of identity: identities are always social products in the sense that they are formed in social arenas and out of resources that lie in those arenas. But 'authenticity' does not have to follow this view: no ethic of the inner self has to be construed so as to commit it to an untenable methodological solipsism.[33]

Taylor's characterization of authenticity, however, runs too far in the opposite direction. For the fact that we need socially derived raw materials for our project of self-definition does not necessarily commit us to living according to the specific norms and practices which predominate in any one particular culture. Of course, the social derivation of selfhood's content will constrain its construction in some way, but it need not entail that the construction must take any specific one of the potentially myriad forms that may be sculpted from such material. Minority, counter-cultural social resources, or resources that are exogenous to a particular culture (the products of other societies), are all 'socially derived raw materials' that may be used to attempt to live distant from, in opposition to, the prevailing cultural traditions and, to that extent, live individualistically. The claim that the value we attach to our self-defining activities has to be drawn from sources exogenous to the self if our lives are going to acquire and sustain an adequate sense of meaning also does not necessarily mean that we have to identify rigidly with any one set of cultural norms. Societies today typically have many potential sources for horizons of significance. Once again, we can find value in identifying with the counter-cultural, the oppositional, and do so perhaps in a very eclectic way.

To develop the claim made by Alasdair MacIntyre that 'the good life ... is the life spent in seeking for the good life', it is far from clear that an adequate good life in Taylor's sense cannot be lived as an exploration of various ways of living, drawing value and learning from the variety that this would bring.[34] Further, if it is suspected that this form of life would encourage an instrumental relationship to the social resources out of which a lifestyle may be fashioned ('I will sample the customs, fashions and tastes of culture X not because I sincerely identify with it but because I wish to see how it suits me for a while'), then we can nevertheless avoid Taylor's central worry over instrumentalism by noting that this would not mean that we necessarily have instrumentalist relations with other human beings, which, for him, would denote an enervated lifestyle.[35] An oppositional, anti-assimilationist attitude to prevailing cultural norms, say, does not itself make one an egoist, a narcissist or a misanthrope. One can be anti-assimilationist without being anti-social: unable to find oneself in the culturally informed identities at hand, one struggles to shape an identity and a life for oneself ('ironically' only in so far as the contingency of its content may become apparent in such projects of self-creation). But non-instrumental relationships with others can still be a vital part of such a life.

The form of life suggested in these remarks is clearly different from that suggested by the multiculturalist version of 'sincerity'. And it is hardly an unfamiliar ethical experience, not only within the kinds of culture which are the central concern of the politics of difference but also within the much more eclectically encultured lives of the modern 'cosmopolitan' approvingly described by Jeremy Waldron.[36] Now it would not be fair to neglect the extent to which Taylor concedes that there are anti-assimilationist tendencies in authenticity.[37] But I would say that his argument about authenticity and the politics of difference threatens not only to 'domesticate' the former by suppressing its resistance to congruence and convention but also, and thereby, to delegitimize certain kinds of ethical experience that are ineradicable and valid in modernity: namely the rejection of the kind of adherence to a specific culture which is the ethical core of the politics of difference.

The political consequences of this conclusion may well be that policies which are designed to uphold certain cultural ways of life, with the intention of encouraging people to affirm or support them, could be defended with reference to an ethic of sincerity but would *not* necessarily produce a social environment that was particularly hospitable to the ethic of authenticity – or at least would not be as conducive as possible to it. This may make no small difference to how certain people end up living their lives. The cultural politics favoured by this version of sincerity may make it much easier for those who identify strongly with given cultural traditions to be able to do so; conversely, it may make it harder for those within that culture who wish to reject its norms to be able to pursue the kind of life they would wish. And a state which declined overtly to support cultural traditions as multiculturalists would wish may be thought to favour authenticity rather more, in that individuals are not as explicitly confronted with cultural norms that are held up as definitive of their identity.

Assessing the ethics of the inner self

Thus we can see that some important ethical choices are unfortunately elided in Taylor's analysis. Should we still seek a politics of difference, now that we can see how its ethical basis favours sincere rather than authentic modes of living? Or is authenticity as it has been characterized here sufficiently attractive for us to think about a politics which might prove to be more hospitable to it? Clearly, political theory cannot avoid entering the debate between the two, and a comprehensive presentation of that contest would be a substantial undertaking, far beyond the scope of this chapter. Yet I think a brief sketch of it may well be enough to suggest that basing a politics on either ethic of the inner self might be ill-advised.

At this point, let us state an important assumption which, for the sake of the present argument, we shall take for granted and set aside, even though some may wish to contest it.[38] That is to say that ethics of the inner self are ill-equipped plausibly to generate their own standards of normative judgement which would be able to specify which forms of authentic/sincere existence should be welcomed or condemned and restrained. (As Taylor himself notes, one of the tensions of authenticity lies in the resistance it may exhibit towards moral conventions.[39]) This is because it is implausible to think that any individual's 'inner self', however it is formulated, can validate its own moral character. For this would entail us assuming that every inner self is 'good', or at least sufficiently moral to permit its expression. Such a theory requires a specific conception of the human self as essentially good, such that manifestations of evil behaviour can be considered as aberrant misrepresentations of one's true self. I think there is sufficient metaphysical scepticism to doubt this equation of inner selfhood and morality. Those who share this scepticism but who, nevertheless, think ethics of the inner self are worth promoting must propose an independent set of moral criteria to identify which forms of inner-self-based life ought in fact to be suppressed. Accepting the need for this moral framework, what might be said for or against either of the ethics we have described?

It should be noted that Trilling thinks that 'sincerity' thus defined has declined in ethical significance, and his view is worth quoting at length:

> If sincerity has lost its former status, if the word itself has for us a hollow sound and seems almost to negate its meaning, that is because it does not propose being true to oneself as an end but only as a means. If one is true to one's own self for the purpose of avoiding falsehood to others, is one being truly true to one's own self? The moral end in view implies a public end in view, with all that this suggests of the esteem and fair repute that follow upon the correct fulfilment of a public role. ... In this enterprise of presenting the self, of putting ourselves on the social stage, sincerity itself plays a curiously compromised part. Society requires of us that we present ourselves as being sincere, and the most efficacious way of satisfying this demand is to see to it that we really are sincere, that we actually are what we want our community to know we are. In short, we play the role of being ourselves, we sincerely act the part of the sincere person, with the result that a judgement may be passed upon our sincerity that it is not authentic.[40]

I suggest the problem described here may be only a contingent, not a necessary, flaw of sincerity. It is not inevitably as other-directed as this. Trilling might appear to be making it out almost to be some sort of *amour propre*, but we should remember how Rousseau strove for much of his life to live sincerely – if only through his voluminous writings – whilst urging constant vigilance against this quite distinct vice. Nevertheless, the experience of feeling as an externally imposed expectation that one *has* to demonstrate to others one's identitarian attachment to the shared community is, perhaps, not a rare phenomenon among the kinds of community with which multiculturalism is concerned. As such, there may be a lurking danger that sincerity in practice may be prone to self-subversion.

The desire to 'know oneself' and live as best one can in the light of this knowledge is a pronounced feature of modern culture in general and, in its 'talk-show' manifestations and the like, it is perhaps not always one of its more edifying spectacles. Moreover, we have realized at least since Freud just how complex and opaque 'the self' can be, which inevitably problematizes the very idea of what it means sincerely to affirm one's inner self. Even when we think we can grasp this self in our perceptions such that we know to what it is we seek to be true, the whole project can be enormously demanding even or perhaps especially when balanced against the other demands (moral, relational) that may be levied on the self, particularly in modern life. To cleave doggedly to it in the face of such pressures may be no guarantee of a life that is satisfying, fulfilling or flourishing. In this regard, Trilling reminds us of the fate of the eponymous hero

in Goethe's epoch-forging novella *The Sorrows of Young Werther*.[41] Rigidly earnest
in his sincerity, he finds himself incapable of overcoming the love he has for the
married, unattainable Lotte (the deepest commitment of his inner self) and eventually his life disintegrates towards his suicide even as 'he struggles to be true to
the self he must still believe is his own'.[42] He lacks the ironic detachment which
authenticity bequeaths to us and with which one might cope with the vicissitudes
of life: detached from any such fixity of commitment as its definitive content, the
self may avoid such a collapse from within when such commitments would
otherwise prove unrealizable in the maelstrom of human circumstance.

Yet it would obviously be wrong to conclude that all ethical agents are likely
to be unduly constrained by the ethic of sincerity. Some obviously value the
particular sources of sense of worth or meaning in life that sincerity may bring
and which Taylor celebrates in his work. Even in modernity, personal identification with settled values and practices in a wider social context is a familiar mode
of flourishing for many: this, indeed, is one of the lessons of the politics of
difference. We can see here the basis of the familiar communitarian argument
that the self is at least partially embedded in specific cultural traditions and
would thereby become alienated if it were to be somehow cut loose from them.[43]
So an ethic of authenticity is likely to prove somewhat inhospitable to such
lifestyles. And some who try to live authentically – ironically detached from
settled identifying commitments, playfully experimenting with lifestyles, living life
'in and for itself' without thinking one has to subordinate oneself to any particular rigid format or meaning – may find such a life cannot ultimately provide
them with a suitably enriched sense of self.

Unless one is to 'drop out' of society altogether, to the extent that one is able
to live authentically in typically modern circumstances its possibility may only be
realized fragmentarily (perhaps similarly to the way in which genuine autonomy
is possible only on occasion in a typical life). The image of Rorty's 'private
ironist' springs to mind here as an expression of this mitigated ideal: self-creation
in the private sphere, solidarity with communal norms and practices in the
public.[44] We might suspect that this kind of life overly compromises the
authentic ethos in a similar way to Taylor's own domesticated characterization of
it. Its constraint by such a strong public/private divide certainly looks to be
something that authenticity would resist. Admittedly, there could still be a significant difference between a lifestyle in which one lived conventionally in the public
sphere (holding down a job, living within the law, and so on) and sincerely
according to a set of traditions in the private sphere, and one which is conventional in public and more authentically free-flowing in private. Further, perhaps
any degree of authenticity in living promises some crucial creative power: it may
(indirectly) force traditions to change from within, or utilize the *mélange* of social
influences to fashion new modes of living, thinking, and so on. Yet, as Taylor is
always keen to remind us, in its resistance to congruence, codification and the
restraints of fixity, authenticity may always be in a perplexing tension with other
demands, including the regulatory morality we have conceded that any ethics of
the inner self needs. It may not necessarily abandon reflection, as Larmore

erroneously suggests;[45] the authentic person can still practically reason on how one still might cope with life's conflicting demands, but even this is no guarantee that a satisfyingly liveable and/or socially sustainable life can be achieved from the attempt to live authentically.

Against ethical impartialism in politics

From this brief overview, it is not difficult to conclude that whilst some people may find fulfilment through sincerity, others may find it through authenticity (and I leave aside the issue of other possible modes of living). In short, there is more than one viable way of living according to an ethic of the inner self – and this may readily lead us to the conclusion that no account of politics ought explicitly to privilege either one or the other. Taylor's authenticity-based case for a politics of difference therefore seems to fail. Now this failure seems to occur for reasons which support impartialist liberalism: because of ethical plurality, the state should seek to act only on the basis of autonomy in order to respect the right of citizens to choose their own mode of living (within the framework of justice) for themselves. One might concede the points raised in the opening section that even a preference for autonomy embodies certain substantive ethical priorities, but contend that these are unavoidable and we should resist the temptation to be any more ethically prescriptive (as we would be in any further picking and choosing between ethics of the inner self).

This reversion to impartialism, or anti-perfectionism, is too rapid, however, and I conclude by outlining two reasons for this claim. The first is that a difference-based politics of recognition is a serious option, and perhaps a necessity, for some societies. We need to take very seriously the point that a politics which encourages communitarian identification with one's specific culture may be privileging not, or not just, autonomy but a more specific mode of being: *contra* Taylor, it is sincerity rather than authenticity. Despite the bias this represents against other types of ethic, it may well be that the advantages of a difference-based politics outweigh whatever costs such bias brings. The desire for as much ethical impartiality as possible should not be treated as the invariably uppermost political priority. We should anyway not over-estimate the actual obstacles generated to the pursuit of alternatives, particularly in a generally democratic environment, simply because certain of the state's policies have a specific ethical orientation. Neither its intent nor its effects when it has such an agenda are likely to be so overbearing that other ethical opportunities in civil society and private life will be significantly frustrated.

The second point draws attention to some implications of the social-dialogical account of identity's origins which are in a way more radical than those developed here. The present discussion has proposed that it is perfectly intelligible to talk of ethical experiences of the 'inner self' as genuinely profound and personal whilst, at the same time accepting that this self is forged in social interaction from a *mélange* of social and cultural influences. Now if we look at this in a quasi-Foucauldian way in terms of these influences constituting the self, our attention is immediately directed to the questions of which social forces have contributed to the construction of the self, and how.[46] Whether through desistance or active intervention, the state is one of many social institutions implicated in the particular configuration taken by these forces. We can identify and scrutinize the ethical norms underpinning these effects in the social construction of the self – and the way may be open to consider alternative norms and a reconfiguration of some of the ways in which identities are forged. Think in particular of how state-sponsored educational curricula try to produce in pupils certain types of behaviour: there are substantive ethical agendas at work here, a practice which we may have good reason to welcome even where we may contest the particular content in question.[47]

So, even if we wish to reject an ethics of the inner self as the basis for politics, impartialism is not the only alternative. A neo-Aristotelian political concern with the quality of individuals' character which asks how we might *externally* and *internally* influence (if only modestly, partially and cautiously) the very *content* of (inner) self may also be in play.

Notes

I am grateful for helpful comments to the participants at the conference on 'Identity, Legitimacy and Rights' at the University of Wales Cardiff (July 2002) and to Anne Evans for careful inspection of the final draft.

 1 J. Rawls, *A Theory of Justice*, Oxford: Oxford University Press, 1972, pp. 395–439.
 2 For examples of overtly ethical ('perfectionist') liberalisms, see W. Galston, *Liberal Purposes*, Cambridge: Cambridge University Press, 1992; G. Sher, *Beyond Neutrality: Perfectionism and Politics*, Cambridge: Cambridge University Press, 1997; and M. Evans, 'Prolegomenon to a Liberal Theory of the Good Life', in M. Evans, ed., *The Edinburgh Companion to Contemporary Liberalism*, Edinburgh: Edinburgh University Press, 2001, pp. 299–312.
 3 J. Raz, *The Morality of Freedom*, Oxford: Clarendon Press, 1986.
 4 C. Taylor, *Multiculturalism and 'the Politcs of Recognition'; An Essay*, Princeton University Press, 1992; and C. Taylor, 'The Politics of Recognition', in A. Gutmann, ed., *Multiculturalism: Examining the Politics of Recognition*, Princeton: Princeton University Press, 1994, pp. 25–75.
 5 Taylor, *The Ethics of Authenticity*, chs 1–3. Cf. C. Lasch, *The Culture of Narcissism*, New York: Norton, 1978.
 6 L. Trilling, *Sincerity and Authenticity*, London: Oxford University Press, 1972.
 7 My title is, of course, evocative of Adorno's (T. Adorno, *The Jargon of Authenticity*, trans. K. Tarnowski and F. Will, London: Routledge and Kegan Paul, 1986). His critique of Heidegger highlights the essentially mystificatory use of 'authenticity'. I do not believe that is the effect of the term's usage in this context, but I suggest there are unclarities and confusions in this 'buzz word' in multiculturalist discourse which gives an unfortunate impression that it is indeed 'jargon' in its pejorative sense.
 8 J. Golomb, *In Search of Authenticity*, London: Routledge, 1995.
 9 Trilling, *Sincerity and Authenticity*, pp. 58–73 and 93–4.
10 M. Berman, *The Politics of Authenticity*, London: Allen and Unwin, 1971.
11 A. Melzer, 'Rousseau and the Modern Cult of Sincerity', in C. Orwin and N. Targov, eds, *The Legacy of Rousseau*, Chicago: University of Chicago Press, 1997, pp. 274–95.
12 Although one runs the risk of losing something valuable from an author's thought by pigeon-holing it, it does no great violence to Rousseau to say that most of his life was

spent trying to live sincerely, as is most evident in his *Confessions* (J. J. Rousseau, *The Confessions*, trans. J. M. Cohen, Harmondsworth: Penguin, 1953). But his life also exhibits how difficult this is. Social life always threatens to compromise the sincerity of the individual, rending the self (the apparent sincerity of life at Clarens as depicted in *La Nouvelle Héloïse* in fact masks its complete failure to facilitate the overcoming of the feelings that Julie and St Preux retain for each other: J. J. Rousseau, *Julie, or La Nouvelle Héloïse*, trans. P. Stewart, J. Vaché, Hanover, NH: University Press of New England, 1997). Hence Rousseau's eventual retreat to the authentic – because unencumbered – celebration of the immediate contact between the solitary self and *le sentiment de l' éxistence* in his *Reveries of the Solitary Walker*, trans P. France, Harmondsworth: Penguin, 1979.

13 Taylor, *The Ethics of Authenticity*, pp. 25–6; Taylor, 'The Politics of Recognition', p. 28.
14 Taylor, *The Ethics of Authenticity*, p. 28; Taylor, 'The Politics of Recognition', pp. 28–9.
15 Taylor, *The Ethics of Authenticity*, p. 29; cf. Taylor, 'The Politics of Recognition', p. 30.
16 Taylor, *The Ethics of Authenticity*, p. 29; cf. Taylor, 'The Politics of Recognition', p. 31.
17 Taylor, *The Ethics of Authenticity*, p. 33; cf. Taylor, 'The Politics of Recognition', p. 32.
18 A. Tocqueville, *Democracy in America*, vol. 1, trans. G. H. Reeve, New York: Schocken, 1961.
19 Taylor, *The Ethics of Authenticity*, pp. 47–9; Taylor, 'The Politics of Recognition', pp. 34–6.
20 Taylor, *The Ethics of Authenticity*, pp. 49–50; Taylor, 'The Politics of Recognition', p. 36.
21 Taylor, *The Ethics of Authenticity*, pp. 35–7.
22 Ibid., pp. 40–1.
23 Taylor, 'The Politics of Recognition', p. 57.
24 Ibid., p. 38.
25 C. Taylor, *Philosophical Arguments*, Cambridge, Mass.: Harvard University Press, 1995, pp. 257–87.
26 M. Cooke, 'Authenticity and Autonomy: Taylor, Habermas and the Politics of Recognition', *Political Theory* 25, 2, 1997, pp. 258–88.
27 Trilling, *Sincerity and Authenticity*, pp. 2 and 27.
28 See the discussion in C. Larmore, *The Romantic Legacy*, New York: Columbia University Press, 1996, ch. 3.
29 Trilling, *Sincerity and Authenticity*, pp. 99–100.
30 The ironic life is not the same as the authentic life, but the two are not opposed in the way suggested by Larmore, *The Romantic Legacy*, p. 83. Whereas irony is a reflective attitude, for Larmore authenticity is essentially unreflective: an immediate mode of being, unconstrained by any reflectively preconceived project (ibid., p. 93). It is true that authenticity is not a 'project' in this sense, but that does not mean that ironic reflection is absent from the authentic mode of life.
31 Trilling, *Sincerity and Authenticity*, pp. 120–1.
32 See Jerry Cohen's relevant autobiographical discussion both of the (insincere) concealment of a communist childhood from his schoolboy peers and the contradictory experiences of ethnic discrimination in G. A. Cohen, *If You're an Egalitarian, How Come You're So Rich?*, Cambridge, Mass.: Harvard University Press, 2000, ch. 2.
33 Even Rousseau's solitudinous perception of the sentiment of existence is, as David Gauthier stresses, *post-* as opposed to pre- or non-social: Gauthier, '*Le promeneur solitaire*: Rousseau and the Emergence of the Post-Social Self', in E. F. Paul, F. D. Miller, Jr and J. Paul, eds, *Ethics, Politics and Human Nature*, Oxford: Blackwell, 1991. Cf. Rousseau, *Reveries of the Solitary Walker*, p. 89.
34 A. MacIntyre, *After Virtue*, 2nd edn, London: Duckworth, 1985, p. 219.
35 Taylor, *The Ethics of Authenticity*, pp. 52–79.
36 J. Waldron, 'Minority Cultures and the Cosmopolitan Alternative', in W. Kymlicka, ed., *The Rights of Minority Cultures*, Oxford: Oxford University Press, 1995, pp. 93–102.

Of course, 'authenticity' would not support the purely consumerist, fashion-led versions of the cosmopolitan lifestyle that appear to be an increasingly dominant cultural form. But note that what could distinguish the authentic from the inauthentic lifestyle is not so much its content as the attitude taken to it by the agent; this, indeed, seems to be the reason why Waldron suspects some communitarian-culturalist lifestyles may be 'inauthentic'.

37 Taylor, *The Ethics of Authenticity*, p. 65.

38 A. Ferrara ('Authenticity and the Project of Modernity', *European Journal of Philosophy*, 2, 3, 1994, pp. 241–83) is one author who reworks a conception of authenticity with the intent of making it normatively self-contained, able to generate its own standards of moral evaluation. It will be clear that I find this implausible, but I lack the space to develop the reasoning for this any further.

39 Taylor, *The Ethics of Authenticity*, p. 66.

40 Trilling, *Sincerity and Authenticity*, pp. 9, 10–11. The term 'authentic' here is perhaps unfortunate, as Trilling clearly intends not to refer to the particular moral experience he understands by it. Here, the word denotes the idea that sincerity led thus is not a genuine experience of the self, merely a role it has, for whatever reason felt it necessary to play.

41 J. W. Goethe, *The Sorrows of Young Werther*, trans. M. Hulse, Harmondsworth: Penguin, 1989.

42 Trilling (*Authenticity and Sincerity*, p. 32) notes this gloriously simple metaphor for sincerity: Werther dies in what is apparently his unchanging mode of dress: dark blue coat, buff waistcoat and breeches, and knee-length boots: Goethe, *The Sorrows of Young Werther*, p. 134, cf. p. 92. It is certainly ironic that this costume became the uniform of the young men swept up in the Werther cult of late eighteenth-century Germany.

43 See M. Sandel, *Liberalism and the Limits of Justice*, Cambridge: Cambridge University Press, 1982, for one of the founding statements of the contemporary communitarian position.

44 R. Rorty, 'Private Irony and Liberal Hope', in his *Contingency, Irony and Solidarity*, Cambridge: Cambridge University Press, 1989, pp. 73–95.

45 See n. 30 (above) and Larmore's discussion of Stendhal in Larmore, *The Romantic Legacy*, pp. 86–91.

46 Note that one reason for calling this a *quasi*-Foucauldian account is to emphasize a constitutive rather than repressive conception of power. Thus we become who we are as results of such power. To use a Foucauldian term, the technologies of the self which are central to an ethic of the inner self – 'which permit individuals to effect by their own means or with the help of others a certain number of operations on their own bodies and souls, thoughts, conduct, and way of being, so as to transform themselves in order to attain a certain state of happiness, purity, wisdom, perfection, or immortality' – are techniques learned in and imparted through social processes: Foucault, *Technologies of the Self*, ed. L. Martin *et al.*, London: Tavistock, 1989, p. 18. This does not imply, however, that talk of the genuinely personal, which is integral to the 'inner self', is redundant.

47 See Evans, 'Prolegomenon to a Liberal Theory of the Good Life', for an elaboration of the ethical politics outlined here.

6   Theorizing recognition

Jonathan Seglow

In this chapter I seek to give a partial vindication of what has come to be called a politics of difference or politics of recognition. The central claim of such a politics is that group-differentiated rights, laws and policies are justified on the grounds that membership of groups is an important aspect of persons' well-being. The legal recognition of groups comes within the ambit of social justice. Often, however, the politics of recognition is represented as making a further claim: that marginalized or disadvantaged groups should be publicly affirmed or esteemed in order to correct their subordinate status and put their members on the same footing as members of mainstream society. This second, wider type of recognition, referring as it does to citizens' attitudes towards one another is, I think, different from the former, more narrow question of legal or policy changes, and in this chapter I seek to explore the difference between them. I would like to begin by setting out the types of claims that are made under the banner of (what I shall call) narrow recognition, and the criticisms made of them, before moving on to consider 'wide recognition' later in the chapter. What sorts of claims does narrow recognition make? We can, I think, classify them into five broad types:[1]

(i)   Measures which limit the toleration of practices that offend the dignity and hence threaten the public standing of marginal groups. This is exemplified by laws against racist, sexist and homophobic speech, expression and behaviour – or 'hate speech'.

(ii) Measures which release members of minority groups from the demands of state laws on the grounds that, given their cultural identity, they find them peculiarly burdensome. Examples include exemptions on headwear, dress codes, drug laws, animal slaughter and universal education requirements.

(iii) Measures which seek to give members of minorities special assistance, legal or financial, so as to rectify the social disadvantages they endure. Examples include bilingual schooling for children of recent immigrants; affirmative action programmes which help under-represented groups such as ethnic minorities gain jobs and university places; and public resources to benefit minority communities (such as building cultural or religious centres).

(iv) Changes to laws or public conventions in order that they no longer discriminate against members of minority communities. This type includes the legalization of same-sex marriage, as well as revisions to dates and times of public holidays and work practices; changes to the symbolism in flags, currencies, anthems and constitutional declarations; and revisions to curricula in schools so that they promote a positive image of minority communities' histories and achievements.

(v) The final category encompasses a number of claims centred on the ideas of government or self-determination. It includes measures to give minorities quota places or guaranteed seats in legislatures (though these might better be seen as an extension of [iii]). More radically, it encompasses claims for devolved power and what Galeotti calls 'collective liberty':[2] the collective right of a group to the non-intervention of the state in its communal life. Some Aboriginal peoples' demand that an indigenous legal tradition take precedence over the Australian legal code is an example. At the limit, category (v) includes demands for independence and outright secession.

Now all these claims are, to state the obvious point, highly controversial. Category (v) is, however, the most controversial of all. Claims for collective liberty, self-government and secession are all pleas for recognition of a sort. But there is an important difference between a group enjoying recognition as a distinct political entity, with different norms and laws to the larger society from which it seeks some separation, and the recognition that a group has a distinct identity while its members, nonetheless, remain members in full standing of that larger society. The former challenges the very integrity of a political community; the latter challenges only its constitutive rules. Moreover, and this is a second difference between (i)–(iv) and (v), collective liberties and self-government can be illiberal in so far as they license the oppression of vulnerable members of a minority group by depriving them of the protection in law which other citizens unproblematically enjoy. One argument against acceding to claims for independence and secession is that powerless members of the incipient society may now be coerced by laws and rules that were kept in check when it was part of larger, more liberal political community. But in cases (i)–(iv) those laws and rules still apply. Conflicts between minority communities' coercive aspects and the liberalism of the larger society have to be resolved in favour of the latter.

In this chapter, therefore, I shall restrict myself to discussing categories (i)–(iv) of recognition, which all represent appeals made by minority groups to the larger political community which they inhabit for group-differentiated laws and policies that recognize their specific group identities, but fall short of outright separatism. But this does not get us very far. For many critics, claims to recognition (i)–(iv), far from having any moral basis, are merely interest-group politics by another name. So let us begin by surveying the key criticisms which are made of narrow recognition from a liberal point of view.

Criticisms of the politics of recognition

The first criticism says that the politics of recognition arbitrarily privileges the wants and interests of certain minority cultural groups, and hence cannot be justified from an impartial moral perspective.[3] Besides philosophical discussion, this attitude is often found in common complaints about the injustice of affirmative action, quotas, bussing and (as recently experienced in the UK) claims by whites that Asians living in the same town get priority treatment from welfare and housing agencies. In his *Culture and Equality*, Brian Barry offers a sophisticated restatement of the liberal impartialist point of view. Barry concedes that laws on headscarves, protective helmets, drug use and the slaughter of animals, for example, place a disproportionate burden on religious groups whose traditional practices run contrary to current law. But special exemptions for Muslims, Sikhs, Jews and Rastafarians are ruled out on the grounds that '[t]here is no principle of justice mandating exemptions to generally applicable laws for those who find compliance especially burdensome in virtue of their cultural norms or religious beliefs'.[4] The core of liberal impartiality is equal treatment, and that applies just as much in dismissing special pleading for recognition, as it does in rejecting discriminatory evils such as racism, sexism and homophobia.

A second argument says that recognition is illiberal in the straightforward sense that it denies the value of individual liberty. We have already encountered the charge of illiberalism when we saw how easily it could be made against collective liberty claims – type (v) above. However, the argument comes in a number of further versions which apply to (i)–(iv) as well. In one version the argument is a complaint at the politicization of culture that recognition entails. Thus, Iris Marion Young calls for a 'cultural revolution' where 'no aspect of everyday life would be exempt from reflection and potential criticism', and where, moreover, 'no social practices or activities should be excluded as improper subjects for ... collective choice'.[5] In contrast to the equal respect which citizens can quite easily show each other in a liberal democracy, recognition demands that we affirm the unique value and specificity of every last collective identity. Instituting this demand in everyday life can only be experienced as coercive. The second version of the illiberalism argument is directed more narrowly at the members of minority groups who are to be the beneficiaries of policies of recognition. As Appiah points out in his critique of Charles Taylor, some recipients of recognition might object that it is not they who are receiving it, but just some attribute of theirs – first language, skin colour – which they invest with no special significance. Many members of minority groups may nonetheless regard themselves first and foremost as free agents. 'It is at this point that someone who takes autonomy seriously will ask whether we have not replaced one kind of tyranny with another.'[6]

The third argument is that recognition, whatever its other merits or demerits, is logically incoherent. Cultures, religions and ways of life (among other things) embody certain values. Recognizing them, in the sense usually intended by advocates of this position, involves affirming their values. However, the values of cultures directly conflict: some ways of life believe that gay relationships should be celebrated, for example, whilst some religious cultures are convinced homosexuality is a sin. The two sides cannot both be right. Hence one cannot affirm both cultures so long as that involves valuing their values. As Peter Jones puts it:

> The fundamental problem with the demand for recognition ... is the contradictory commitments it asks people to accept. People are allowed to believe in the worth of their own culture including the beliefs and values it embodies, yet they are also required to believe that others' cultures, embodying different and conflicting beliefs and values are of no less worth. How can we expect people to embrace that absurdity?[7]

Only, answers Brian Barry in *Culture and Equality*, 'with a great deal of encouragement from the Politically Correct Thought Police'.[8]

The fourth criticism is that the assertion of group identity at the heart of the politics of recognition is tribalistic, fragments political communities and undermines the sources of civic solidarity. Though made in the name of equality and inclusion, the demands of minority cultural and other groups in fact assert their own values and interests at the expense of peaceful co-existence, which is the *sine qua non* of successful multicultural societies. The more pluralistic a society, the more citizens have to work to build solidarity and common loyalty. Endorsing group-based claims to recognition, however, subverts this process because members of minorities (or at least their leaders) will be encouraged to press their own claims rather than work towards the common interest. This can only increase conflict, suspicion and resentment among different social groups and erode the construction of a common political identity.[9]

In summary, the politics of recognition is, according to its critics, over-partial, illiberal, incoherent and tribalistic. Underlying and animating these accusations is, I think, a further thought: that the various claims to recognition I catalogued briefly are, however forcefully made, really no more than everyday political demands. Groups always demand things in politics, but most of their demands are not genuine claims of justice (which is not to say they are unjust). For the liberal who is sceptical towards recognition, the desire of minorities to channel public money for them to celebrate their identity or change the school curriculum, for example, are not issues of justice on a par with basic rights like freedom of speech or the right to welfare. Moreover, some claims to recognition, like affirmative action or exemptions from otherwise universally applicable laws, are arguably quite unjust from the liberal point of view. In order to vindicate any version of the politics of recognition, therefore, we need not just to take issue with the four critiques; we need also, more positively, to show how recognition belongs to justice in a way that is cogent and persuasive. That is what I try to do in the rest of this chapter.

Two kinds of justice

I want to suggest that there are two distinct kinds of claim to which advocates of recognition appeal. Both are credible, but only one has as its immediate object the types of recognition I outlined in (i)–(iv) above. In each case there is a different principle of justice that is being appealed to, though each principle has its limitations.

The first kind of justice that minorities seem to be appealing to is a principle of non-discrimination. The basic idea here is that members of a group should not systematically receive a lesser share of social opportunities or a greater share of social burdens merely on the basis that they happen to belong to one group rather than another. Put another way, it is unjust for any particular group of people to be discriminated against in the distribution of social benefits and burdens on the arbitrary basis of their group affiliation.[10] It is not difficult to see how many of the claims I listed might be assimilated under this principle. Type (i) claims, where we lower the threshold of toleration to avoid offence to marginalized groups, can be conceived of as equalizing the degree of offence which any group can reasonably be asked to bear by incorporating into law the extra/special offence suffered when one's ethnic or sexual identity, for example, is assaulted. Type (ii) claims, which make exceptions for minority groups to otherwise universal laws, can similarly be seen as releasing them from the burden of compliance which they, on account of their group membership, uniquely suffer. Allowing Muslim schoolgirls to wear headscarves, for example, is recognition of the special burden that would be placed on their identity were they to be forced to abandon their traditional dress in favour of school uniform. Claims of type (iii) which, on the surface, give minorities special assistance, also however come under the rubric of non-discrimination. For they simply seek to distribute a social benefit – access to one's own language, for example, or funding for public places of worship – that the majority in society unproblematically enjoy. Type (iv) claims differ from type (ii) in that an explicitly non-universal law – for example, that public holidays reflect the Christian religion or (more controversially perhaps) that marriage is a sacred union only between two people of the opposite sex – is modified so as not to exclude those whose group identity is not reflected in the original law. Once again, non-discrimination is the key to amending such laws.

However, although non-discrimination is a prima facie principle of justice, it cannot reasonably be presented as a universal principle to be applied *carte blanche* to every single case of a failure of recognition. This is so for at least four reasons. To begin with, we all suffer from some kinds of discrimination on the basis of memberships that we had little choice in making. Place of residence, nationality, even physical characteristics, can all result in unchosen burdens, but not ones there is necessarily a case in justice to correct. When it comes to culture, the principle of non-discrimination glosses over questions about the responsibility that members bear for their culture and the reasonable demands that might be made of them in the name of assimilation. (Such thoughts underlie the first – partiality – critique I sketched in the previous section.) Second, members of a culture are not unthinking bearers of a primordial essence that can be identified with a precise range of sacrosanct cultural practices. On the contrary, cultures evolve in response to the circumstances they find themselves in, and some change should be expected in a culturally pluralist society. In fact, the principle of non-discrimination, if applied in a crudely uniform way, will tend to make cultural groups present themselves as unique, authentic essences at risk from being assimilated into a majoritarian mould not of their making. Third, the principle does nothing to prevent the phenomenon whereby each group sees itself solely on its own terms, thus stifling just the kind of cross-cultural engagement and accommodation that any successful multicultural society needs.[11] Finally, it will encourage cultural groups (or their leaders) to press for as many benefits, exemptions and kinds of special treatment as they can possibly get, thus dissipating the moral values at work in the politics of recognition, reducing it to interest-group politics and, in the process, fragmenting the civic bond which ideally should hold disparate groups together. As we saw with the fourth criticism, recognition risks subverting the construction and maintenance of a common political identity.

In his discussion of the injustice of discrimination, Steven Lukes writes that, in addition to the denial of advantages resulting from discrimination, there is an additional injustice done to groups who lose out, namely they suffer 'rejection from the dominant culture of mutual recognition'.[12] Taking up this idea, I want to suggest that, separate from the burden of discrimination imposed by partisan laws and conventions, members of groups who demand recognition are also appealing against a further kind of injustice, that of being excluded from the dominant norms, mores and standards of the society of which they are legally members. At stake here is the need to have one's collective identity publicly acknowledged and accepted for what it is, and not, on account of it, be marginalized, excluded and disregarded. I shall say more in defence of this need later on. The kind of recognition does not concern in the first instance the kinds of legal and policy measures as detailed under claims (i)–(iv). Rather, its object is the symbolic value of being included as a full member of society, given the ascriptive differences which one bears. That the value of inclusion is not always manifest is evident when one considers the salient circumstances of the politics of recognition. Struggle for recognition occurs when value conflict between the majority and minorities in the same society results in the traits, beliefs and values of the minorities being labelled as different and inferior to the majority's and a threat to traditional public standards (as defined by the majority) – and hence when minorities' values are effectively excluded from the public sphere. Beyond inequalities of legal treatment, therefore, minorities suffer an additional harm of exclusion.[13] They occupy a marginalized and subordinate position, and demand equal public standing and acceptance for their distinct identities. Their object of claims to recognition here is to ensure that previously excluded minorities, invisible or devalued in the public sphere, will be able to relate to their collective identities with the same ease and confidence as members of the majority because they regard themselves to be members of society in full standing. Toleration as recognition will have succeeded when 'different' minorities identify with the prevailing normative standards in society, are symbolically included within them and, like the majority, are able to adapt and revise their identities without fear.[14] Wide recognition seeks to redress the asymmetry involved in the power to label. Inclusion is its over-arching value.

Wide recognition concerns the values and attitudes that citizens of different backgrounds evince in their day-to-day interactions with each other. Wide recognition also refers to the normative standards of public life more generally, including the kinds of discourse employed by politicians, the portrayal of different kinds of groups in television and the print media, in literature and in school curricula. If a group enjoys recognition in this wide sense, it does not mean that people go around affirming its values or praising its achievements. What it does mean is that the particular minority identity in question is publicly accepted and acknowledged as having its own particular perspective and view of the world that is different from the majority's. Wide recognition is, as Galeotti puts it, 'content-independent':[15] the majority need only affirm that the minority identity is different from their own, is valuable at least on its own terms and is a distinct source of political claims, and hence that some political accommodation may be required. A failure of wide recognition is when the agents of public and political discourse either ignore or, more commonly, actively disparage, demean or humiliate the minority identity in question.

I have tried to show that there are two distinct modes of justice to which advocates of recognition appeal, encapsulated by two different moral principles: non-discrimination and inclusion. While the former is familiar to us from many non-cultural issues of justice, the latter is more controversial. Interpreted as the means by which citizens can regard themselves as members in full standing of their political community, inclusion is clearly a value. Securing the conditions which underlie a felt sense of inclusion must be a political imperative of some kind. But I cannot here mount a full defence of inclusion's status as a part of justice. Suffice it to say that feeling oneself a member of the political community that one shares with fellow citizens must be part of what a fulfilling life involves. And justice is what citizens owe to one another in order that each can lead a fulfilling life.

Wide recognition

In the remainder of this chapter, I shall defend wide recognition, and then (a democratic version of) its narrow counterpart. The first question to ask, in conducting this defence, is whether wide recognition is subject to the four critiques of recognition I outlined above. I suggest that there is no special difficulty with the first and the fourth critique, but that the second and the third are more problematic. The first critique said that recognition is over-partial. But recall that this critique arose in the context of policies, like affirmative action, that treated some citizens differently from others. Wide recognition, by contrast, is a need that is shared by all. Failures of recognition occur when public discourse is normatively structured in such a way that minority identities are not properly acknowledged. Acknowledging them is a way of correcting that in the name of impartiality. Nor need wide recognition encourage social fragmentation, the fourth critique. Its object is to make excluded groups feel they belong to the political community. This is the opposite of fragmentation.

The second and third critiques, illiberalism and incoherence, present more difficulties. I shall address them at greater length in this section, and in doing so elaborate further the meaning of wide recognition. However, rather than rehearse the two critiques again, I shall examine two anti-recognition arguments that are inspired by them.

The first argument, which draws on the illiberalism critique, is that recognition, as compared to equal respect, is over-demanding and intrudes upon the liberties of those citizens required to meet its obligations. A good example of this argument can be found in Nancy Rosenblum's *Membership and Morals*. Wide recognition, as she interprets it, involves 'taking responsibility for others' and 'active solicitude for their sense of self-worth'. But, she argues, 'carefully calculating social status, making fine cultural or racial distinctions, and taking exquisite pains to avoid slights are wholly out of keeping with democracy in everyday life'.[16] Democratic interaction calls for 'easy spontaneity' with others, and this means citizens have to be thick-skinned at times and tolerate being misunderstood or, at least, others' indifference. There are minimal standards of civility which citizens are obliged to show one another, but these are encapsulated by what liberals typically understand by mutual respect: upholding rights, avoiding harm and engaging in a process of democratic justification to determine those coercive norms strictly necessary for a well-functioning polity.

In so far as wide recognition, interpreted here as a civic duty, does indeed demand that citizens take (some) responsibility for each other's sense of self-worth, it plainly does circumscribe their liberty. And wide recognition is clearly incompatible with Rosenblum's conception of robustly vigorous democracy (though I shall argue in the last section of this chapter that wide recognition is a prerequisite for the appropriate conception of democracy in multicultural societies). The case for treating wide recognition as a civic duty in the first place stems from acknowledging that recognition, just like respect, is a basic human need. And that in turn rests upon a theory of the person which regards self-reflexivity (along with autonomy) as a central feature of our being. On this view, developed by Charles Taylor and Axel Honneth in recent years, human beings do not form goals and preferences out of nowhere but, rather, are beings who relate reflexively to their own identities and the qualitative conditions of their lives.[17] Values, beliefs, intentions and, crucially, the sense of one's own capacity for agency are structured and oriented by one's own fundamental sense of self-identity. Self-reflexivity, then, is the first premise of this theory. The second is that the practical construction of reflexive self-identity is critically dependent on the attitudes and evaluations of other human beings. Only through the secure receipt of recognition by others are human agents able to achieve an adequate relation to self. Personal recognition is a basic need, and its bestowal on people is, consequently, a moral requirement. Honneth even goes so far as to identify morality with 'the quintessence of attitudes we are mutually obligated to adopt in order to secure jointly the conditions of our personal integrity'.[18] Whether or not we identify recognition with morality, what we have here is a philosophical argument which connects the acknowledgement of social differences to a people's sense of identity and self-respect, and the latter to their own faith in their efficacy as properly functioning social agents. Once this linkage is accepted, one can see how failures of wide recognition represent injustices, ones manifest in psychological harms. It is more difficult to function effectively as a social agent, and to make use of whatever legal opportunities are open to one, if one is publicly disregarded and categorized as beyond the norm.[19] The sense of inclusion which wide recognition brings helps previously disregarded groups to achieve autonomous agency and function effectively in the public sphere.

This compressed account of the philosophical theory of recognition raises several critical questions in its turn. How much recognition is needed? How much in the public political as opposed to private sphere? Is it individuals as members of cultures we recognize or individuals on their own account? Given the unlimited degree to which we could affirm each other's identities, are there not principled limits to the scope of public recognition – especially given the crucial human need for freedom which plainly stands in some tension with it? I have suggested that recognition is necessary in the political domain, not as a positive evaluation of others' distinct identities but at least as their acknowledgement. Furthermore, while recognizing others is a demand on free agents, it is also necessary for the recipients' sense of personal agency and thus for their own capacity for freedom. Nevertheless, even granted these points, the rationale of Rosenblum's argument is that wide recognition inflates the standard liberal lexicon of moral harms beyond what it can reasonably bear. On her view, citizen's obligations towards one another are simple, clear-cut and best defined negatively. They are to avoid force, coercion, manipulation, violations of laws and rights and similar injustices, and breaches of common standards of decent behaviour, including the grosser forms of offence. On this view, recognition is a strictly supererogatory virtue, and best reserved for the private and perhaps associational domains. But I think this liberal argument can be turned on its head. For once *some* harms to identity are included within the ambit of illegitimate harms – ones citizens must strive to avoid – it becomes very hard to hold the fort at only one class of such harms – gross offence, say – and not include other harms to identity such as humiliation, rejection and marginalization. The point is not that all these must be precisely defined and then codified in law. Rather, acknowledgement that they are indeed harms goes on to inform an account of what wide recognition as a civic duty involves. Though not a legal imperative, wide recognition is nonetheless something citizens are encouraged to demonstrate in their public interactions. And in so doing, they recognize that in a society in which some are in subordinate positions, the category of harm does require expansion, though on principled grounds and informed by the philosophical-psychological theory just outlined.

Let us now consider a contrary argument, signalled above, that wide recognition is not only a vital human need, but it also requires us not merely to accept or acknowledge but to positively affirm, esteem and valorize the identities of others. Recognition as mutual esteem seems to be Taylor's position in 'The Politics of Recognition', where the point of intercultural dialogue is to fuse the value horizons of different groups in order that they can appreciate the collective goods of one another – something each side has a duty to do. Similarly, Young writes that '[g]roups cannot be socially equal unless their specific experience, culture and social contribution are publicly affirmed'.[20] This line of thinking is the object of the third critique of recognition, that it is incoherent simultaneously to affirm the contrary value commitments of different cultures. The critique is, however, off-target in so far as Taylor, Young and Tully[21] employ a quasi-aesthetic notion of value according to which the value of cultures lies in their uniqueness and authenticity. There are no contradictions between different instantiations of uniqueness. Nonetheless, wide recognition, even interpreted as mutual acknowledgement, is highly demanding, and even perhaps impossible, at least in so far as it appears to mandate affirming those values of others which one does not hold oneself.

However, to say that wide recognition is a civic duty leaves it open as to how that duty is best discharged. It need not be a matter of citizens going round affirming each other (which is easily parodied). What wide recognition enjoins us to do in practical terms, in our day-to-day contact with others, and in public life more generally, is not to demean or disparage the values of others, and to accept that their form of life is valid – at least for them. This idea – recognition as acknowledgement – is more demanding than tolerating others, but it is still very far from actively esteeming them. Its object is to ensure that no form of life is publicly rejected or considered beyond the pale. In this sense it helps secure the important good of inclusion – a good, I maintained, that is part of social justice. For the diehard politics of recognition advocate, however, acknowledgement may appear not to go far enough: the solution to misrecognition, on this person's view, must be actively to esteem and affirm minority ways of life. Affirmation, however, must be a voluntary act. And it is indeed incoherent to affirm others' values to which one does not subscribe oneself. Acknowledgement, by contrast, does make sense as a civic duty. A society in which citizens do acknowledge one another's ways of life – a society which practises wide recognition – is one whose public culture and public values are democratized and opened up. Though these values are incompatible and competing, none are marginalized simply by virtue of being a minority view. Wide recognition means, for example, that Islam is not disparaged as a religion and belief system; that non-European art is not considered primitive and savage; that speakers of Punjabi are not looked down upon; that gay relationships are not considered intrinsically inferior. Now suppose a 'community of recognition' is clustered around values that are not systematically degraded by the wider society. Individuals who hold these values can then be affirmed and esteemed by others in that community (if not by the wider society) for achieving the distinctive excellences and virtues that their way of life defines. So one can gain the esteem and affirmation of one's community of recognition as a good Muslim, a talented African artist, a scholar of Punjabi, a person who exhibits the skill of maintaining a gay (as any) relationship. When a person achieves some of the virtues that a way of life defines, then others who share that way of life (and perhaps even a few who do not) can offer positive recognition for that achievement. In this way, recognition in the relatively weak sense I have outlined can help maintain the conditions where persons can be positively recognized by, and on the terms of, their relevant communities.

Let me end this section by asking a final question: what would a society without wide recognition be like? In many respects it could be a perfectly liberal society. It could be a society that guaranteed each of its members an equal degree of legal freedom. It could be one where coercive norms were universally publicly accepted and justified. It could be a relatively affluent society, and one enjoying a reasonably equitable distribution of wealth and property. But it would also, I suggest, be one absent a significant dimension of social justice: the dimension that begins with the normative attitudes that citizens evince towards one another, and ends with the sense of inclusion. Given the need for others' recognition in order to achieve an adequate relation to self, a society that actively disparaged certain minority groups would be an unjust one. A society that did practice wide recognition would give to minority collective identities what the majority unproblematically enjoys: a secure sense of their own identity. As Galeotti puts it:

> One should feel at ease with one's collective identity, choosing to stress or to dismiss any particular aspect of it, to exhibit or to keep private a cultural practice. ... In short, members of minority groups should relate

to their social identity just as members of the majority have always done.[22]

Narrow recognition and democracy

I now want to take up, finally, the justice of claims to narrow recognition with which I began. To recall: these all involve changes to laws, policies, public conventions and state funding which seek to accommodate the specific needs and identities of minority groups. Our question is: are they justifiable? And what is the best perspective to make a reasoned judgement about whether they are justifiable? I have defended the notion of wide recognition. Could any form of narrow recognition likewise be vindicated? Three sets of considerations signal against its justifiability. The first concerns impartiality and non-discrimination. I suggested above that narrow measures of recognition could be defended on the grounds that no group should systematically receive a lesser share of social opportunities or a greater share of social burdens merely on the basis that they happen to belong to one group rather than another. On the other hand (and here we return to the impartiality critique), the principle of non-discrimination is too blunt an instrument to apply to every unchosen social burden, ignores the reasonable demands that might be made of cultures and minority groups to modify their practices for the sake of universally applicable laws, and indeed encourages them to press for as many kinds of special treatment as they can get. The second consideration revolves around issues of liberty. In particular, members of minority cultures who benefit from policies of recognition often prefer to be treated as autonomous individuals with their own projects and not as cultural dupes who need recognition in order to function. Resentment at affirmative action, even by its beneficiaries, is the archetypal example of this. Third, policies of narrow recognition arguably fragment the political community and undermine the sources of civic solidarity in so far as they accentuate difference and encourage separatist group-based thinking.

I want to address these critiques by clarifying the relationship between wide and narrow recognition. Which should come first? Though two dimensions of the same general phenomenon, the relationship between them is dynamic and causally complex. A concrete measure of narrow recognition is likely to fuel a change in wide recognition, although precisely what change will depend on the circumstances to hand. The introduction of Muslim schools in the UK, for example, might boost the public status and inclusion of Muslims in this country, or there might be a backlash where it encourages separatism and anti-Muslim feeling. Unless a group is publicly acknowledged and at ease in the wider society, policies of narrow recognition are all too likely to be resented – and to be subject to accusations of partiality, illiberalism and separatism. On the other hand, a more accepting attitude by mainstream society can sometimes follow on the heels of changes in the law. For these reasons, I suggest that wide and narrow recognition must proceed in tandem; neither should precede the other. While an ethos of wide recognition should ideally underlie measures of narrow recognition, it is not always politically expedient for legal and policy changes to wait until that ethos is forthcoming; on the contrary, the public debate they stimulate could help foster a sense of inclusion.

Wide recognition – acknowledging others in their full particularity and accepting them on their own terms – is, I have suggested, a basic human need. Politically speaking, its aim is to ensure that the public culture is a reflexive one: citizens from all backgrounds understand that that culture is made by them and its normative standards are up for democratic negotiation and debate.[23] I have also suggested that others' acknowledgement of one's particular identity is necessary for effective political agency. This includes the exercise of the deliberative democratic virtues of argument, empathy, accommodation and compromise. Indeed, the successful exercise of democratic agency – effectively presenting one's views, having them taken seriously by others and (when they are most just in the circumstances) translated into policy – can only boost the group esteem of the minorities involved. In different ways, then, wide recognition seeks to create the background conditions against which claims of narrow recognition may be democratically resolved.

When a political theorist says that some thorny problem must be resolved democratically by the parties concerned, there must be the suspicion that this is because he does not have an answer himself. So, to avoid this accusation of intellectual abnegation, let me supplement my claim that narrow recognition must be settled democratically with two guiding principles which, I believe, should help structure participants' deliberations. The first of these is our friend non-discrimination. It is a principle that expresses the equality of all citizens. Non-discrimination plainly informs deliberative democracy in the fundamental sense that each citizen, whatever her or his background and group affiliation, is equally entitled to participate on the same terms as every other. But, beyond that basic sense, it is also an orienting guideline for her or him to evaluate substantive measures of recognition. I earlier sketched the basic idea that members of a group should not systematically receive a lesser share of social opportunities or a greater share of social burdens merely on the basis that they happen to belong to one group rather than another, and I suggested that claims to narrow recognition can make an appeal to this principle. It is for co-deliberating citizens to decide how far this holds, and how far to the contrary there are reasonable demands to be made of cultures and minority groups to modify their practices for the sake of universally applicable laws.

The second guiding principle is inclusion. This might seem inappropriate as an over-arching principle in the context of democratic debate because it may appear to embody a substantive view of the character of a political association when that is precisely what participants are to settle themselves. However, a principle of inclusion should be admitted into our account of democratic deliberation on the grounds that it works to strengthen collective deliberation itself.[24] The more that minority groups feel included in the political community, the more effectively they will be able to engage in that public process of evaluating laws and policies of narrow recognition. Excluded groups make less good advocates. Moreover, inclusion functions as a guideline for assessing the justice of recognition in the sense that questions which participants should ask of any particular law or policy of narrow recognition are: will it tend to make its beneficiaries more or less a part of the political community? Will it work to build bridges or to erect borders between majorities and minorities? Again, the answers to these questions will vary according to the case in hand. I gave an example of this with the case of Muslim schools. If their introduction, far from fuelling separatism, in fact boosted the public standing of Muslims in the UK and made them more effective contributors to democratic deliberation – which they may – then that would be a strong consideration in favour of the introduction of such schools.

We are also now in a position to say something in reply to the fourth critique: that narrow recognition encourages political fragmentation. Though this is a real danger, we should not accept it *simpliciter* without a thorough analysis, including empirical investigation, of the sorts of loyalties different sub-communities actually do exhibit in different states, and in different contexts and circumstances. Some, David Miller for example, maintain that there is no contradiction involved in citizens having a dual identity (and dual loyalty), towards both the national community and their own local community.[25] Moreover, the claim that political recognition encourages fragmentation invites analysis of whether *not* recognizing a range of sub-groups is less conducive to generating loyalty to the larger state.[26] There is at least some logic behind the contrary claim that acceding to claims for narrow recognition will more effectively foster an inclusive ethos and bring minority groups into the democratic political process than resisting their demands in an undemocratized public culture. It is also worth emphasizing that the civic solidarity so necessary in plural societies is itself fostered and strengthened by the very activity of engaging in democratic interchange with one's fellow citizens. Civic solidarity need not always rest on a common identity, or indeed any *thing* in common. But it can be promoted by the actual practice of collective debate, exchanging arguments and reasons and having one's views taken seriously by fellow citizens. In sum, while wide and narrow recognition do not necessarily overcome the problem of tribalism, there is no a priori reason to claim that they encourage it.

There is a further, deeper reason why claims to narrow recognition can only ever be settled by the collective deliberations of the citizens of a political community themselves. This is that the practice of argument and discussion over such claims, as well as the political consequences of policies of narrow recognition and evolving attitudes of wide recognition, will themselves tend to change the identities of recognition's advocates and critics. If relatively static groups pressed consistently for the same sorts of recognition, on the same sorts of grounds, and if they were likewise opposed by an unchanging majority with fixed objections, then it might make sense for the political theorist to arrive at a principled solution which settled the issue once and for all. This is not, however, the situation on the ground. Recognition is not just a moral value and a human need, but also an ongoing political process. The collective identities at issue are constructed and reconstructed in part-response to a prevailing legal and normative climate, one which affects the very nature and extent of the claims to recognition minority communities will make, and the rest of society's response to them. Whether cultural leaders push for measures of narrow recognition or whether they will settle for more assimilationist policies, and how far mainstream society is sympathetic to their claims, these issues cannot be settled by the logic of justice and recognition alone. They are political questions. How much citizens who are ascriptively members of some minority group actually identify with that group and work to give it a political presence, for example, and how much they regard themselves conversely as autonomous citizens whose group identities are peripheral and unimportant, is a question whose answer is a function of the dynamics of the democratic process itself. Similarly, members of a group who feel included in a political community may not press so hard for group-differentiated policies of narrow recognition precisely on account of those feelings. Lobbying for legal and policy recognition is often a defensive reaction by groups who are not properly involved in political decision making. In sum, the practices of wide and narrow recognition, in the context of deliberative democratic exchange, will have a recursive effect on what sorts of claims minority groups will tend to make, and how others will react to them. The philosopher cannot predict the results of this ongoing, dynamic process, far less legislate for it. Legislative and policy changes are for citizens themselves to make. Simple arguments, both for and against political recognition, are undercut just because it changes its own bases. The final assessment of those arguments must be left to the citizens who will actually be affected by them.

Notes

1   This list is adapted from A. E. Galeotti, 'Neutrality and Recognition', in R. Bellamy and M. Hollis, eds, *Pluralism and Liberal Neutrality*, London: Frank Cass, 1999, pp. 44–5.
2   A. E. Galeotti, *Toleration as Recognition*, Cambridge: Cambridge University Press, 2002, pp. 209–19.
3   The four criticisms in this section, together with the thought that recognition is not part of social justice, can all be found in B. Barry, *Culture and Equality: An Egalitarian Critique of Multiculturalism*, Cambridge: Polity, 2001. In her chapter in this volume, Andrea Baumeister offers a related rejoinder to Barry's criticisms of multiculturalism, especially his first criticism, on impartiality. See also John Horton's and Margaret Moore's contributions to this volume.
4   Ibid., p. 321.
5   I. M. Young, *Justice and the Politics of Difference*, Princeton: Princeton University Press, 1990, p. 87; cf. Barry, *Culture and Equality*, pp. 269–70.

6 K. A. Appiah, 'Identity, Authenticity and Survival', in A. Gutmann, ed., *Multiculturalism: Examining the Politics of Recognition*, Princeton: Princeton University Press, 1994, pp. 162–3.

7 P. Jones, 'Political Theory and Cultural Diversity', *Critical Review of Social Philosophy and Policy*, 1, 1, 1998, p. 45.

8 Barry, *Culture and Equality*, p. 271.

9 D. Miller, *On Nationality*, Oxford: Oxford University Press, 1995, pp. 130–49; Barry, *Culture and Equality*, pp. 77–90. Cf. W. Kymlicka, *Multicultural Citizenship: A Liberal Theory of Minority Rights*, Oxford: Oxford University Press, 1995, pp. 173–92.

10 See A. Patten, 'Equality of Respect and the Liberal Theory of Citizenship', in C. McKinnon and I. Hampsher-Monk, eds, *The Demands of Citizenship*, London: Continuum, 2000, pp. 193–212.

11 N. Fraser, 'Rethinking Recognition', *New Left Review*, 3, 2000, pp. 107–20.

12 S. Lukes, 'Humiliation and the Politics of Identity', *Social Research*, 64, 1, 1997, p. 45.

13 Cf. I. M. Young, *Inclusion and Democracy*, Oxford: Oxford University Press, 2000, ch. 3.

14 Galeotti, *Toleration as Recognition*, p. 222.

15 Ibid., p.104.

16 N. Rosenblum, *Membership and Morals: The Personal Uses of Pluralism in America*, Princeton: Princeton University Press, 1998, pp. 351–3.

17 A. Honneth, *The Struggle for Recognition: The Moral Grammar of Social Conflict*, Cambridge: Polity, 1995; A. Honneth, 'Recognition and Moral Obligation', *Social Research*, 64, 2, 1997, pp. 17–35; C. Taylor, *Sources of the Self: The Making of Modern Identity*, Cambridge: Cambridge University Press, 1989; C. Taylor, 'The Politics of Recognition', in Gutmann, ed., *Multiculturalism*, pp. 25–75.

18 Honneth, 'Recognition and Moral Obligation', p. 28.

19 Galeotti, *Toleration as Recognition*, p. 98.

20 Young, *Justice and the Politics of Difference*, p. 174.

21 J. Tully, *Strange Multiplicity: Constitutionalism in an Age of Diversity*, Cambridge: Cambridge University Press, 1995.

22 Galeotti, *Toleration as Recognition*, p. 106.

23 Cf. Fraser, 'Rethinking Recognition', pp. 113–20.

24 Cf. S. O'Neill, 'The Politics of Inclusive Agreement: Towards a Critical Discourse Theory of Democracy', *Political Studies* 48, 3, 2000, pp. 503–21.

25 Miller, *On Nationality*, pp. 135–9.

26 Patten, 'Equality of Respect', pp. 204–5.

7 Identity, equality and power

Tensions in Parekh's political theory of multiculturalism

Paul Kelly

Bhikhu Parekh's contribution to both the political theory and practice of a multicultural politics is considerable and wide-ranging. The recently ennobled Emeritus Professor of Political Theory at Hull University has been associated with the politics of cultural integration for many years. The publication of the report in *The Future of Multi-ethnic Britain*[1] – inevitably known as the Parekh Report – is only a further public culmination of his long-standing concern with the broad and complex agenda of multicultural politics. Yet 'multiculturalism' is not only a political problem for modern ethnically plural societies; it is also a problem for political philosophers – indeed, many would argue it has become *the* problem for political philosophers in the last decade. The traditional concern of political theorists with issues of justice, equality, rights and freedom (traditional at least since the mid-1960s, but perhaps for much longer) has been disrupted by the intervention of multicultural theorists, with their challenge of 'whose conception of justice, rights or equality?' Theory, just as much as political institutions and practices, is tainted by cultural presuppositions. Consequently, theory cannot provide the neutral language with which to address and direct politics and policy in this area. Parekh's contribution in this field is as considerable as his engagement with public policy; indeed, his own recent career has embodied the interconnection of both the theoretical problem of multiculturalism and its political manifestations. The publication of *Rethinking Multiculturalism*[2] at about the time of the Parekh Report marked a notable and distinctive contribution to the debates about multiculturalism in political theory. Parekh emerges from both works – for even the Report bears the imprint of his own political theory, albeit the work of many distinguished hands – as a unique and original voice in these debates. His is a voice that takes seriously the issues of multiculturalism and group recognition but does not merely develop the pervasive liberalism of much contemporary political philosophy. Equally importantly, he does not collapse into the fashionable postmodern ironism about multiple identities and the fluidity of identity-conferring groups. He explicitly draws a distinction between what he calls 'self-chosen' practices and those which follow from a distinct way of life.[3] For Parekh, cultural membership and the beliefs systems that go with them are deeply important to their members and are not merely part of the add-on colour and diversity of postmodern pluralist democracy. Not everything we do in life counts as a 'culture'. This robust refusal to merely follow the fashions of 'cultural' theory whilst resolutely defending the claims of 'cultural groups' is only one illustration of Parekh's distinctiveness. Culture matters in his political theory, but it is not the only thing that matters. Parekh is also a thinker of the left and is committed to the ideal of equality. Indeed, it is this commitment which inspires his work against both racial discrimination and disadvantage. His multiculturalism, like that of other 'left' multiculturalists such as Will Kymlicka or Iris Marion Young,[4] is offered as a way of developing a richer and more substantive account of what equality demands than that associated with the liberal egalitarianism of John Rawls or Brian Barry.[5]

However, squaring the claims of cultural authenticity and equal treatment is a problem that goes to the heart of all multiculturalist theories.[6] This pervasive problem for multiculturalist theories is peculiarly acute for Parekh because of the Oakeshottian character of his argument. The long shadow cast over Parekh's multicultural theory by the quintessentially English 'conservative' political philosopher is, from a biographical point of view, unsurprising as Michael Oakeshott was a teacher of Parekh during his graduate studies at the London School of Economics in the late 1950s. However, I want to suggest that from a theoretical point of view (as any Oakeshottian will claim, this is not a 'philosophical' matter), this Oakeshottian legacy is not simply the curiosity of a peculiarly 'English' theory of multicultural accommodation, but potentially vitiates the inclusive and tolerant multicultural politics that Parekh wants to build on it. The Oakeshottian legacy provides him with the resources from which to build his critique of the prevailing liberal-egalitarian orthodoxy of John Rawls and Brian Barry. However, as Parekh is concerned with providing not merely a 'culturalist' critique of liberal egalitarianism but also a normative multicultural theory that can assist in guiding the politics of intercultural evaluation and change, this Oakeshottian legacy becomes a liability and sets up a fatal tension between the claims of cultural authenticity and equal treatment. Consequently, the Oakeshottian character of Parekh's multicultural theory sets out the wrong agenda for 'the future of multi-ethnic Britain', and this is a concern for those who wish to defend much that is in the Parekh Report and take it further in building a decent, just and inclusive country.

Parekh and the 'multiculturalists'

To understand the 'Oakeshottian' character of Parekh's multicultural theory, we need to locate his position in the broader multiculturalist assault on the liberal discourse of distributive justice. Political liberals of a Rawlsian character see the claims of cultural groups through the prism of 'fair equality of opportunity'. John Rawls's famous *A Theory of Justice* provides the defence of an account of 'fair equality of opportunity' that is followed with subtle but

often minor variations by many British and American liberal political theorists. In his later work, Rawls moved away from the position of *A Theory of
Justice* and adopted a more contextualized or political defence of liberalism.[7]
However, the early Rawls still receives robust support from political philosophers such as Brian Barry.[8] For thinkers such as Rawls and Barry, the
problem of group recognition and cultural integration in ethnically plural
societies is simply a particular case of a broad general category of injustice
as unfair treatment, where unfair treatment is the denial of equality of
opportunity or discrimination in terms of the violation of basic civil and
political rights distributed by the norm of 'fair equality of opportunity'.
Cultural groups are seeking 'justice', and the norm of equality derived from
liberal theories determines what justice requires and what, therefore, must be
given to these groups seeking justice. Indeed, the substance of Barry's recent
critique of multiculturalist theory in *Culture and Equality* argues that the
claims of multiculturalism either fall under the remit of liberal egalitarian
principles of justice or else they are bogus. There is no alternative space for a
multicultural theory of justice.

The multiculturalist critique grows out of two dissatisfactions with this
liberal approach. Critics of liberalism and multiculturalist theorists, such as
Will Kymlicka, James Tully, Iris Marion Young, Charles Taylor and Michael
Walzer, all suggest that the liberal approach reinforces relationships of dependence and domination and fails to take account of the cultural specificity of
the original norm of equality of opportunity. The first part of the critique
takes the view that the liberal model entails a centralized juridical state as the
distributive agency dispensing justice.[9] As such, liberal egalitarianism cannot
take seriously the important political function of associations and groups in
constituting moral and political goods. Among such groups and associations
will be cultural and ethno-national groups in multi-ethnic and multi-national
societies, all of which will have conceptions not only of what justice requires,
but also of the institutional structures and norms through which it should be
delivered. More radical theorists such as Iris Marion Young want to open the
category of cultural groups to include any identity-conferring group, not just
ethnicity or national cultural groups, and consequently broaden the remit of
multiculturalism.

The second dissatisfaction is with the apparent cultural blindness or false
neutrality of liberal norms of justice and inclusion. It is argued by multiculturalist critics that the form of liberal norms of inclusion is already culturally
biased, in that they prescribe equality of opportunity in terms of having and
exercising certain primary goods. These goods are things one needs, whatever
else it is that one wants or values – such things as civil and political rights, the
minimum conditions of self-respect and some level of economic well-being.
As general headings these may well seem fair enough – who possibly could
object to civil and political rights? The problem arises with the specification of
these rights and goods. If these rights are premised on a liberal conception of
autonomy, then they may well run up against the internal norms of a culture

which, whilst it values freedom, does not privilege autonomy as a source of a good life. Similarly, if fair equality of economic opportunity is achieved by encouraging (or requiring) women to enter the workforce as equal competitors in the job market, this will undermine cultural groups who attach special roles to women in the home and family. Many liberals, and most feminists, might well say, so much the worse for traditional cultural norms that exclude women from the labour force. However, whatever view one takes about such norms, liberals are left with the task of providing reasons to the cultural groups for why their perception of unfair exclusion is or is not legitimate. The privileging of liberal freedoms over cultural traditions cannot simply be justified on the grounds of 'this is how we liberals do things around here'. Liberals either have to have a principled reason for rejecting a cultural practice or have to acknowledge that such a response unduly favours the liberal majority in deciding a society's norm of inclusion, and thus fails to treat cultures equally. For multiculturalists, liberal egalitarianism is simply a further set of historically conditioned social and political practices. There is no conception of liberal primary goods which is not already pregnant with liberal cultural values and presuppositions, such as the ethical priority of individuality and individual judgement. In such circumstances, it is unsurprising that cultural groups and minority nations see the claims of liberal egalitarianism as merely the preferences of the dominant majority. Multicultural theorists connect the theory and practice of multiculturalism by drawing the lessons of multicultural politics into the realm of an apparently complacent liberal philosophical discourse. The multiculturalist critique argues that the politics of negotiation must precede the aspirations of liberal theory.

This general line of critique is reflected in Parekh's scepticism about the false neutrality and universalism of liberalism and extends into his rejection of the idea that traditional liberal political theory can have much to contribute to the accommodation of cultural group differences. Indeed, the first chapter of *Rethinking Multiculturalism* involves a sustained critique of classical liberalism from Locke through Bentham to J. S. Mill for offering a monistic liberal theory which places a certain conception of individual human nature and flourishing at the centre of its politics. This conception of human nature and flourishing, according to Parekh, is closely tied to theories of colonialism and the civilizing mission of the liberal European Enlightenment. In support of this interpretation, Parekh is able to point to Mill's views about the backwardness of other races and Locke's equivocal views about slave-holding and colonialism. Like James Tully in *Strange Multiplicity*, Parekh wishes to draw attention to the ambiguous legacy of liberalism over the last three centuries. More importantly, however, he wants to show that the endorsement of racial and cultural superiority are not merely historical accents and temporary lapses from good taste by otherwise benign liberal philosophers, but rather that this ambiguity goes to the heart of the liberal project, which cannot be separated so easily from its history. It is this rejection of the contribution of normative theory as supposedly above ordinary politics and his consequent reliance on what he calls a society's 'operative public values'[10] that best illustrates the 'Oakeshottian' character of Parekh's multiculturalism.

The elements of 'Oakeshottian' multiculturalism

The English political philosopher Michael Oakeshott is not someone who is immediately or easily associated with the issue of multiculturalism. Yet his influence was both subtle and pervasive among British political theorists, for a number of reasons. Oakeshott was primarily a philosophical sceptic, albeit one of an idealist orientation; as such he was a great debunker of the pretensions of philosophy or theory to either do or change things.[11] This is famously expanded in his critique of the rationalist in politics.[12] The critique of rationalism results in an assault on those who hide their political interests beneath the mantle of philosophy and, consequently, in a rejection of the idea of normative political theory of the post-Rawlsian variety. For Oakeshott, political philosophy is not supposed to provide people with a handy theoretical tool-kit for solving practical political problems. This is the kind of hubris associated with arch-rationalists such as Jeremy Bentham.

There can, therefore, be no universal principle which will provide a way of arbitrating the claims of cultural groups seeking recognition in the wider society. But if there is no prospect of appeal to abstract universal principles or reason, where does this leave political and moral justification and critique? In one sense this is precisely the kind of question that Oakeshott wanted to dispense with. Only a rationalist could ask for advice from anything as vulgar as a theory when confronting a real issue of political concern. Instead, moral and political issues and problems can only be addressed from the internal perspective of a moral and political tradition. Solutions, or at least ways of dealing with practical concerns, are found by pursuing the intimations of such traditions. These moral and political traditions are complex and organic and are, therefore, not reducible to any finite system of rules. Instead they take the form of a conversation which has no other purpose than the internal one of carrying on.

These aspects of Oakeshott's perspective have been particularly attractive to political theorists of a sceptical, anti-theoretical kind. Oakeshott provides an armoury for those who wish to deflate the pretensions of normative political theory to have a principled answer to problems of politics. Like many multiculturalist critics of liberal political theory, Oakeshott's position supports the primacy of politics over political theory – at least to the extent that it collapses the high pretensions of normative theory into simple political advocacy. We see what normative political theory really is, shorn of its philosophical pretensions. But Oakeshott's conception of the limitations of political theory does not simply support a retreat from normative political theory. In its elevation of a practice-based account of moral and political life as the backdrop to practical reflection, it opens up the possibility of thinking about cultural inclusion in a different way from that offered by liberalism.

This is precisely how Parekh develops the Oakeshottian legacy in his approach to multicultural inclusion and his understanding of the nature and identity of cultural groups. He draws on both strands of the Oakeshottian legacy to build a communitarian response to the issue of multicultural inclusion. First, he rejects the possibility of an appeal to universal principles or norms as a way of reconciling or arbitrating between cultural groups. He also turns to the substantive Oakeshottian position of 'operative public morality' to provide a way of determining how far we should include the practices of other cultures. It is this latter idea that is developed and expanded in *Rethinking Multiculturalism.*

Parekh also uses the 'Oakeshottian' idea of practices that are constitutive of a way of life as a means of distinguishing the relevant groups for the purposes of multicultural inclusion from those which are merely lifestyle choices and, therefore, voluntary. Cultural practices provide the background against which choices can be made and, as such, these practices cannot merely be validated by their endorsement by individuals contrary to the way lifestyle choices are validated. In contrast to Iris Marion Young, who wishes to challenge the essentializing tendency of some multicultural discourse and collapse the distinction between lifestyle choices and cultural groups, Parekh forcefully reasserts the distinction but without collapsing it into a crude essentialism.[13] Lifestyle choices are voluntaristic and therefore place responsibility on the choosing agent for any costs that might be incurred. Culture, on the other hand, shapes personality such that it makes the whole concept of opportunity subject-dependent. Thus, for Parekh, it does not really make sense to say that Jews have the opportunity to eat pork, or Sikh males to abandon the turban. Opportunity is subject-dependent and subjectivity is an historical and cultural achievement, not merely a choice.[14]

Before turning to consider Parekh's account of 'operative public morality' and its implications for multicultural politics, I want to rehearse the arguments underlying Parekh's critique of liberalism to show how they reflect the sceptical communitarianism that is the legacy of Oakeshott's assault on rationalism. Parekh's arguments against the liberal impartialist approach are familiar and involve three related claims, which parallel neo-Hegelian or communitarian criticisms of abstract universalism.

The liberal impartialist solution to multiculturalism requires the justification of universal moral principles that are neutral between conflicting moral claims. Liberalism is supposed to provide an external, neutral perspective from which it can adjudicate between cultures. Without such a perspective, contemporary liberalism is merely one other tradition or view and, as such, of no greater authority than any other cultural practice or set of beliefs. Parekh claims that this enormously demanding project remains unredeemed, despite the best efforts of Immanuel Kant and subsequent generations of philosophers down to the likes of John Rawls and Brian Barry in the present. In this he is no doubt right, to the extent that no impartialist theory has as yet acquired universal consent – although how important the fact of such universal consent is remains controversial. But Parekh is not merely pointing to the fact that as yet we do not have a philosophical consensus on the basis of the liberal principle of impartial inclusion. He claims that the impartialist perspective is incoherent in the way it presumes that there must be one right ordering of human society and the good life, despite the great variety of different views and practices throughout human history. Given the fact of difference, the very presumption that there should be one single right way of doing things needs both explanation and justification. For Parekh, this is merely one further example of the fundamental monism of modern liberalism. Liberalism is monistic in the sense that it offers a single unitary account of the good life for man, and this is true across time and space. Admittedly, liberal impartiality tries to give a thin account of this conception of the good in terms of rights and liberties, but this merely disguises the monism that underlies the apparent tolerance of modern liberalism. Although the set of rights and titles that liberals agree upon is supposed to encompass a very broad range of lifestyles and conceptions of the good, the set of rights and titles, according to Parekh, reflects a particular conception of the person or moral subject. In this way liberal pluralism is only apparent and obscures the fundamental monism that lies at the heart of the liberal Enlightenment, for what underlies the liberal self is an historically contingent and culturally parochial conception of the person.

Parekh's critique of moral monism turns on the idea, familiar from communitarian criticisms of liberal individualism, that it presupposes an atomized or abstract conception of the self or personhood. In contrast to this view, he asserts the hermeneutic thesis that conceptions of the self are always embedded in social and historical contexts. The embeddedness thesis supports the conclusion that cultural commitments or cultural identity cannot simply be separated from the authentic moral identity of the person. Thus Parekh rejects the liberal egalitarian's claim that culture can be separated from moral subjectivity in the way that liberal egalitarians claim. And if this separation is ruled out, then the idea of a single unified conception of the moral good is incoherent, as subjectivity and culture will always be interconnected and necessarily plural. This is as true for what might be called comprehensive liberalisms, such as those of Locke or Mill, as it is of contemporary liberal impartialism of the sort we find in Barry and Rawls. But this problem of monism does not only apply to contemporary liberalism in its impartialist variety. Parekh goes on to extend his critique to perfectionist liberals such as Will Kymlicka and Joseph Raz, who try to accommodate the idea of pluralism in a constitutive rather than a voluntarist sense.[15] Voluntarist pluralism collapses into the idea of a plurality or diversity of individual wants which people may pursue. This is the kind of pluralism that underpins Rawls's *A Theory of Justice*. Constitutive pluralism, on the other hand, recognizes the plurality of constitutive conceptions of the good or forms of life out of which different conceptions of the self emerge.

Although Kymlicka and Raz attempt to overcome the criticism of Rawls's unencumbered moral subject by situating their accounts of moral autonomy in social and cultural contexts, both make the case that the liberal ideal of autonomy does not involve the abandonment of constitutive attachments and thus does not entail atomism. This idea of constitutive pluralism and liberal autonomy is precisely what underpins Kymlicka's liberal multiculturalism. Against this reconciliationist thesis, Parekh argues that Kymlicka and Raz still adopt the idea of a transcendental autonomous subject in order to support their liberal multiculturalism and perfectionism. Whilst both Raz and Kymlicka represent an advance of Rawls and Barry, and a considerable advance on Locke and Mill, they are still all implicated in the same monistic enterprise of reducing the plurality of moral and cultural perspectives into a single general form that privileges the claims of moral autonomy over all other moral considerations.[16]

As we have seen, the fact of pluralism, for Parekh tends to suggest a more substantive moral pluralism in which cultural practices are given a primary value because they are constitutive of personhood and moral agency. Whereas liberals wish to separate persons and their cultures when they confer equality of concern and respect on people, for Parekh the egalitarian aspiration to treat people equally must entail equal respect for cultural practices as part of what it means to treat people equally.

But even if we are unconvinced by these considerations and accept the liberal aspiration of universalism, we are, according to Parekh, still left with two other problems which render the liberal project problematic. The first of these considerations is the motivation problem. Even if we could find a philosophical foundation for a universal liberal norm of inclusion, we might still have a problem of providing a motive to act on such a norm that is sufficiently overriding in the face of competition from other, less impartial moral and political commitments. Here Parekh rehearses the familiar charge that universal first-order moral principles are simply too demanding for mere mortals, with their partial commitments and special obligations. It is only through our more substantive commitments to particular individuals through complex social relations and practices that we can have the idea of overriding moral motives. The abstract perspective of moral universalism, were it even possible, is just too thin to support demands of obligation to our fellows.

The third part of the objection to moral universalism follows from the need to interpret universal principles. Parekh's example of a universal moral principle that needs interpretation is 'respect for human life'. Many, perhaps all, cultures can be said to endorse this principle, but on its own it does not entail any single authoritative interpretation. Does it entail merely negative liberty rights, or the positive provision of welfare? Is it something that is the responsibility of the whole community? Such a moral principle can be cashed out in many ways in culturally diverse societies, such that appeal to the principle will not in itself do any real work. As Hegel and all communitarian philosophers since have been quick to point out, abstract moral principles, because of their abstraction, have to be actualized in a concrete form of ethical life. Such a form of ethical life will always be particular and local; there is no single universal form of ethical life that will satisfy all people, as we can see from the fact of reasonable pluralism. For an Oakeshottian, this sceptical conclusion marks the limit of political philosophy. It can tell us what we cannot have and thus set limits on the philosophical authority of those who wish to claim more.

Because we have no philosophically uncontroversial moral principles, and because they would not, in themselves, provide much help in facing the problem of multicultural inclusion, we need another approach. It is here that Parekh turns to the second aspect of the Oakshottian perspective: 'operative public values'.

'Operative public values' and the terms of inclusion

The 'operative public values' of a society are the public moral and political rules that bind a particular group of people into a common society. Without such 'operative public values' the different and often conflicting components of a society could not exist as a cohesive body. They have no higher origin than that they constitute the overlapping common bonds of the various different groups, classes and interests that make up a political society. Their only authority is that they have become part of the received structure of social relations. They are in effect 'how we do things around here'. And their acceptance and broad acknowledgement is their only claim to authority. These values constitute a common form of life among people who otherwise differ; they do not prescribe the final structure or content of a human life or a common set of goals towards which a society is progressing. They are merely the unwritten terms of a common practice within which various particular forms of life are pursued and reconciled. This conception of a shared form of life manifests itself in the constitutional framework of a society as well as its laws, both municipal and moral. It also manifests itself in the civic relations of its members. These unwritten rules of conduct include the good manners of a particular society, that is, ways of behaving that share a common but unarticulated understanding of how to act.

'Operative public values' constitute and embody a shared form of public life; they are not derived from a thick conception of the moral life or of the human good, but they are inevitably influenced by such a perspective. As such, they provide the particular content for the Oakeshottian form of the modern state as a civil association.

How do these operative public values help with the issue of multicultural inclusion? Parekh clearly suggests that we should turn to these operative public values as a means of establishing and negotiating multicultural inclusion. When faced with a claim for the recognition of a practice by a minority group, the wider society does not merely assert its operative public values as if these were static and beyond reproach. Instead, it uses the operative public values as the basis for opening a dialogue with the minority group. This dialogue involves both a defence of the operative public values through a process of reason giving and, if necessary, an attempt to explain why the minority practice offends against those values. The minority must try to defend its practices and show why these ought to be recognized by the wider society. This process is supposed to be dialogical in that both parties learn from and transform their understanding of their respective values. The apparent advantage of the dialogue between the operative public values of the wider society and the beliefs and practices of the minority claiming recognition is that they provide clear terms within which the minority can articulate its position in order to persuade the multifarious views of the broad public. In the absence of operative public values, the minority would need to convince each group, interest or individual of the consonance of its beliefs and practices with their fundamental moral views.

When liberals such as Rawls or Barry offer equalitarian norms and rights as the basis of the terms of social co-operation, they are, according to Parekh, merely offering interpretations of the operative public values of particular societies such as the United States and Britain. Rawls seems to concede this point in later works such as *Political Liberalism*.[17] Yet Parekh is much more explicit in his historical situation of liberal egalitarianism. He is not claiming that the operative public values of British and American political culture are indeed liberal. Rather, these liberal theorists are actually providing a liberal interpretation of the operative public values of a particular political society. Of course, anti-liberals will contest these interpretations and offer other, perhaps more conservative, interpretations of the operative public values of a society.

Given Parekh's rejection of universalism, there is no other perspective from which we can construct a better way of dealing with group recognition and multiculturalism. But, in the end, does Parekh provide an adequate approach to the problems of multicultural inclusion and recognition? Or does his hasty and familiar rejection of the false neutrality of liberal impartialism leave him with nowhere else to go in confronting the problem of cultural recognition than asserting that 'this is how we do things around here', that is, merely doing precisely what is supposed to be wrong with liberal impartialism? It should be pointed out that, for Oakeshott, this *is* a sufficient justification for carrying on in a certain way in the realm of practice. Does this Oakeshottian aspect of Parekh's argument vitiate his attempts to provide an adequate vocabulary for dealing with the recognition of cultural practices? And if so, where does this leave the defence of the provisions of the Parekh Report, which are critical of many of our less than satisfactory operative public values?

The dangers of Oakeshottian multiculturalism

Whereas many multiculturalist critics who reject an impartial or external principle of inclusion are left with no other means of accommodating the claims of identity groups than reintroducing such principles through the back door, Parekh seems to make a virtue of this position. Clearly he wants there to be dialogue between the operative public values and the claims of the minority group. But what grounds has he got for assuming that there will be such a dialogue and that it will not merely be distorted by the current distribution of power in society? Surely, one of the common concerns of multiculturalists on the ground is the absence of such dialogue. Yet, even if we are more optimistic about the dialogue taking place, there is still a major problem with Parekh's theory that leaves unaddressed the real concern of multicultural politics.

The whole thrust of Parekh's perspective privileges the received operative public values of a society. In this he does not even disguise his concern to endorse 'how we do things around here', for there is no other perspective from which to start. Remember that, following Oakeshott's account of cultural practices and traditions, there is no other possible basis (or need) to defend the authority of a tradition than to show that it is the way of doing things of particular groups. To argue against the legitimacy or authority of the British political and constitutional tradition is to engage in a category mistake and to lapse into rationalism.

Parekh's apparent endorsement of this approach might well be seen to be fine if we start from a liberal society, although multiculturalists have generally been thought to be critics of the merely apparent neutralism or impartiality of liberalism. But why should we start from such a society, and which society is ever fully liberal in terms of living up to standards of equality and respect for the person of the sort we find in liberal theories of justice? What about the shared forms of life of those societies which are less tolerant of difference than an *ideal* liberal democracy, precisely those forms and practices which are the subject of the Parekh Report?

Although Parekh is pushed towards adopting the operative public values as the basis of negotiating recognition and inclusion because of his Oakeshottian rejection of liberal universalism, there remains something curious about appealing to a society's internal self-understanding as a means of dealing with multicultural claims. Parekh does not assert that the operative public values of a society guarantee complete homogeneity; that would surely be wrong. However, the operative public values are supposed to embody a conception of society as sufficiently stable. So we are not expecting uniformity, but neither are we expecting total diversity. This presents a picture of the circumstances of modern pluralistic societies as relatively homogeneous but open to inclusion of the correct sort. (Incidentally, there doesn't seem to be any imperative that the 'operative public morality' should be inclusive of 'lifestyle' groups seeking recognition of their sexuality – so much the worse for opponents of Clause 28.) Yet one of the characteristic features of multicultural societies is not merely the request by minority groups for recognition but a challenge to the idea of an uncontroversial account of the 'operative public morality'. What is at issue in debates about multiculturalism is precisely what

Parekh assumes as the starting point for addressing the problem, namely an uncontroversial norm of inclusion. This is not to assert some facile post-modern ironism, but merely to point to the fact of pluralism that underlies the politics of multiculturalism. Parekh's endorsement of this Oakeshottian stance results in his starting to address the claims of groups for recognition from the wrong place. For Oakeshott, this is deliberate, as the whole point is to endorse a broadly conservative approach to political institutions and practices. But for Parekh, who wants to ground the enlightened political reforms of the Parekh Report, this is fatal.

The other crucial way in which Parekh's reliance on operative public values seems to misconstrue the issue of multiculturalism is that it resolutely tends to conceive of the issue as one of assimilation. The whole point of the dialogue with the operative public values of a society is to identify ways of including some cultural practices into the terms of the operative public morality. Yet, in conceiving of the issue in this way, Parekh appears to have replicated one of the key problems posed by the liberalism he rejects. The cultural group seeking recognition is dependent upon the wider society for what it needs, and it is up to the wider society through its operative public morality to grant or withhold what is needed. This institutionalizes the group's inequality of status. It also advantages the majority culture in granting or withholding recognition. There is no allowance for the multicultural group to seek to challenge the terms of inclusion, which are set by the 'operative public values' of the majority. Assimilation is offered on the best terms that the wider society can make, but the real issue of injustice to cultural minorities is often that the best terms they can achieve will merely reflect their numerical weakness or lack of bargaining power. What is left unaddressed by focusing on the operative public values of a society, or its conception of itself as a community embodying a shared form of life, is the unequal and possibly unjust power relationships that exist within that society. If the multiculturalist is seeking fair terms for negotiating inclusion, that is, terms which do not advantage one particular group merely because of numbers or history, then Parekh's approach ceases to be multiculturalist, because on this key issue it has nothing to say. His approach has no way of distinguishing dominance, oppression and injustice from the way 'things are done around here'. Indeed, the whole question ceases to make sense as we collapse into a strong relativism. Against the dangers of such a relativism we are merely offered a hope that the wider society will be tolerant and open to inclusion.

In the end, Parekh's Oakeshottian multicultural theory is simply too communitarian. It places too much emphasis on 'how we do things around here' in order to address concerns about the impartiality and the false neutrality of liberalism, with its unfortunate history of imperialism. But as such it leaves no theoretical resources for dealing with the core multicultural concern with fair terms of inclusion. Parekh's theory, as is true of all genuinely communitarian theories, has nowhere to go but the internal view of a particular society and culture. Yet it is precisely the authority of such internal perspectives that the multiculturalists wish to challenge in their quest for recognition and inclusion.

Equality, power and the spectre of liberalism

As we saw at the beginning of this chapter, Parekh is not simply an Oakeshottian; he is also a left egalitarian and believes that the familiar liberal concern with equality of opportunity is too narrowly restrictive in its failure to take account of the problem of cultural recognition. Yet the hermeneutic aspects of Oakeshott's legacy on Parekh's thought leaves him with two major problems. If he is to avoid the charge that his reliance on operative public values does not collapse into the endorsement of the majority perspective and the assimilation of minorities, he needs to provide a conception of the egalitarian norm which does some critical work. However, the hermeneutic perspective seems to have deprived him of the possibility of constructing such a principle. This becomes all the more problematic when that principle is used for coercive regulation or even prohibition of cultural practices. Parekh has done much to challenge the liberal critic of multiculturalism's preoccupation with the more lurid issues of genital mutilation, ritual scarring or forced marriages, on the grounds that on these issues most multiculturalist theorists agree with liberals and that these issues are a diversion from the many benign aspects of cultural practices that are rendered unduly costly by liberal societies.[18] That said, there remain many areas where society has to make hard decisions that cut across the cultural norms and practices of certain groups. This is precisely where the hermeneutic perspective derived from Oakeshott is of no help to Parekh. Whilst Oakeshott can and does simply assert the need to rely on our received operative public values, that strategy effectively undermines Parekh's egalitarianism. One is left with the question: why should we bother about equal treatment?

Parekh uses the hermeneutic perspective to expand a conception of equality, and his extended discussion of the concept in *Rethinking Multiculturalism* involves the discussion of issues and cases in which a more nuanced application of egalitarian norms is required. Yet that hermeneutic perspective does not provide any ground for adopting the perspective of equality in the first instance. This leaves Parekh with two choices: either he can say that the norm of equal treatment is a cultural preference but one that is widely shared, or he can search for an independent account of his basic commitment to equality.

If we adopt the former position, then equality is merely a value relative to a particular community and does not provide a normative justification for action to those who do not form part of that community. This equality cannot provide a fair basis of social interaction between those who regard the sexes as not equal but different, and those who regard sexual equality as a primary moral commitment. In practice one might be able to arrive at a *modus vivendi* defence of equality. One might, for instance, convince a cultural group to accommodate itself to the demands of sexual equality on the grounds that it cannot impose its will on all others and therefore wishes to preserve itself from total assimilation. This approach might be one way of reading Parekh's strategy of intercultural evaluation and justification. However, such *modus vivendi* arguments are always contingent on the balance of power and advantage and thus can change at any time. Unless there is a principled commitment to equality of treatment, then whatever relations are agreed between cultural groups will merely reflect the existing distribution of power. As we have seen, that is not what Parekh wants, and it is an inadequate basis for multicultural recognition. But that then leaves only the external perspective from which to defend a norm of equality. This is what liberal egalitarianism aspires to in offering egalitarianism as a free-standing principle, that is, one that might have a particular cultural root, but which is not dependent on its origins for its justification and authority. However, it has to be conceded that the inadequacies of the internal perspective of a particular society do not of themselves vindicate the case for universalism or impartialist egalitarianism, although they might explain why the quest for an impartialist view is attractive to those of a liberal persuasion. Without commencing a full defence of impartiality here, it is possible to object that Parekh's rejection of the demandingness of first-order impartiality does not dispense with the impartialist perspective. Furthermore, the issue of philosophical foundations remains open, as Parekh's two other criticisms of universalism (which includes liberal egalitarianism) are far from devastating if impartiality is confined to the second-order level of the distribution of decision-making power and the terms of inclusion.

Yet whether modern liberal theory has been able to redeem its basic promise remains a side issue because Parekh's own position cannot avoid the kind of abstraction from the situated or internalist perspective of a cultural group if he is to seek norms of social integration that have any authority. His rejection of externalism seems to rest on a peculiarly realist conception of universal justification. Unless we can find a neutral third language into which we can translate the claims to two cultures, we cannot have a neutral perspective from which to arbitrate their claims. Yet liberal universalists do not have to be as naïvely realist as this. The whole thrust of contemporary liberalism has sought to construct a language that is thin enough to obtain the consensus of the broad majority of conceptions of the good. Whether this has indeed been achieved is an open question, but whether it is as naïve as Parekh suggested earlier is much more controversial. Parekh seems to want to replace this abstract and monological (or one-sided) conception of philosophical justification with a more situated and democratic or dialogical conception of justification. But this turn to dialogue begs the question at issue. The whole point of liberal egalitarianism's turn from the primacy of politics to the primacy of justice in the basic structure of society is that politics is open to the existing distribution of power. In the real world of politics, groups and their interests compete or co-operate in accordance with their relative bargaining positions. This distribution of power and positional advantage is historically contingent, so it cannot form the basis of a fair agreement on the basic norm of social inclusion. The whole point of the primacy of justice over politics is that it tries to confront the existing distribution of power and advantage. But it can only do that by abstracting the issue of moral and political justification from the normal processes of politics. Liberal norms of equality are supposed to provide a regulative ideal against which we can criticize and assess fair terms of social co-operation. These norms cannot emerge from the normal processes of political interaction.

Parekh wishes to avoid the unduly abstract perspective of liberal egalitarianism by advancing a conception of intercultural dialogue and agreement, but this dialogical enterprise cannot provide the terms of its own exercise. Implicit in Parekh's view, as in other attempts at establishing a democratic resolution of intercultural disagreement, is a norm of inclusion that is not itself subject to such an agreement but which regulates all such agreements.[19] This does not have to be a substantively liberal norm, but it will have the features that Parekh finds so problematic in the case of liberal norms, namely their universalism, abstraction and thinness. What it must have, however, is an authority that extends beyond the boundaries of a particular culture or society's way of doing things, otherwise it provides no justification for the coercive regulation of relations between different groups.

Parekh accepts the possibility of abstraction from cultural context to the extent that he denies that our identities are rigidly determined by our situation. This is certainly borne out by his willingness to engage in the critical judgements of certain cultural practices such as genital mutilation in the chapter of *Rethinking Multiculturalism*, on the logic of intercultural evaluation. But once he has accepted that possibility of abstraction, he has opened the door precisely to the arguments of Kymlicka and Raz which, as we saw, he wished to reject for their residual monism. If we are culturally situated but not determined, we can interact with and transform our identities and we can ask probing questions about the structures and power within which we find ourselves. But acknowledging this also has the effect of weakening the claims of culture because it allows for a distinction between a person and his or her context. This does not necessarily entail a liberal multiculturalism such as that of Kymlicka and Raz unless we also add a liberal commitment to equality or autonomy. But unless we add some such external norm we have no basis from which to engage in cultural and political criticism. If we want the latter, as Parekh does, then we need to disengage social criticism from the interpretation of an existing practice or form of life because the authority of particular cultural practices is precisely what is at issue in debates about cultural accommodation. If we are to provide fair terms of social interaction between cultural groups, even if those terms are negotiated in some intercultural dialogue, that dialogue must itself be located in a set of norms which are external to the cultural practices of a particular group – at least to the extent of being free-standing. In terms of the logic of intercultural accommodation there is simply no third way between internalism, or cultural relativism, and, externalism. That Parekh does recognize that, at the level of particular issues of group claims there is a surprising convergence between his own multiculturalism and Brian Barry's anti-multiculturalist egalitarianism, merely reinforces the idea that for Parekh, as for Iris Marion Young and James Tully, there is the spectre of a suppressed liberalism lurking beneath the surface of his theory.[20]

Conclusion

In conclusion I would suggest that Parekh's critique of liberalism actually misconstrues its character and disguises the extent to which he too is committed to a residual liberal egalitarianism. This problem is exacerbated by the Oakeshottian character of his critique of liberalism and defence of cultural practices. Yet this aspect of his theory is ultimately unsatisfactory because it brings the cultural presuppositions of the majority community not only into the open, but also into a position of dominance. To the extent that Parekh is prepared to continue to endorse this Oakeshottian defence of cultural practices, he cannot defend his egalitarianism as anything other than a cultural prejudice. And to the extent that he defends his commitment to egalitarianism, he weakens the significance and authority of cultural norms and practices. This does not entail that there is no choice between cultural relativism and Brian Barry's liberal egalitarianism; but it does suggest that there is no third way between those who attach ultimate significance to either culture or equality. Parekh is a genuinely decent and tolerant person and many of his committee's recommendations reflect this; however, the theory we are offered in *Rethinking Multiculturalism* has no such necessary implication. As such it not only fails to support such inclusive and genuinely pluralist conclusions, but it also provides ammunition for those (perhaps the unreflective majority) who would wish to undermine and reject them.

Notes

This is an expanded version of ' "Dangerous Liaisons": Parekh and "Oakeshottian" Multiculturalism', *Political Quarterly*, 72, 4, 2001, pp. 428–36. The author is grateful to the editors of *Political Quarterly* for permission to reproduce parts of the original article.
1   *The Future of Multi-ethnic Britain*, London: Profile Books, 2000.
2   B. Parekh, *Rethinking Multiculturalism: Cultural Diversity and Political Theory*, Basingstoke: Macmillan, 2000.
3   Ibid., pp. 142–3.
4   W. Kymlicka, *Multicultural Citizenship: A Liberal Theory of Minority Rights*, Oxford: Clarendon Press, 1995; and I. M. Young, *Justice and the Politics of Difference*, Princeton: Princeton University Press, 1990.
5   J. Rawls, *A Theory of Justice*, Oxford: Oxford University Press, 1971; and B. Barry, *Culture and Equality: An Egalitarian Critique of Multiculturalism*, Cambridge: Polity, 2000.
6   See the introduction to Kelly, ed., *Multiculturalism Reconsidered*, Cambridge: Polity, 2002, pp. 1–17.

7   See R. Martin, 'John Rawls', in D. Boucher and Kelly, eds, *Political Thinkers*, Oxford: Oxford University Press, 2002, pp. 496–515.

8   B. Barry, *Justice as Impartiality*, Oxford: Clarendon Press, 1995; and *Culture and Equality*.

9   This view finds its most forceful statement in the work of James Tully, see *Strange Multiplicity: Constitutionalism in an Age of Diversity*, Cambridge, Cambridge University Press, 1995; and his response to Brian Barry in 'The Illiberal Liberal: Brian Barry's Polemical Attack on Multiculturalism', in Kelly, ed., *Multiculturalism Reconsidered*, pp. 102–13.

10   Parekh, *Rethinking Multiculturalism*, pp. 264–94.

11   The best short introduction to Oakeshott's philosophy is David Boucher, 'Oakeshott', in Boucher and Kelly, eds, *Political Thinkers*, pp. 459–79.

12   M. Oakeshott, *Rationalism in Politics and Other Essays*, London: Methuen, 1962.

13   The most forceful statement of the distinction between cultural practices and lifestyle choices is to be found in an earlier paper, B. Parekh, 'The Logic of Intercultural Evaluation', in J. Horton and S. Mendus, eds, *Toleration, Identity and Difference*, Basingstoke: Macmillan, 1999, p. 163. Here Parekh writes: 'unlike such self-chosen practices or life-styles as cohabitation and homosexuality, cultural practices are part of a way of life, have a normative authority and are generally regarded as binding by the members of the community concerned'.

14   Given what Parekh says about the subjective nature of opportunity, it is perhaps surprising that he can describe 'homosexuality' as a lifestyle choice. Whilst it might make sense to say that a homosexual has a choice whether to indulge or not in sexual activity, in the same way that anyone else does, it is surely much less plausible to suggest that homosexuals choose to be homosexual. This is much more likely to be a case in which ideas of choice and opportunity are subjective in a similar way to Parekh's account of cultural identity. For a discussion of Parekh on the subjectivity of opportunity, see D. Miller, 'Liberalism, Equal Opportunities and Cultural Commitments', in Kelly, ed., *Multiculturalism Reconsidered*, pp. 45–61.

15   See W. Kymlicka, *Liberalism, Community and Culture*, Oxford: Oxford Univesrity Press, 1989; and J. Raz, *The Morality of Freedom*, Oxford: Clarendon Press, 1986.

16   Parekh, *Rethinking Multiculturalism*, pp. 109–13.

17   J. Rawls, *Political Liberalism*, New York: Columbia University Press, 1993.

18   For a multiculturalist thinker who is far more tolerant of such controversial practices, see C. Kukathas, 'Are There Any Cultural Rights?', in W. Kymlicka, ed., *The Rights of Minority Cultures*, Oxford: Oxford University Press, 1995, pp. 228–55.

19   See especially Young, *Justice and the Politics of Difference*; and Tully, *Strange Multiplicity*.

20   B. Parekh, 'Barry and the Dangers of Liberalism', in Kelly, ed., *Multiculturalism Reconsidered*, pp. 147–8.

8 The limits of universalism

Andrea Baumeister

In his recent book *Culture and Equality*, Brian Barry aims to refute the case for a differentiated citizenship, which seeks to accommodate the claims of cultural diversity through a broad range of group rights. For Barry, the liberal commitment to civic equality is best achieved through a unitary citizenship, which removes religious and cultural differences from the political sphere and grants all citizens an identical set of rights and liberties. While citizens should be free to pursue a broad range of lifestyles, the state should not employ its powers to promote a particular religion or way of life. Consequently, Barry concludes that liberalism neither can nor should accommodate demands for 'deep cultural diversity'. That is to say, the state should not grant group-differentiated rights – be they legal exemptions or self-government rights – designed to maintain or perpetuate a particular culture or religion. To do so would be to depart from the principle of state neutrality.

However, not only does Barry underestimate the extent to which all liberal regimes are thickly embedded in a particular cultural context, but the assumptions that underpin his defence of state neutrality also remain contested. Whereas Barry contends that it is possible to construe a point of view which all reasonable people can be asked to accept, liberal value pluralists such as Stuart Hampshire, Richard Bellamy, John Gray and Bhikhu Parekh reject this preoccupation with universal reason.[1] For these writers, moral life is characterized by a plurality of values which cannot be harmoniously combined in a single life or a single society. Thus, in contrast to Barry's emphasis upon universal human needs and interests, these value pluralists view human identities as inherently diverse, each expressing a distinct set of values and virtues. For value pluralists, therefore, political life is characterized not by the search for a 'common standard', but by the inevitable conflict among incommensurable cultures and values. Consequently, liberal value pluralists will be attracted to a 'differentiated' citizenship, which acknowledges the political implications of cultural membership and recognizes a broad range of group-differentiated rights.

This chapter sets out to clarify the dispute between Barry and liberal value pluralists. It argues that, contrary to Barry, liberal value pluralism is not insensitive to the fact that human flourishing requires certain values and commitments, such as, for instance, some form of justice. However, whereas Barry seeks to define these norms through a conception of impartiality, value pluralists believe these norms manifest themselves in a variety of ways, each historically and culturally specific. Furthermore, while Barry fears that the recognition of group-differentiated rights will reinforce cultural differences and thus hinder the development of a common standard or shared point of view, value pluralism need not imply such a commitment. On the contrary, value pluralists such as Parekh expressly stress the importance of dialogue and mutual adaptation.[2] The chapter concludes that, by employing imaginative institutional mechanisms such as 'transformative accommodation', liberal value pluralism can uphold a differentiated citizenship which recognizes the demands of deep cultural diversity, while safeguarding typically liberal concerns for individual well-being, freedom and equality. The value pluralist challenge cannot therefore be as easily dismissed as Barry suggests.

The case for universal citizenship

In *Culture and Equality* Barry seeks to challenge the key assumptions of what is variously referred to as 'the politics of difference', the 'politics of recognition' or 'multiculturalism'.[3] These views rest on the premise that in the face of cultural diversity a commitment to equality and liberty entails a differentiated citizenship that grants a broad range of group rights. Barry, however, argues that the liberal Enlightenment model of unitary citizenship which endows all citizens with an identical set of common citizenship rights can adequately respond to questions of ethnocultural diversity. As Barry notes, 'the liberal commitment to civic equality entails that laws must provide equal treatment for those who belong to different religious faiths and different cultures.'[4] On the unitary model, such equal treatment is best achieved by removing religious and cultural differences from the political arena. Thus the state should not employ its powers to promote a particular religion or way of life, but should seek to adjudicate fairly between the conflicting demands of the various groups that constitute the polity. That is to say, the state should remain impartial. Hence, all citizens should enjoy the same rights and be subject to the same constraints. For advocates of a unitary model, the fundamental rights of individual citizens typically protect universal interests shared by all human beings. It is this vision of equal rights and a unitary citizenship that provides the foundations of Barry's liberal egalitarianism. Consequently, Barry rejects demands for a broad range of group-differentiated rights, including widespread legal exemptions on cultural or religious grounds and laws designed to secure the survival and maintenance of a particular way of life.

While exemptions from generally applicable laws may on occasions be justified, especially where a law bears particularly harshly on some people due to their religious or cultural commitments, Barry believes that such cases will be rare.[5] In particular, he rejects the notion that because a specific law impacts differentially upon some citizens, the state, as a matter of justice, must make special provisions for them. Here he distinguishes between the range of opportunities open to people, and the limits on the choices that people may make within that particular range of opportunities. While a person's particular beliefs and preferences will 'bring about a certain pattern of choices from among a set of opportunities that are available to all who are similarly placed', it does not affect the range of opportunities as such.[6] For example, your opportunity to read a range of books is determined by literacy and appropriate access to books. If the Christian sect you belong to teaches that it is sinful to read any book other than the Bible, 'you will choose not to avail yourself of this opportunity. But you still have exactly the same opportunity to read books as someone who is similarly placed in all respects except for not having this particular belief.'[7] While, for liberal egalitarians, justice requires that the state secures equal rights and opportunities for all citizens, it does not demand equality of outcomes. On the contrary, in a society characterized by genuine diversity it is to be expected that members of different groups will 'observe different customs, emphasize different values, spend their leisure time differently and perhaps have a tendency to cluster in different occupations'.[8] Provided all gratuitous barriers have been removed, there is no reason for regarding such an outcome as unfair.

Just as Barry rejects the notion that egalitarian justice requires a broad range of legal exemptions for members of cultural and religious groups, he is opposed to cultural rights that seek to secure the maintenance or survival of a particular culture or religion. To grant such rights would be to depart from the principle of state neutrality and the prohibition on enforcing a particular way of life. If groups seek special political status as self-governing entities, they must 'observe the constraints on the use of political power that are imposed by liberal justice'.[9] Thus, for Barry, sub-state polities such as the Pueblo Indians in the United States should not be permitted to use their self-governing rights to try to perpetuate their traditional culture and religion by discriminating against members who adopt a different way of life. On liberal egalitarian grounds a Pueblo sub-state, constituted on the basis of Pueblo ethnicity, would have to be neutral with regard to religion. By denying Christian converts communal resources like housing benefit made available to adherents of the traditional religion, the Pueblo tribal government is violating the typically liberal commitment to freedom of religion. This is not to suggest that those citizens who wish to follow an illiberal lifestyle should not be free to do so. Membership of associations and communities clearly plays an important role in the well-being of normal individuals. Furthermore, if associations and communities are to flourish, they will need to be able to determine their own affairs. For instance, groups must be free to decide whom to admit and whom to exclude. Given the typically liberal commitment to freedom of choice and freedom of association, this implies that groups must be free to adopt internal structures that do not conform to liberal principles. However, 'liberals cannot turn a blind eye to the potential that associations and communities have for abusing, oppressing and exploiting their members'.[10] The liberal state therefore has to take steps to ensure that the rights of individuals are safeguarded. Hence, in addition to upholding the constraints on the use of political power imposed by liberal justice, the state must ensure that all groups – including illiberal ones – are voluntary associations. As Horton notes in this volume, this is not to deny that membership of some groups may originally have been unchosen. However, for Barry, such attachments are only of continued value if individuals voluntarily endorse them. This implies that group members should have the capacity to 'make well-considered and well-informed choices from a range of realistically available options'.[11] Consequently, 'all participants should be adults of sound mind' and 'should be free to cease to take part whenever they want to'.[12] To leave a group will in most cases entail certain costs. To determine whether membership is voluntary requires an assessment of the type of costs incurred. Here Barry distinguishes between intrinsic costs, associative costs and external costs. Intrinsic costs are those costs that are inevitably associated with a loss of membership. These are costs that the state can neither prevent nor ameliorate. For instance, the state cannot alleviate the distress felt by a devout believer who has been excommunicated from the church she regards as her only route to salvation. Associative costs refer to penalties such as the loss of social relations with members of one's former group. While the state could potentially address these costs, they are the result of people engaging in activities that the liberal state ought to permit. However, the state can and should seek to alleviate external costs of exit. These are costs that groups cannot legitimately impose upon members who wish to leave the group or are expelled from the group. For example, an employer should not be permitted to fire an employee because the church they both belong to has excommunicated her. A careful analysis of the costs of exit places significant restrictions upon the demands that groups can make upon members. For instance, although a significant number of Amish successfully leave the group, Barry argues that the Amish fail to satisfy the criteria of a voluntary association, since the opt-out they have negotiated from social security provisions makes it extremely costly for members to leave the community late in life. In the absence of pension entitlements, members of the Amish community are dependent upon community provision in their old age. This constitutes a very significant disincentive to leave the group. In addition the Amish fail to meet minimal liberal requirements for the education of children. If membership of the group is to be voluntary, children must be brought up in a manner that 'will eventually enable them to leave behind the groups into which they were born, if they so choose'.[13] The Amish, however, have sought to limit the higher education of their children and have successfully fought for the right to keep their children out of local high schools (*Wisconsin* v. *Yoder*, 1972). The limited education provided by the Amish does not prepare children for employ-ment outside the community in anything but a narrow range of occupations. Hence it places significant barriers on the ability of Amish children to leave the community they were born into.

While the unitary model of citizenship advocated by Barry enables citizens to pursue a range of lifestyles, including illiberal ones, it implies that the state should uphold a uniform system of liberal laws. Consequently, Barry concludes that liberalism neither can nor should accommodate demands for 'deep cultural diversity'. That is to say, the state should not grant group-differentiated rights –

be they legal exemptions or self-government rights – designed to maintain or perpetuate a particular culture or religion. To do so would be to depart from the principle of state neutrality.

The case for cultural rights

As Barry is keenly aware, his model of a unitary citizenship runs counter to the aspirations of many religious and cultural groups currently campaigning for recognition. Not only do the exemptions sought by religious groups such as the Amish violate his criteria for voluntary group membership, but measures such as the language laws adopted by Quebec or the self-government rights sought by many non-liberal indigenous communities in Australia, Canada, New Zealand and the United States also violate the strict limits he imposes upon the exercise of political power. For Barry, the fact that his model cannot accommodate such demands does not imply that it fails to be neutral. A commitment to neutrality does not entail that the liberal state must accommodate the demands of all world views to an equal degree. Liberalism will inevitably conflict with some values and beliefs. All that state neutrality requires is that all groups are subject to the same rules and none is given preferential treatment.[14]

However, this ideal of equal treatment may prove more difficult to attain than Barry acknowledges. All states must reach a decision on a range of questions, such as what official language(s) to adopt, how to draw internal political boundaries, what powers to assign to sub-units, what public holidays to observe and what state symbols to recognize. As Barry notes, the principles of universal citizenship and state neutrality do not preclude liberal states from filling in the 'thin liberal code' of fundamental rights and liberties with a range of conventional rules, such as rules regulating traffic or norms that stipulate that all citizens have to contribute to the cost of collecting household waste. Since the general observance of these norms

> creates a public good that benefits most of the population – and especially where non-compliance with the norm by even a small number destroys the benefit – it is perfectly reasonable to enforce it on all, including those whose culture is such that they do not appreciate the benefit.[15]

However, Barry is mistaken to assume that decisions as to which official language to adopt or which public holidays to recognize are similarly mere conventions.[16] Language, for instance, has deep cultural resonance. It is because of these cultural meanings that minorities have fought hard to have their language recognized. Liberal regimes will therefore be much more thickly embedded in a particular cultural context than Barry acknowledges. As Kymlicka notes, in culturally diverse societies minorities may subsequently find themselves unfairly disadvantaged in the cultural marketplace. Minorities will frequently be in danger of being 'outbid or outvoted on resources and policies that are crucial to the survival of their societal cultures'.[17] Unlike the majority culture, minority cultures are vulnerable to the decisions of the majority. Consequently, members of a minority culture may incure costs to secure the cultural membership that makes sense of their lives, while members of the majority culture effectively obtain the good of cultural membership for free. Members of minority cultures suffer this disadvantage regardless of the particular life choices they make. As Margaret Moore argues in this volume, culture therefore is inevitably politicized.

While Barry insists that a commitment to liberal principles implies that individuals are responsible for the choices they make on the basis of their cultural and religious convictions, he stresses that liberal egalitarianism is not opposed to compensating people for disadvantages for which they are not responsible. Since members of minority cultures are disadvantaged regardless of the particular life choices they make, they arguably suffer a disadvantage due to circumstances they do not control.[18] Minorities can therefore be said to be entitled to compensation for these disadvantages. However, not only does compensating minorities for the disadvantage they suffer in the cultural marketplace potentially imply granting minorities group-specific rights designed to shield them from the political and economic power of the larger society, but some of the most effective measures may also entail rights that violate the restrictions Barry wants to place on group rights. For example, provisions such as collective ownership of traditional home-lands or restrictions on the sale of property held by group members were integral to many of the native reserves established in the USA and Canada. While historical evidence suggests that this may be the most effective way of protecting indigenous communities from the greater political and economic power of the larger society, such measures not only restrict the citizenship rights of the majority but also limit the freedom of group members. To insist, as Barry does, that groups which want to adopt the principle of collective ownership must pay all members who wish to leave the community their share of the assets, may not only place an unacceptable economic burden upon minorities with limited economic resources, but may also weaken the very principle of communal ownership. These worries regarding the disadvantages suffered by minorities highlight potentially significant weaknesses within Barry's conception of neutrality. The degree to which this undermines his case against group-differentiated rights will in part depend upon the plausibility of the assumptions that underpin his defence of state neutrality.

The value pluralist challenge

Possibly the most radical challenge to the underlying assumptions inherent in Barry's picture of the limits to religious and cultural diversity in a liberal state comes from liberal value pluralists. Central to Barry's defence of state neutrality is the belief that it is possible to construe a view which all reasonable people can be asked to accept. It is from this point of view that the conflicting demands of groups can be evaluated and fairly adjudicated. Thus Barry expresses the hope that 'eventually a common standard of reasonableness will prevail over a certain range of ethical questions, in a way similar to that in which the acknowledgement of the soundness of the physical sciences diffused through the world'.[19] Therefore, for Barry, there is 'nothing straightforwardly absurd about the idea that there is a single best way for human beings to live'.[20] While this does not commit Barry to the view that any one of the particular ways of life currently pursued is indeed the best way of life, his belief that it is not absurd to think that there might be one best way of life for human beings differs significantly from the position of liberal value pluralists such as Stuart Hampshire, Richard Bellamy, John Gray and Bhikhu Parekh.[21] These writers reject the preoccupation with universal reason and the subsequent quest for universal principles that underpins Barry's position. For liberal value pluralists, moral life is characterized by a plurality of values that cannot be harmoniously combined in a single life or a single society. Not only are ultimate values frequently incompatible, they are often incommensurable: that is to say they 'cannot be compared with one another in ultimate value'.[22] This is not to suggest that value pluralists are relativists. On the contrary, for these writers, ultimate values and goods have objective worth. However, 'while there are a limited number of human goods and evils, these underdetermine the possible forms of human flourishing'.[23] From a value pluralist's perspective, ways of life and cultures are therefore inherently diverse, each expressing a distinct set of values and virtues. Thus in contrast to Barry's vision of shared standards of reasonableness, value pluralists reject the idea that rational organization can harmonize all values. Given a particular set of circumstances, values and commitments, it may well be rational to pursue one option rather than another. However, value conflicts cannot be settled by an appeal to the kind of abstract principles of rational choice favoured by Barry. As Raz notes, while an action may well be rational in as far as it is based upon what a particular individual or group takes to be an undefeated reason, for value pluralists this does not imply that it is 'action for a reason which defeats all others'.[24] Choices among incommensurables are therefore underdetermined by reason. Since for value pluralists our common humanity does not determine our nature, the values we pursue will in part be a reflection of our particular historical, political and cultural heritage. Therefore, just as clashes between ultimate values are likely to persist, so conflicts between distinct and incommensurable cultures and identities constitute a pervasive feature of human existence. Hence, whereas Barry seeks to ensure equal treatment by excluding the claims of culture and religion from the political sphere, value pluralists contend that this search for a neutral point of view is misguided. On the contrary, for value pluralists, political life is characterized not by the search for a 'common standard', but by persistent conflict among incommensurable cultures and values. The management and peaceful resolution of such conflict requires institutions and procedures that facilitate negotiation and aid the search for compromise. Therefore, in contrast to Barry's search for a common standard of reasonableness, value pluralism entails a commitment to 'hear the other side' and implies that we respect that 'people can be reasonably led to incommensurable and incompatible values and interests and seeing the need to engage with them in terms that they can accept'.[25] While this commitment to 'hear the other side' requires that all members of society should be able to participate on fair terms in the deliberation of public issues and the formulation of public policy, these principles 'underdetermine what counts as equal and fair dealing in the widely various contexts of negotiation'.[26] Thus the institutional character of the procedural framework is liable to vary according to historical and social circumstances. Hence the shared institutions, procedures and values that help contain conflict within a particular political community should be regarded as the product of a practical political agreement.

Value pluralism, liberalism and group rights

This recognition of the inevitability of value conflict and the acknowledgement that the procedures for negotiating this conflict will inevitably be thickly embedded in a particular culture and history have far-reaching implications for the manner in which liberal value pluralists respond to the demands associated with religious and cultural diversity. From a value pluralist perspective, liberalism is best seen as one of a range of worthwhile ways of life, with its own specific ranking of values. While core liberal ideals such as toleration, autonomy, rights and equality allow for the recognition of a plurality of values, value pluralism does not privilege liberalism. Indeed, given 'that not all values can be pluralistically combined and that some become very pale in too much pluralistic company', pluralist liberal societies, in all their diversity, will only reflect a limited range of possible values.[27] For value pluralists, non-liberal societies that shelter worthwhile ways of life constitute an expression of the diversity of fundamental values and as such are entitled to seek to preserve their way of life.[28] Consequently, liberalism grounded in value pluralism is distinguished by its 'agonistic character, its acknowledgement of an irreducible diversity of rivalerous goods'.[29] In contrast to Barry's attempt to provide universal justifications for the core values and principles that define a liberal society, value pluralists base their defence of liberalism upon the social milieu and historical circumstances that have given rise to liberal societies. From such a perspective, liberalism is best seen as the product of a particular political settlement, which gradually emerges from the long controversies surrounding religious toleration that accompanied the Reformation and its aftermath.[30] Allegiance to liberalism should therefore not be conceived as allegiance to a set of abstract, universal principles, but is best regarded as the expression of a specific shared culture.

Not only does value pluralism favour a historicist defence of liberalism, but it also gives rise to a liberalism that accepts the dynamic of value conflict. Apart from the inevitable conflict between itself and other ways of life, liberalism must, on this analysis, also realize that the core values and commitments at the heart of its theory are open to a range of conflicting and at times incommensurable interpretations. For example, in addition to being potentially incommensurable, the values of liberty and equality contain conflicting elements leading, in the case of liberty, not only to tensions between positive and negative conceptions of liberty, but also to conflicts among different negative liberties.[31] Since for value pluralists the persistent conflicts between incommensurable values, cultures and ways of life can only be settled in the political sphere, a liberalism informed by a commitment to value pluralism will acknowledge the primacy of the political. Consequently, while liberal value pluralists endorse the typically liberal commitment to individual well-being, liberty and equality, they regard the nature and extent of basic liberties, the content of fundamental liberal rights and specific, substantive principles of justice as subject to political debate. Thus the restraints on liberty and the precise content of fundamental liberal rights are liable to change over time and from place to place. What is distinctly liberal about this approach is the belief that all groups should have an equal chance to participate and be heard in the political debate that shapes this specific constitutional settlement.

Liberal value pluralism directly challenges Barry's picture of the limits to cultural and religious diversity in a liberal state. Whereas his defence of state neutrality and a unitary conception of citizenship leads him to conclude that liberalism neither can nor should accommodate demands for deep cultural diversity, liberal value pluralists regard deep cultural diversity as the expression of a conflict of values that cannot be resolved via an appeal to universal principles and thus is liable to persist. While the demands by religious and cultural minorities for legal exemptions and group-specific rights to protect their way of life may conflict with existing interpretations of fundamental liberal rights, or may even entail a rejection of key liberal commitments, such antagonism and disagreement should not be seen as an extraordinary threat to well-established liberal societies, but should be viewed as instances of the unavoidable tensions between different cultures and value systems. Therefore, whereas Barry sets out to remove religious and cultural differences from the political arena, value pluralists seek to engage religious and cultural minorities in political debate and negotiation. Since liberal value pluralists recognize that liberal regimes are thickly embedded in a particular cultural and historical context, they are liable to be sympathetic to demands by minorities for group-specific rights to protect their culture and way of life. Here, value pluralist liberals are likely to be particularly sensitive to the disadvantages suffered by minorities whose culture differs significantly from that of the larger society. Given their typically liberal commitment to equality, the recognition of deep cultural diversity will lead liberal value pluralists to favour a differentiated citizenship, which is sensitive to the different political identities of the groups that constitute the state and recognizes a range of group-specific rights. This is not to suggest that liberal value pluralism will countenance all claims made by religious and cultural minorities. Since a commitment to individual well-being, liberty and equality is definitive of a commitment to liberalism in general, in a liberal society the decision-making procedures and the values embedded in these procedures will clearly be shaped by these ideals. Thus while liberal value pluralists will be sympathetic to demands for group-specific rights, as liberals they will nonetheless be concerned to uphold the fundamental liberties of all citizens, including those who belong to illiberal religious and cultural minorities. Liberal value pluralists will therefore seek a balance between the requirements of liberal justice and the demands of cultural diversity. The manner in which such a balance can be struck will clearly in part depend upon the particular circumstances of individual cases. In the concluding section of the chapter I will outline some institutional mechanisms that can facilitate such processes.

The case for a differentiated citizenship

In the light of the challenge posed by value pluralism, Barry bases his defence of a unitary citizenship on an appeal to universal basic human needs and interests. Furthermore, he contends that the type of differentiated citizenship favoured by liberal value pluralists is liable to reinforce difference and thus may lead to fragmentation and political instability.

As Barry notes, all human beings share certain basic needs and interests which must be met for a decent human life. Thus, all human beings require adequate nutrition, clean water and shelter. All typically desire good health, the ability to pursue their way of life and seek a just political order. The idea that there is a 'universal human nature which gives rise to certain physiological and psychological needs' is strengthened by people's actual choices and preferences.[32] As Barry notes, 'with rare exceptions that can normally be explained by highly unusual beliefs or circumstances, people strongly prefer life to death, freedom to slavery, and health to sickness'.[33] However, while Barry is right to note that all human beings share certain needs and interests, this in itself does not provide sufficient grounds to support his defence of state neutrality and universal citizenship. After all, liberal value pluralists like Hampshire and Bellamy explicitly acknowledge that ultimate values are objective and knowable and that 'there are a limited number of goods and evils'.[34] Although different individuals and societies develop and cultivate different values, we are nonetheless capable of recognizing what is of value in other lifestyles and patterns of social organization.[35] However, as Raz acknowledges, this appreciation of other ways of life always co-exists with a degree of rejection and dismissiveness.[36] Thus, value pluralism inevitably gives rise to tensions, which cannot always be easily resolved. For value pluralists, therefore, our common humanity only partially determines our nature. Here Hampshire invites us to distinguish between our common human potentialities and the equally human drive for diversity, which leads to these common needs being realized and satisfied in many different ways.[37] Thus, while the structure of human thought is shaped by categories or norms such as fairness, truth, and so on, these can manifest themselves in a great variety of ways, each historically and culturally specific. Consequently, these categories or norms can never be specified or fixed once and for all.[38] For example, while the recognition of some form of justice may be essential to all valuable forms of human association, different societies have developed a wide variety of frequently incompatible conceptions of justice. This is not to suggest that for value pluralists all ways of life are of equal value. While common human potentialities and needs can be realized in many different ways, some ways of life do not respect these fundamental basic human needs and interests. For example, according to Hampshire, value conflicts should not be resolved by resort to brute force, domination and tyranny. Therefore some ways of life, such as Nazism, which deliberately aimed to 'eliminate all notions of fairness and justice' in favour of physical conflict and violence, are absolutely evil.[39]

While value pluralism can be shown to be sensitive to the fact that human flourishing requires certain values and commitments, the worry remains that the emphasis value pluralists place upon cultural diversity and the pervasiveness of conflict will give rise to a desire to ossify cultures and hinder the development of mutual understanding and solidarity. Thus Barry fears that to grant a broad range of group-specific rights designed to maintain the culture and way of life of minorities will undermine a sense of common citizenship. Yet such a sense of fellowship and belonging is vital in order to motivate citizens to make sacrifices for the common good. However, the differentiated citizenship favoured by liberal value pluralists will not inevitably lead to fragmentation or reinforce cultural differences. On the contrary, a differentiated citizenship can be a means of building a genuinely inclusive citizenship. As Galeotti notes, a policy of public neutrality, which views all differences as equally different, fails to recognize 'the distinction between traits, characteristics, behaviour [and] options which are perceived as "normal" and those which are singled out as "different" '.[40] Yet this distinction is vital to the public consideration as a member of the political community. To belong to a group whose 'different collective identity is socially invisible, erased or despised' usually leads to a lack of confidence and a lack of self-esteem. This in turn undermines the capacity of individuals to take advantage of the resources and opportunities society has to offer and thus makes it much more difficult to become a functioning social agent and full citizen.[41] The public recognition and protection of differences can play an important role in facilitating the full inclusion of minorities within democratic citizenship. Not only is a differentiated citizenship sensitive to the subtle barriers which prevent minority groups from becoming full members of the polity, but also the public recognition of difference need not lead to the ossification of cultures.

While in a multicultural society the recognition of diversity may entail granting some minorities a range of legal exemptions and group rights designed to accommodate demands for deep cultural diversity, for Parekh a differentiated citizenship must be accompanied by an open-minded, morally serious dialogue between the majority and minority.[42] Such dialogue must search for common ground and aim at mutual adaptation. In this search, neither majority nor minority can expect all its existing cultural practices to remain unchanged. Where the current practices of the majority and minority conflict, intercultural dialogue must probe the nature and importance of existing cultural practices and must encourage reflection and debate, not only between communities but also within the various communities themselves. Thus, communities must consider whether contentious cultural practices are essential to their way of life, or whether they could safely be abandoned. For example, on Parekh's account, many of the most contentious cultural practices regarding the treatment of women, such as female circumcision, are arguably not essential to the way of life and values of the cultures that practise them and therefore could be abandoned without threatening the survival of these cultures.

To promote such serious intercultural dialogue, value pluralists will have to develop institutional mechanisms which facilitate exchange between minority and majority and which actively encourage reflection upon existing practices. Critics of liberal value pluralism frequently express the fear that because of its emphasis upon the inevitability of conflict and its rejection of abstract rational criteria for conflict resolution, value pluralism will ultimately give rise to political settlements that simply favour the views of the majority. If such fears are to be averted, the institutional framework will have to ensure that minorities can participate in dialogue and political negotiation on equal terms. This may in part be achieved through models of joined governance, which divide jurisdiction between several political actors. Since effective political decision making will frequently require co-operation, the division of political authority promotes dialogue between the various political actors. Such models can be employed to strengthen the political bargaining position of minorities, while at the same time safeguarding the fundamental rights of all citizens. Here, liberal value pluralists may find the notion of transformative accommodation as developed by Ayelet Shachar particularly interesting.[43] As Shachar notes, many contested social areas such as, for example, family law or criminal justice, are internally divisible into distinct yet interdependent sub-matters or functions. On the model of transformative accommodation, both the minority group and the state are given authority over part of the sub-matter, but neither is allowed to control all aspects of the contested social area. For example, in the case of marriage the minority group may manage the demarcatory function, which controls changes in marital status and entitlement to community membership, whereas the state regulates the distributive function, which includes the rights and obligations of marriage partners and economic and custodial matters. To take account of the power asymmetry between the state and the group, the presumptions in the negotiations regarding the initial allocation of areas of authority should be in favour of the group. Thus the group may, for example, be given the opportunity of setting the agenda for negotiations or it may be given priority in the allocation of the sub-matter it regards as the most crucial. Since a legal dispute in a particular social area can only be fully resolved if these sub-matters are addressed together, neither party has complete control over its members. Such an arrangement promotes dialogue and co-operation between the state and the minority group and encourages both parties to be responsive to the needs of their members.

The latter aspect is reinforced via the final feature of transformative accommodation: the establishment of clearly delineated choice options. At predefined reversal points, individuals are to be given the choice whether to remain within the jurisdictional authority of the original powerholder. On this model, individuals are justified in 'opting out' if the current powerholder in a particular sub-matter systematically fails to address their concerns. Such reversal options allow individuals to bring pressure to bear on the groups that represent them and thus create a strong incentive for powerholders to address in-group problems. For instance, if the rules of divorce systematically discriminate against women by granting husbands the right to unilaterally divorce their wives or by insisting that in order to obtain a divorce a wife must gain the consent of her husband, women may choose to 'opt out' of the group's jurisdiction in this particular matter.[44] Since such an 'opt-out' or partial exit only applies to a particular issue, vulnerable group members do not have to give up their overall group membership in order to seek redress. At the same time, groups have a strong incentive not to risk alienating their members. Consequently, groups may decide to reinterpret the existing rule to accommodate the concerns of disaffected members. Transformative accommodation therefore combines the recognition of group rights and the protection of individual liberties. This makes it a potentially useful model for resolving the disputes associated with deep cultural diversity. However, it clearly will not be suitable in all areas. For example it is not well suited to disputes concerning children, since as minors children are not able to exercise the choice option. Nonetheless the mechanisms employed in this model suggest interesting ways forward in many potentially problematic areas.

Conclusion

The case for a differentiated citizenship rooted in a liberalism informed by a commitment to value pluralism suggests that Barry's defence of state neutrality and a unitary citizenship remains problematic. While Barry bases his argument upon an appeal to universal human needs and interests, value pluralists are not insensitive to the fact that human flourishing requires certain values and commitments. However, in contrast to Barry, value pluralists believe that these norms manifest themselves in various ways, each historically and culturally specific. Consequently, whereas Barry maintains that a liberal state should not grant group-differentiated rights designed to maintain or perpetuate a particular culture or religion, liberal value pluralists recognize that the full inclusion of minorities in the liberal polity may require the public recognition and maintenance of group identities. By employing imaginative institutional mechanisms such as transformative accommodation, liberal value pluralists can uphold a differentiated citizenship which recognizes the demands of deep cultural diversity while safeguarding the typically liberal concern for individual well-being, freedom and equality. The value pluralist challenge therefore cannot be as easily dismissed as Barry suggests.

Notes

1   S. Hampshire, *Justice is Conflict*, London: Duckworth, 1999; R. Bellamy, *Liberalism and Pluralism*, London: Routledge, 1999; J. Gray, *Two Faces of Liberalism*, Cambridge: Polity, 2000; B. Parekh, *Rethinking Multiculturalism: Cultural Diversity and Political Theory*, Basingstoke: Macmillan, 2000.
2   Parekh, *Rethinking Multiculturalism*.
3   B. Barry, *Culture and Equality: An Egalitarian Critique of Multiculturalism*, Cambridge: Polity, 2001.

4   Ibid., p. 24.
5   On Barry's account, the state may grant exemptions in some cases for prudential or political reasons. For example, given the very great number of Sikhs working in the construction industry, a case can be made for granting at least those Sikhs currently employed in the building trade an exemption from legislation which makes it compulsory to wear hard hats on building sites. The imposition of such legislation upon Sikh construction workers who wear turbans could give rise to high levels of unemployment within the Sikh community and thus may prove socially disruptive. However, such exemptions are not based upon considerations of justice, but merely constitute temporary arrangements based on an assessment of the balance of advantage, given a particular set of circumstances.
6   Barry, *Culture and Equality*, p. 36. As John Horton notes in his chapter in this volume, Barry's rejection of the rule-and-exemption approach rests in part upon his denial that there are any relevant differences between beliefs and preferences. For Horton, this is to seriously misconstrue the status and significance of people's fundamental ethical and religious convictions.
7   Ibid., p. 38.
8   Ibid., p. 71.
9   Ibid., p. 189.
10 Ibid., p. 117.
11 Ibid., p. 147.
12 Ibid., p. 148.
13 Ibid., p. 149.
14 For a detailed discussion of Barry's account of liberal neutrality, see Margaret Moore's chapter in this volume.
15 Barry, *Culture and Equality*, p. 287.
16 Another two of Barry's examples, 'public order' and 'decency', are equally contentious. For a discussion of these two examples see John Horton's contribution to this volume.
17 W. Kymlicka, *Multicultural Citizenship: A Liberal Theory of Minority Rights*, Oxford: Clarendon Press, 1995.
18 Many liberals accept that individuals who are disadvantaged due to *circumstances*, such as social environment or natural endowment, deserve to be compensated. As Horton notes in this volume, whereas Barry repeatedly stresses the importance of the voluntariness of group membership, the very value of culture arguably depends at least in part on it being non-voluntary. Yet if cultural membership is to a significant extent non-voluntary, then, on the principles of liberal egalitarianism defended by Barry, minorities are entitled to compensation. Barry may well be attracted to the rather implausible picture of culture as somehow freely chosen, because he is keenly aware that if he acknowledges the non-voluntary character of cultural membership, as a liberal egalitarian he has to consider the question of compensation.
19 Barry, *Culture and Equality*, p. 262.
20 Ibid.
21 See note 1 above
22 Gray, *Two Faces of Liberalism*, p. 63.
23 Bellamy, *Liberalism and Pluralism*, pp. 3–4.
24 J. Raz, *The Morality of Freedom*, Oxford: Clarendon Press, 1986, p. 339. A helpful discussion of the value pluralist account of the role of reason is offered by I. Berlin and B. Williams, 'Pluralism and Liberalism: A Reply', *Political Studies*, 42, 2, 1994, pp. 306–9.
25 Bellamy, *Liberalism and Pluralism*, p. 121.
26 S. Hampshire, *Innocence and Experience*, London: Penguin, 1989, p. 75.
27 B. Williams, 'Introduction', in I. Berlin, *Concepts and Categories*, London: Hogarth Press, 1978, p. xvii.

28 Non-liberal societies need not deny the idea of a plurality of values. As Gray notes, most non-liberal societies are particularist rather than universalistic in their outlook and consequently justify their way of life, not by an appeal to universal premises but on the grounds that this is their existing way of life, with which they identify deeply. Furthermore, non-liberal societies need not be hostile to diversity. For instance, under the Ottoman empire Muslims, Christians and Jews were all viewed as self-governing units, thus allowing minority religions to exist alongside the dominant one.

29 J. Gray, *Berlin*, London: Fontana Press, 1995, p. 145.

30 In contrast to this contextual argument for liberalism, some value pluralists have tried to argue that value pluralism implies liberalism, since 'pluralism gives us a reason to value diversity' and 'diversity is best accommodated by liberalism' (G. Crowder, 'From Value Pluralism to Liberalism', *Critical Review of International and Political Philosophy*, 1, 1998, pp. 2–17; p. 9). However, such an attempt to establish a strong link between liberalism and pluralism fails to acknowledge the extent to which the typically liberal commitment to individual liberty and autonomy places limits upon the diversity that can be accommodated within a liberal society. For a discussion of both the contextual and the universal argument from pluralism to liberalism, see ibid.

31 For instance, freedom of information may conflict with the right to privacy. In a similar vein, the ideal of equality entails the incommensurable ideas of equality of opportunity and equality of outcome.

32 Barry, *Culture and Equality*, p. 285.

33 Ibid.

34 Bellamy, *Liberalism and Pluralism*, pp. 4–5.

35 Individuals are often keenly aware of the opportunities they have forgone by following their chosen lifestyle. Thus, for example, a great artist who, in the pursuit of her art, has abandoned many normal human interests, such as, for instance, a stable family life, may nonetheless recognize the values inherent in these general human interests and may regard this as a price that had to be paid for the lifestyle she desired.

36 J. Raz, '*Multiculturalism: A Liberal Perspective*', Dissent, Winter 1994, pp67-79.

37 Hampshire maintains that his position regarding human nature is 'close to Hume's: that opinions about substantial justice and other virtues arise from, and are explained by, natural and widespread human sentiments greatly modified by very variable customs and social histories' (*Justice is Conflict*, pp. 41–3). However, in contrast to Hume, who holds that humanity has a tendency towards consensus, Hampshire holds that diversity and, subsequently, conflict are unavoidable.

38 Gray, *Berlin*.

39 Hampshire, *Innocence and Experience*, p. 68.

40 A. E. Galleotti, 'Contemporary Pluralism and Toleration', *Ratio Juris*, 10, 2, 1997, pp. 223–35; p. 229.

41 Ibid., p.230.

42 Parekh, *Rethinking Multiculturalism*.

43 A. Shachar, *Multicultural Jurisdictions*, Cambridge: Cambridge University Press, 2001.

44 For example, under the Muslim form of divorce known as the *talaq*, a husband may unilaterally divorce his wife without recourse to any court or extraneous authority, while under Orthodox Jewish law a woman can only gain a divorce if her husband gives her a *get*, or consent to divorce, 'whereas a man can be granted a divorce without his wife's consent' (Barry, *Culture and Equality*, p. 187). Barry cites both these cases as arguments against granting religious groups greater control over their members. This, however, underestimates the extent to which imaginative institutional mechanisms such as transformative accommodation can provide incentives for internal reform.

9 Canadian indigenous peoples and the transformation of political theory into cultural identity

Mark Francis

Canadian political theorists have focused on cultural identity during the past two decades, and it seems important to analyse their efforts. Of course, in no sense are they a corporate or ideological grouping, but – because they have been grappling with the same questions about national political culture – they possess certain family resemblances. The more prominent of the theorists, Will Kymlicka, Jim Tully and Charles Taylor, also hold considerable international reputations as spokesmen for identity politics and minority rights. When these writers transform basic political theory into the recognition of Canadian cultural differences, this has some universal currency. The words of Jim Tully – currently a professor of Political Science at the University of Toronto – are heard everywhere. His claim is that citizens cannot identify with, or give allegiance to, the Canadian federation until their cultural differences are recognized and affirmed in the Constitution, and in the legal and political structures of Canada.[1] Tully believes that this is not happening. Instead, there is a glacial movement towards disunity and separation in Canada. This is caused by a failure to recognize and to accommodate the aspirations of Quebec, and of First Nations as well as of other cultural groups.[2] This warning is not just to Canadians, but to inhabitants of all nation states.

The prominence given to Quebec and to non-indigenous groups in Canadian constitutional debate had caused indigenous identity to be subsumed under a perpetual Canadian constitutional crisis which has loomed ever larger since the debate over the 1982 Charter of Rights. However, this national context should not occupy all the channels of discourse; indigenous people have a theoretical standing which is separate from other ethnicity issues. First Nations should be considered separately from the imperatives of defending the Canadian identity. In this chapter I will attempt to focus on the theoretical claims made about First Nations without concerning myself too much with the identity of Quebeckers, English Canadians or of the other fragments of the ethnic mosaic. Since theoretical literature of identity politics is usually expressed either as a rights discourse or as a plea for greater participation in politics, I will discuss it under these headings.

I believe that Canadian theoretical discourse has become clouded or occluded, and that when applied to a specific kind of identity – the indigenous kind – it produces few defensible ethical results. The conceptual apparatus of political theory seems to have been pressed into service as a tool for building a personal identity for a nation when, perhaps, nations should remain impersonal.[3] I am suggesting that the identities of indigenous peoples should not be reconciled into a national one, and perhaps that Canadians should ensure that their institutional frameworks are not conflated with national identity. The argument here is that the state should not reflect the fragmented images of its majority and minority peoples as if they were a single identity, but should remain neutral on the subject. It is also suggested that political philosophers and legal theorists become suspect when they engage in nation building. They should not be allowed to surrender their academic independence or to continue using their conceptual tools when these have become contaminated with political bias. Theorists who rely on the remnants of liberalism to dabble in identity politics are particularly troubling. Liberalism has its uses – particularly when it blurs the edges of cruder forms of equity – but it is a cumbersome device when it is used in areas such as the defence of collective rights against individual ones. There are many reasons one could cite as to why liberalism does not invariably produce innovative ways of thinking about ethnic politics, but here I will restrict myself to two of these. First, liberalism came into existence as an ideology designed to attack privileges of a type which resemble collective rights and, therefore, is still difficult to reconcile with those. Second, liberalism says little about the nature of the state, yet it is upon this institution that we rely to protect and enhance the quality of life of citizens.

For these reasons I will analyse Canadian political theory – when it speaks of rights and participation – without placing it under a liberal umbrella. In any case, from my survey of recent Canadian political theory, it would seem that it is unnecessary to discuss liberalism. Often the way in which rights and participation have been used by Canadian writers does not draw upon liberal theory in any essential way, and a detailed discussion of that doctrine is not, therefore, valuable.[4] Even Oxford-trained political philosophers whom one would usually associate with liberalism abandon this in favour of nationalism when they undertake the serious business of rescuing Canada from conceptual confusion. For example, Will Kymlicka's statements in his book of constitutional advice, *Finding Our Way*,[5] are illiberal, but not in the way they used to be. He had earlier tried to re-focus liberalism to protect cultures rather than individuals. However, these early attempts treated aboriginal minorities as if they possessed the same standing as non-aboriginal minorities, and was quite seriously punished.[6] No such criticism would be levelled at him now because, in attempting to reach an accommodation between Quebec's nationalist aspirations and a 'multinational federalism', he has taken up an extreme stance which distinguishes sharply between the normative importance which he gives to 'national communities' in comparison with other ethnic groups. Ordinary attempts at national salvation are rejected by Kymlicka: he is sceptical about claims by his compatriots that Canada can be rescued by increasing the amount of shared political language or of common political values. Instead, he believes the future lies with a form of federalism which will be held suspended over national groups. Three of these groups – the English, the French and aboriginal peoples – seem to him to have priority as founding peoples. Such a suggestion seems startling and almost non-ethical because many philosophers emphasize the liberal tenets of individual choice and consent. However, with Kymlicka the right for self-government seems to be reserved for groups who have lived in Canada at least since the eighteenth century[7] but not those who came afterwards. That is, Quebeçois, Anglo-Saxons and indigenous peoples are given the right to govern themselves but, for example, not groups such as Icelanders, Chinese and Ukranians whose ancestors have lived in Western Canada since the nineteenth century. This is an unintended consequence of Kymlicka's emphasis upon current migration politics. He disregards various well-entrenched ethnic groups because his concern is not with old migrants, but with new ones. He is keen that recent immigrants to Quebec recognize that French is the language of public life in that province. Further, he is sympathetic to the suggestion that English Canadians be encouraged to conduct themselves in a nationalist way which parallels that of the French. That is, the former should construct a linguistically based nation with which to balance the political aspirations of French Canada. The suggestion that large national groups should engage in nation building by forcing new migrants to surrender their own languages is rooted in the ideas of Herder and other nineteenth-century European nationalists. This is the ideal of the organic and natural community. Such an ideal has few of the moral qualities which one would expect to see in the writings of a philosopher currently engaged in constitutional speculation. In particular, Kymlicka's advocacy of the primacy of large groups leaves little space for the cultural independence of less dominant groups even though one imagines that they also value their identities. Kymlicka does not intend to harm indigenous peoples – on the contrary, he explicitly attempts to safeguard their rights to be self-governing – but he narrows their options by not reinforcing rights language in general (few indigenous peoples would actually benefit from his suggestions[8]). As a consequence he leaves little constitutional space for First Nations.[9] These peoples are the bell wethers for other ethnic groups. They seem to be the most deserving but, if their normative claims can be easily set aside, then there is little hope that others will be considered. It is not that Canadian political theorists are badly disposed towards indigenous or other ethnic groups. On the contrary, they show every sign of sympathy with these. It is just that their good intentions cannot survive the theoretical strategies they have adopted. Kymlicka is representative of the process which has affected other Canadian political theorists. In his juggling with identity politics, he has lost sight of those normative standards which are familiar to his colleagues who live outside the peculiar Canadian environment of contested nationalities. Nor is he unique in being entangled in a thicket of identity claims. He is simply the most prolific of Canadian political theorists. Canadian political theory has become odd and eccentric. Perhaps the burden of renegotiating Canadian identity is too heavy for scholars who have exclusively worked inside a formal and quasi-philosophical discourse.

Rights discourse

In recent theoretical work on the rights of indigenous peoples, Canadian political theorists usually make reference to court decisions rather than to the kind of
general political principles which could be addressed through a ballot box or a
parliament. There is a sense in which the courts have become the primary political arenas, while the mechanisms and theories of parliamentary democracy
have been put aside as inoperative, unjust, or as just too vague to be of concern.
On the subject of rights, legal commentators have supplanted political philosophers in providing direction and defence for moral claims. On the surface this is
refreshing: lawyers seem more likely to give practical advice. A typical example
of legally inspired advice comes in Tom Svensson's article in *Études Canadiennes*.
Svensson grapples with rights and autonomy in such a way that they appear as
political remedies rather than moral quandaries. Instead of empty philoso-
phizing, one gets the impression of a successful discovery of an applied
programme of action which will bring relief to aboriginal peoples. In this
programme, 'autonomy' refers not to the complexities of Kantian moral
discourse, but to an actual enhancement of a people's political independence
and the preservation of their traditional cultural base (the land which supports
hunting, fishing and trapping) and, consequently, of their cultural identity.[10]
Svensson's arguments stem from an agreement (finalized in 1975) between
Hydro Quebec and the Inuit and Cree Peoples of the James Bay region, which
guaranteed that the economic base of indigenous peoples would be preserved,
and which provided them with a limited degree of self-determination – including
veto rights.[11] However, optimism about the possibility of legal discourse
resolving the problems of theoretical politics is misplaced. Legal commentary
invokes notions such as rights and autonomy in an ambiguous way. It refers to
practical items, such as economic resources, and to theoretical political concepts,
such as jurisdictional authority, as if they were equal and indistinguishable. The
lack of clarity in distinguishing between different kinds of rights and between
varying degrees of autonomy suggests that constitutional arrangements which
delegate ethnic disputes to the courts might result in politicization rather than
resolution. Since lawyers usually construe claims as specific rights, their ambiguity about these is likely to produce volatile political outcomes.

Rights are particularly difficult to operationalize in legal politics if the object
of these rights is to protect indigenous identity. Since rights language is usually
attached to the idea that individuals should be protected, it tends not to work
well when applied to collectives. It also gives rise to conflict when a collective
asserts its rights over individuals who also make rights-based claims. That is, to
assign self-government and jurisdictional authority to a group in order to protect
their culture raises the spectre of insoluble conflict over rights. There is no
reason to believe that autonomous self-governing groups will restrict their governance solely to preserving traditional economic activities such as hunting, fishing
and trapping, especially when the importance of such activities is seen as subordinate to the goal of maintaining a unique cultural identity. This goal might very
well require that the group attempt to curtail individual rights. This hypothetical

danger is a troublesome commonplace in the proceedings of international meet-
ings of indigenous peoples. When the Mikmaq of the Atlantic Provinces decided
to affirm the universality of human rights at UN conferences in the mid-1980s,
they were isolated by opponents who thought that such a declaration would
restrict self-determination and would spread ideas of gender equality which were
alien to indigenous cultures.[12]

An example of this curtailment of individual rights came in 1992, when the
Coast Salish tribe forcibly initiated David Thomas. They were exercising their
right to preserve their collective identity at the expense of his individual right.
The disagreement was between a collective preparing a tribal number for the
Spirit Dance, and the individual who saw himself as a prisoner. Thomas, though
a member of the tribe, knew little about its religion and practices. He did not
live on the reserve, nor was he brought up on it. Subsequently, he took legal
action against members of the tribe for his forced confinement and fasting.
(Other indignities included a ceremonial bath, and being lifted horizontally by
the initiators so that they could blow on his body to bring out his song.[13])
Thomas won his suit against his initiators because the court found that the Spirit
Dance – for which he was being prepared – was not a central feature of Coast
Salish culture.[14] This decision side-stepped the issue of how one could reconcile
the right of the collective to preserve its cultural identity with the individual's
right to autonomy and freedom of choice.[15] It has been suggested that over-
emphasizing the conflict between collective and individual rights as an
incommensurable one is an unpleasant habit of juridical commentators.[16] That
is, if decision making is transferred from political institutions into courts, and this
is then interpreted as a flawed resolution of disputes that are actually incommensurable, this augers badly for the political future of Canada. Added to this
difficulty is the fluidity of rights language in legal discourse. Legal interpretations
of aboriginal rights were broad and liberal under *R. v. Sparrow* but, in 1996,
under the Van der Peet test, they came to be characterized in terms of specific
activities and were narrowed to focus on an historical dimension. Part of the Van
der Peet test also expands government interference with such rights.[17] The
magnitude of this shift suggests that legal rights are an unsound basis for long-
term identity politics because their meaning is not anchored in the political
culture(s) of Canada.

From the perspective of political theory the most flawed legal intervention
took place in a recent decision about the right to self-government. This is the
case of *Delgamuukw v. British Columbia*, where the appeal by the Gitskan and
Wet'suwet'en people for the self-government of their 22,000 square miles of
northwest British Columbia was rejected because it was made on *general* grounds.
The appeal was regarded as a 'conceptual failure' because it had not referred to
the approved models of self-government in the relevant pages of the Report of
the Royal Commission on Aboriginal Affairs.[18] The court's decision has been
criticized by Jim Tully in *Strange Multiplicity*. However, he himself seems to
struggle on the subject of indigenous self-government. Instead of dwelling upon
the obvious curiosity of a political claim being dismissed because it was made on

general grounds, he focused upon the court undervaluing the aboriginal claim to self-rule 'based on their forms of governance [and] long before the Europeans arrived'. He also objected that the judge in this case, Chief Justice Allan McEachern, had commented that the indigenous people had low-level technology and had customs which included slavery and war. Tully equated these comments with Hobbes's statement that life in a state of nature was 'nasty, brutish and short'.[19] The implication of McEachern/Hobbes is that the traditional behaviour of Gitskan and Wet'suwet'en people demonstrated that they had not possessed a true government and that, therefore, they could not ask for it to be restored.

Part of Tully's objection is based upon the fact that the judge construed First Nations as primitive and violent. In opposition to this, he shaped his own views to coincide with those of the indigenous artist Bill Reid, who envisioned pre-contact indigenous peoples as having advanced cultures. 'Sometimes (the European invaders) found beautiful, gentle, generous people, so they made slaves of them and killed them.' Sometimes they found avaricious peoples with whom they allied themselves until these could also be dispossessed of their goods and cultures.[20] However, part of Tully's objection owes nothing to his expression of solidarity with Bill Reid. That is, he makes an additional point that indigenous forms of governance are legitimate because they were in use before the Europeans arrived. The structures were pre-European and, therefore, for Tully, resonate with qualities such as timelessness, authenticity and changelessness. The coda to this is that these ancient qualities are vital and integral to indigenous identity. This claim is similar to the early modern English view of the 'ancient constitution'.[21] It is a statement that a constitution is owed respect because it is traditional, alive and woven into the fabric of national life. To change it is to cause the dissolution and death of a society. It is possible that Tully has unwittingly borrowed his 'ancient' constitutionalism from John Locke in the same way that the judge, Allan McEachern, borrowed the state of nature from Hobbes. However, whatever its origin, it has the unfortunate consequence of suggesting that self-government is to be valued because it draws upon tradition. Tully's argument seems to be that pre-European concepts of authority varied, but from a modern perspective the quality which they had in common is a negative one. The positive contents of the traditions are unimportant because to specify them would probably result in the elimination of variety and the substitution of a few universal principles of government which would not be acceptable to many indigenous peoples. Tully's position is that we must not subvert the cultures of indigenous people in order to satisfy the reasoned inquiry of European officials and judges, but his stance here carries its own peril. He has rejected the western tradition as relying upon principles which were state-centred and Hobbesian, but he himself has an imperative principle, tradition, which leaves no room to accommodate the cultural changes which both collectives and individuals have undergone. There is a problem here because if historical anthropologists, or First Peoples, were able or willing to specify which aspects of an indigenous culture were traditional and which were modern, it would be unlikely that they would systematically give the former priority when discussing their present needs. Yet Tully's 'ancient' constitutionalism would do this and lock aboriginal peoples into their traditions when they themselves seem to be concerned that a revival of traditional institutions and laws might reinstate practices that discriminate against certain individuals and groups.[22]

Greater participation in politics

Legal commentators and courts – with their rights discourse – occupy the dominating heights in indigenous identity politics. The remaining terrain is taken up by Canadian political philosophers and political scientists who are determined to overthrow juridical views.[23] While the former express their views on cultural identity in a rights language, the latter claim that to focus on rights is to misunderstand cultural identity and, further, is likely to undermine the whole Canadian political tradition, which protects aboriginal citizens as well as majority ones.[24]

One of the chief sources of the anti-judicial theoretical politics in Canada is the work of Charles Taylor,[25] who has attempted to modify liberal democracy to make it fit Canadian needs. In the course of this adaptation he restricts the use of rights because he distrusts the support they give to extreme individualist claims. Essentially, Taylor's mode of operation is to reconcile identity politics with the democratic state by diminishing the role of equity, and by invoking a form of participation which has its roots in classical political philosophy. This form of participation stresses that citizens had a duty to maintain the state. Taylor adds a novelty to the theory by suggesting that both citizens and ethnic groups acquire their identity in opposition to others, and that this identity is an autonomous condition which needs to be protected and nurtured by the state. This form of participatory politics owes little to the way in which actual liberal democratic politics have developed since the nineteenth century but, instead, is rooted in an interpretation of Hegel's *Philosophy of Right*. The substitution of this theory for conventional reality allows Taylor to address himself to a modern polity or state which he sees as composed of legitimate ethnic groups as well as of individuals.

Taylor's critique of conventional politics involves a wide-ranging historical overview of the way in which basic concepts have evolved but, in essence, his position is that modern politics in general (and Canadian politics in particular) have developed in such a way that the functions of government have become more bureaucratically rigid, and more distant from the citizenry.[26] He believes that this is a regrettable outcome because, without a large amount of participation, a society cannot be stable, and the people will be in a condition of tutelage.[27] His procedure is like a teleological analysis which examines the functioning of a political society in terms of the goals which citizens seek when protecting their dignity. Thus, in a rights-bearing society, such as the United States, the dignity of a free individual resides in his or her ability to secure rights – even against the will of the majority.[28] If this philosophical stance is adopted in another country, such as Canada, it will restructure its politics so that they will reflect the demand for rights. To avoid this outcome, Taylor offers a vision of a participatory society where citizens' dignity, and their freedom, depend upon their having a voice in deciding the common laws by which they and other members live.

> This naturally presupposes that the institutions and practices by which the whole corpus of common laws are established, as well as the corpus itself, enjoy a profound respect in the society, so that our identity is defined in relation to them and dignity is conferred by taking part in them. Special importance attaches to the fact that we as a whole, or a community, decide about ourselves as a whole community.[29]

The significant features of Taylor's restructured participatory society are that they emphasize the connection of freedom with dignity rather than with rights, and that they insist that the whole community takes its identity from its law-making capacity.

Taylor's rejection of a rights-based society has deep roots in his own cultural experience. When he refers to 'solitudes' in the title of one of his recent works, he is invoking the title of a classic Canadian novel, Hugh McLellan's *Two Solitudes*, in which the French and English fail to understand each other. The only link between the two communities is the ageing and isolated French Canadian politician, Tallard but, since he is a committed rationalist who is secretly devoted to the memory of Voltaire, he is cut off from the religiosity and nationalism of his compatriots. Taylor's empathetic title *Reconciling the Solitudes* seems designed to avoid the futile hopes of rationalism by appealing directly to the cultural identity of the *patrie*.

Though one can sympathize with Taylor's desire to preserve an idealized corporate life from careless and debilitating appeals to rights, his strategy seems flawed. The type of participation to which he gestures is an unattractive one to a modern audience. While he can appeal to an ancient pedigree of Greek and Roman republicanism for his support, it is unclear why he thinks that this tradition underpins the modern sense of national identity. As Walter Benn Michaels has observed about modern America, identity is now disconnected from citizenship – from the rights and obligations conferred upon the subject by his or her legal status as a citizen.[30] In Canada, too, it would be extremely antique to agree with Taylor that a common identity or common life must be constantly nourished by citizens participating in formal activities such as voting and petitioning.[31]

Taylor, with the assistance of Tully and others, softens his demands that participation involves the whole community when he discusses the politics of difference (roughly defined as the conflicting politics of ethnic identity). His statements about difference politics can be seen as an exception to his general stance that freedom and dignity flow from the practice of taking part in enacting laws for the whole community.

So members of aboriginal bands will get certain rights and powers not enjoyed by other Canadians, if the demands for native self-government are finally agreed on, and certain minorities will get the right to exclude others in order to preserve their cultural integrity, and so on.[32]

The exception for aboriginal bands raises difficulties for Taylor's notion of identity. His politics of difference relies on the potential that each individual and each culture has in forming and defining its own identity,[33] but this leaves him without any way of invoking identity as a value in case of disagreement between an individual and a culture. His theory of identity will fall to the same criticism which renders rights useless if individuals and collectives both make the same claim about them: that is, disagreement would immediately lead to incommensurability.[34] This is not to argue that institutions such as courts should, or should not, balance between 'incommensurable' principles; it is merely to observe that Taylor's identity politics does not anchor political principles in such a way that individuals will see their interests as represented in the culture of a community.

Jim Tully's exposition of the politics of difference does not depend upon Taylor's commitment to a shared identity in which citizens celebrate their mutual recognition of each other by the making of laws. Indeed, Tully finds it curious that a modern nation state would pretend to have a shared identity.[35] In his view, while a nation state possesses unity and power, these attributes should not be used to impose cultural uniformity.[36] This criticism is not the minor disagreement with Taylor which Tully believes it to be. Instead, it signals a major rift because, while they share a common focus upon identity as the basis of politics, they interpret this in very different ways. Tully's notion of cultural identity has little in common with the classical republican motifs admired by Taylor. Instead, Tully takes his idea of culture from the work of James Clifford, who sees this as an overlapping, open and negotiated condition.[37] However, rather than this being a fashionable extension of Taylor's views, it is a disjunctive shift into the descriptive and quasi-scientific discourse of recent cultural anthropology. While Taylor views cultural identities as accompanied by an institutional mechanism which would cause them to recognize each other, Clifford's views are simple products of a critical anthropology which offers no promise of constitutional interaction. It is also important to note that while Clifford seems to advocate a universal discourse of culture, the strand of ethnic identity which most attracts his attention is extremely parochial. For Clifford, the typical story of cultural identity is about one of the Algonquin people of New England, the Wampanoags. In brief, the moral of his narrative is that all cultures are masks which conceal a composite and self-chosen collection of social features. However, this observation is of dubious political value in Canada, where the identity of indigenous peoples is usually more than ethnic nominalism. That is, Clifford's notion of culture is not relevant to the cultural politics of indigenous Canadians.[38]

Clifford's story is an American one which began with his puzzlement that the descendants of the Wampanoags who appeared in the Boston Federal Court in

1977 were required to prove their identity. This request was phrased in such a way that, in order to answer it, they had to prove a continuous tribal existence since the seventeenth century.[39] Since the people in question were descended from a tiny Christian tribal remnant who had survived a brutal racial war in the late seventeenth century, and since their spoken language had long vanished, Clifford was led to conclude that their knowledge of their culture was blurred, and 'overlapped' with that of white New Englanders. This is a reasonable assessment: even by the mid-nineteenth century the inhabitants of Boston only knew of the Wampanoags because of the portrayal of 'King Philip', a seventeenth-century Indian leader, by a white actor.[40] However, the Wampanoags are an extreme case even in the United States, a country whose policies towards Indians were usually strongly integrationist. This example is not relevant to Canada, where segregationist policies and low population densities allowed for the preservation of indigenous historical identities and languages. While the cultures of Canadian indigenous peoples were heavily modified by commercial, missionary and governmental contact, they still would find it easy to give an affirmative answer to Clifford's question as to whether they were something more than a collection of individuals with varying degrees of Native American ancestry.

Even if we accept Clifford's view of culture as universal, and decide that all cultures are overlapping, open and negotiated, why should we consider them as political in the conventional sense of that word? Are we obliged to obey a culture as if it possesses authority? If cultures overlap and are open, what institution would have the authority to coerce others into obedience? The fact that these sorts of questions seem meaningless suggests that Tully was mistaken to co-opt an anthropological definition of culture into his constitutional theory.[41] Or, alternately, his attempt to add a constitutional dimension to Clifford's notion of culture relies upon a belief that a desirable form of political participation occurs if culturally dissimilar peoples exchange stories or narratives. Participation is thus defined as learning to appreciate the differences between cultures. Tully imagines that this process is a matter of uttering speech acts of the following kind: 'Let me see if I understand what you said' and 'Is what you said analogous to this example in my culture?'[42] He believes that this process will allow disparate groups to reach accommodation or to become reconciled in a way which would not be possible for principled people who were not engaged in such a dialogue.[43] The former groups would understand claims and reach accommodation, while the latter would misunderstand, and view other cultural groups as opponents. There is no reason, however, to accept Tully's statement as a normative one; it is a faulty empirical statement. People who negotiate are as likely to acquire suspicion and hostility towards their interlocutor as they are to acquire sympathy and understanding. In the psychological literature on conflict and negotiation, the latter outcome is called 'autistic hostility'.

Tully's views on political negotiation rest upon an analogy with individuals attempting to achieve self-recognition in their struggles with other individuals. He explicitly attributes this idea to Hegel.[44] However, this analogy is flawed, for two reasons. First, it is not clear that Hegel intended his comments upon self-recognition to be used in constitutional debates. Indeed, since his own extensive constitutional writings on England were unaccompanied by such analysis, it is reasonable to assume that he does not provide authority for this. Second, modern conflict literature does not provide backing for Tully's idea that an 'Hegelian' negotiated constitutionalism would lead to moral outcomes. That is, while it seems to be true that negotiation is more successful when no parties use threats while bargaining, it is also successful when only one party (rather than both parties) uses threats.[45] The success of negotiation may, or may not, result from moral behaviour such as refusal to engage in threats or insistence upon equity.

When Tully refers to 'overlapping forms of self-government', he cites Taylor's *Reconciling the Solitudes*[46] as if he agrees with that work's appeal for a state-centred identity. However, I suggest that it would be a more generous act of homage if Tully refrained from mentioning Taylor's name, and abandoned the politics of identity. While his argument for identity politics is based on a clearly stated premise, it does not produce a cogent basis for his two consequential suggestions that the nation state will be preserved if it follows his constitutional analysis. Tully's premise is that Canadian citizens cannot identify with their government unless their cultural differences are recognized. His first suggestion is that there should be a revision of the vocabulary and institutions of political identity which are associated with the modern nation state.[47] Tully then reaches beyond this to make a second suggestion that the recognition of diverse strands of identity in Canada will prevent the disunity and the disintegration of the nation state.[48] At this point he is on weak ground. His adoption of a modern anthropological definition of culture with which to replace Taylor's notion of the state as the centre of culture diminishes the rationale for the politics of recognition. That is, if there is no shared political identity, then how can the diverse strands of Tully's culture recognize each other, and why would they do this? What had been explicit as a psychological mechanism in *Reconciling the Solitudes* no longer functions. Taylor's theory of political identity was a conventional one with Hegelian connotations which reinforced an idea that one's own individual identity was a response to the recognition of others. By analogy, individuals also were supposed to recognize themselves in the state. While this explanation of identity is archaic, it provides *an* explanation of why people could recognize a common constitutional idea – the state. However, when Tully asks the question, 'Why is the first step of mutual recognition so difficult?'[49] there is no answer – only an unconvincing reference to diverse ideologies which were constructed to exclude others. While Tully remains an advocate of participation, there is no reason why a member of an indigenous minority should agree with him. Tully's speech acts might end in hostility. Further, while the word 'participation' might have pleasant connotations to a liberal democrat, it is unlikely to be attractive to an indigenous citizen whose very identity can be altered by the state, and whose collective persona might be too demographically insignificant to exert electoral power.[50]

The conflict between collective and individual rights in the David Thomas case discussed above raises a further difficulty with identity politics. That is, it appears that the identity of the rights-bearing collective, the Coast Salish, was determined by the court: an external authority objectively determined whether or not the collective's focus on a ritual such as a Spirit Dance or a Potlatch was a central component of their culture. This would seem presumptuous even if the history of race relations in British Columbia had not always involved European authorities attempting to identify and to extinguish the central components of tribal culture. Even the very existence of a collective might be determined in this way. For example, in 1991 the Supreme Court of Canada found that linguistic evidence demonstrated that the Matachewan and the Temagami were aboriginal peoples of their part of Ontario because the root words of their language differed from the neighbouring North Temiskaming and Nipissing peoples. The separate identity of the Matachewan and Temagani was successfully established – though their claim was disallowed on other grounds.[51] This sort of procedure suggests that the theoretical claims of indigenous people are not treated as having comparable weight with those of individuals. No similar burdens of proof of identity could be put upon individual citizens. For example, one would not find an individual claim more appealing if it had been expressed in the same language for several decades. Or, similarly, one would be puzzled if individuals were considered more deserving if they differed from their neighbours. If identity is something which can be assigned or modified by expert outside advice, then there is no persuasive reason to believe that it carries any intrinsic moral weight. Further, one would doubt that an indigenous people would voluntarily place their cultural 'identity' in the hands of a non-indigenous decision-making process unless their existence was already threatened. First Nations have a history of resenting government by outsiders. There is no evidence that they feel more inclined to accept decisions because these could be defended by reference to principles such as judicial impartiality. One suspects that indigenous people will not be content to have their future cultural identities shaped by judicial officials any more than they were happy to have their pasts arranged by Indian agents or, more recently, by civil servants.

In the past, Canada's indigenous peoples defined the state as 'a group of strangers who demand obedience. It is inherently intrusive, coercive and restrictive.'[52] This is still true. The state does not represent their identity; it is foreign and its ideas are alien ones. Whether it is W. P. Kinsella in *Born Indian*[53] writing about officials in Alberta, or Garry Potts writing about Ontario bureaucrats, the narratives do not distinguish between elected and appointed officials. All were government functionaries who behaved as if the people were children. Conventional appeals to normative ideals seemed meaningless. 'But they also have words at their disposal. "Democracy" means that they are your government, and they play on that. "We speak for the people".'[54] It is clear to Potts that the 'people' for whom they speak are not indigenous ones.

Both Canadian discourses – rights and participation – do not serve the interests of aboriginal peoples. The identity upon which their rights are based is an objective category assigned by courts which assesses linguistic and anthropological evidence before determining the degree of autonomy, the shape of local administration and the nature of rights. The last of these, rights, seems especially fluid and can direct indigenous peoples to focus alternately upon a progressive future or a traditional one without reference to their welfare and their wishes. Like rights language, participation also threatens the identity of aboriginal peoples. It means either participation in the state to which they are hostile, or ethnic membership in one of a variety of overlapping cultures, which means that they are likely to lose their unique standing.

Given the lack of clarity in the current Canadian discussions of rights and participation, it could be prudent to step back from the literature and ask how rights and participation function. On the first of these, one should ask how many rights there are and how participation will benefit aboriginal peoples. Given that one cannot enumerate or specify indigenous rights, the only general principle which might apply is that rights are correlative to duties assigned to other individuals and groups. This, of course, is difficult to accept because indigenous political activity is not part of a balanced world where duties and rights are reciprocated. The rights referred to by indigenous peoples are usually associated with claims to autonomy and self-government and, thus, not based on claims against other citizens. Participation also fails. There are two reasons for this. First, it relies on democratic theory which indigenous people, as a permanent minority, can scarcely be expected to incorporate as part of their identity. Second, in Taylor's form, participation would mean adherence to the state as a meta-ethnic identity. This, however, would run into the difficulty that First Nations have often forged their cultures as opponents of governments not as participants in them. To put the matter in Taylor's Hegelian language, indigenous people may recognize that their own identity was absorbed by the state, but in the future they may perceive the state only as the 'other'.

Notes

1   J. Tully, 'The Crisis of Identification: The Case of Canada', *Political Studies*, XLII, 1994, p. 78.
2   Ibid., p. 91.
3   In making this comment I am extending a suggestion by Amy Gutmann ('Introduction', in Gutmann, ed., *Multiculturalism: Examining the Politics of Recognition*, Princeton: Princeton University Press, 1994, pp. 4–5) when she suggests that Charles Taylor and others are mistaken to ascribe an identity to the state. I take her suggestion to mean that we should not think of the state as a unifying focus of group identity after the fashion of a national sport such as baseball or soccer.
4   Exceptions to the statement are Darlene M. Johnston (she offers a liberal defence of indigenous group rights in 'Native Rights as Collective Rights: A Question of Group Self-Preservation', in W. Kymlicka, ed., *The Rights of Minority Cultures*, Oxford: Oxford University Press, 1995) and Will Kymlicka, in his *Liberalism, Community, and Culture*, Oxford: Clarendon Press, 1989, esp. pp. 142–57. In this early work Kymlicka acts as a philosophical minority attempting to persuade his fellow Canadians that indigenous peoples would benefit from the application of liberalism. More recently his position has become more attenuated and closer to the views of his former opponents.
5   Will Kymlicka, *Finding Our Way: Rethinking Ethnocultural Relations in Canada*, Toronto: Oxford University Press, 1998.

6 See J. R. Danley, 'Liberalism, Aboriginal Rights, and Cultural Minorities', *Philosophy and Public Affairs*, 20, 2, 1991, pp. 169 and 182.

7 Kymlicka, *Finding Our Way*, p. 115. When Kymlicka discusses the merits of group-based representation, he focuses upon the fact that only aboriginal peoples and the Quebecois were self-governing nations prior to incorporation. Since the English were doing the incorporation, it follows that there are three founding groups.

8 One of Kymlicka's sympathizers, Michael Murphy, thinks that the Inuit in Nunavut, various Yukon First Nations and the Nisga'a in British Columbia would form 'national communities' but not other indigenous peoples. M. Murphy, 'Culture and the Courts, A New Direction in Canadian Jurisprudence on Aboriginal Rights?', *Canadian Journal of Political Science*, 34, 1, March 2001, p. 114. The test for a 'national community' seems to be a territorial one where a group was contiguous in settlement and of the same ethnicity. However, since such a test might also include descendants of immigrants, it might be insufficient. Further, as Danley originally observed in reply to Kymlicka, it might lead to 'Balkanization' not to a unified set of *national* communities.

9 Will Kymlicka's political speculations are not restricted to the Canadian Constitution, nor does he attempt to be consistent on the role of indigenous peoples within modern nation states. In his most recent book (W. Kymlicka, *Politics in the Vernacular: Nationalism, Multiculturalism, and Citizenship*, Oxford: Oxford University Press, 2001, pp. 128–9) Kymlicka is both tentative and pragmatic on this subject.

10 T. G. Svensson, 'Litigation as Ethnopolitical Action: A Means of Attaining Improved Land Rights', *Études Canadiennes*, 20–1, 1986, p. 33.

11 Ibid., p. 35.

12 R. L. Barsch, 'Indigenous Peoples and the Idea of Individual Human Rights', *Native Studies Review*, 10, 2, 1995, pp. 35–6.

13 A. Eisenberg, 'The Politics of Individual and Group Difference in Canadian Jurisprudence', *Canadian Journal of Political Science*, XXVII, 1, March 1994, pp. 3 and 15.

14 Ibid., p. 15. To claim that a particular ritual, such as a dance, lacks cultural centrality suggests that the court imagines that such practices are more authentic and more defensible if they are ancient and changeless. This, however, is to impose an impossible legal test upon the authenticity of ritual; it is an anthropological commonplace that such dances have changed in the past. See, for example, the comment on the dances of the Coast Salish neighbours, the Kwakiutl, in A. Jonaitis, ed., *Chiefly Feasts*, Vancouver: Douglas & Macintyre, 1991, pp. 113–14.

15 Eisenberg ('The Politics of Individual and Group Difference', p. 16) notes that the court would have had even more difficulty with its decision if Thomas had had a conventional upbringing on the reservation, or if his personal security had not been threatened.

16 Ibid., pp. 11 and 14.

17 C. Bell, 'Introductory Note' to *Canadian Supreme Court: Delgamuukw v. British Columbia* [11 December 1997], 37 ILM 261, pp. 261–2. The change in constitutional direction from the Sparrow and Sioui precedents to the Van der Peet one is viewed by Michael Murphy ('Culture and the Courts', pp. 109–29) as a serious diminishment of the legal and political status of aboriginal people.

18 *Delgamuukw v. British Columbia*, pp. 318–19. The idea that a court should decide on important issues of cultural identity – such as the format of a tribe's autonomy and its organization – undermines the sense in which *identity* is invested with moral importance. For example, individual identity is often admired because it signals that an autonomous individual possesses the ability to reason and to make choices. Without such attributes it would be difficult to ascribe moral qualities to an individual. The models referred to are those of nation, public government and community of interest ('Report of the Royal Commission on Aboriginal Peoples', vol. 2, *Restructuring the*

Relationship, Part One, Ministry of Supply and Services Canada, 1996, pp. 250–79). However, the Report of the Royal Commission of Aboriginal Peoples repeatedly makes it clear that all indigenous people giving evidence to the Commission regard the right to self-government as an 'inherent' one. Therefore, it could be regarded as a general right by anyone referring to the Report.

19 J. Tully, *Strange Multiplicity: Constitutionalism in an Age of Diversity*, Cambridge: Cambridge University Press, 1995, p. 132.

20 Ibid., pp. 19–20.

21 Tully's views on the similarity of traditions are not those of the Gitskan and Wet'suwet'en people. He sees their ancient traditions as similar to common law, while they see their rights in opposition to this. See *Restructuring the Relationship*, p. 110.

22 Ibid. p. 137.

23 This division between lawyers and political theorists would not be accepted by T. M. J. Bateman ('Rights Application Doctrine and the Clash of Constitutionisms in Canada', *Canadian Journal of Political Science*, 31, 1, March 1998, pp. 3–29), who sees conventional constitutional lawyers as liberals, and political theorists, such as James Tully, as 'post-liberal' constitutionalists. In other words, he regards lawyers and political theorists as engaged in a debate over the liberal interpretation of the Constitution. I see this view as over-emphasizing the importance of liberalism for both groups and as misguided in its connotation that the political theorists are seriously concerned with criticizing legal theorizing.

24 It would be wrong to assign the entire blame for the division in Canadian theoretical politics to the Charter of Rights. The pioneer of the charter, F. R. Scott, had an account of politics which fell in between Charles Taylor's two models of a rights society and a participatory society. On this see A. Mills, 'Of Charter, Rights and Freedoms: The Social Thought of F. R. Scott, 1930–1985', *Journal of Canadian Studies*, 32, 1, Spring 1997, p. 60.

25 There are, of course, other important Canadian voices on the politics of cultural identity. For example, A. Cairns (*Charter versus Federalism: The Dilemmas of Constitutional Reform*, Montreal and Kingston: McGill-Queen's University Press, 1992, p. 59) advocates the nurturing of cultural identity as a necessary symbolism needed to flesh out theoretical citizenship.

26 C. Taylor, *Reconciling the Solitudes: Essays on Canadian Federalism and Nationalism*, Montreal and Kingston: McGill-Queen's University Press, 1993, p. 89. Cairns (*Charter versus Federalism*, pp. 116–17) could be seen as taking the opposite stance to Taylor. Cairns argues that the Charter of Rights eroded the leadership of executive federalism in formal constitutional change. It also meant that aboriginal groups no longer see themselves as supplicants. Both these changes could be construed as ones which increased participation.

27 Taylor, *Reconciling the Solitudes*, p. 90.

28 Ibid., p. 94.

29 Ibid.

30 W. B. Michaels, *Our America: Nativism, Modernism and Pluralism*, Durham, NC: Duke University Press, 1995, p. 15.

31 See Taylor's *Reconciling the Solitudes*, p. 97.

32 C. Taylor, 'The Politics of Recognition', in Gutmann, ed., *Multiculturalism*, pp. 25–75.

33 Ibid., p. 42.

34 When Eisenberg raised this difficulty with the rights language in Canadian jurisprudence, this was done in conformity with Taylor's criticism of rights. Presumably Eisenberg did not notice that a similar difficulty resides in Taylor's notion of identity.

35 Tully, *Strange Multiplicity*, p. 45.

36 Ibid., p. 198.

37 Ibid., p. 46. Tully also finds sources for his 'overlapping' cultures in the work of Michael Carruthers and Wittgenstein (pp. 10 and 139). In 'The Crisis of Identification', p. 90,

Tully describes political identity as having a 'tangled' nature, and suggests that cultures and legal forms 'overlap' and interact.

38 That is, it is often plausible in Canada to assert self-determination on the grounds of 'territorial predominance'. See *Restructuring the Relationship*, pp. 179–80.

39 J. Clifford, *The Predicament of Culture: Twentieth-Century Ethnography, Literature, and Art*, Cambridge, Mass.: Harvard University Press, 1988, pp. 7–8.

40 On the recent past of Wampanoags, see J. Lepore, *The Name of War: King Philip's War and the Origins of American Identity*, New York: Vintage Books, 1998.

41 Clifford bears no responsibility for the use of his ideas by political theorists. When he uses the world 'authority' he is primarily referring to whether or not texts and anthropological evidence possess authenticity. He does not apply the term to demands for obedience or to rational acceptance of constitutional arrangements.

42 Tully, *Strange Multiplicity*, p. 133.

43 Ibid., p. 134.

44 See J. Tully, 'Diversity's Gambit Declined', in C. Cook, ed., *Constitutional Predicament: Canada after the Referendum of 1992*, McGill-Queen's University Press, 1994, p.183. Later Tully (in 'Struggles over Recognition and Distribution', *Constellations*, 7, 4, 2000, pp. 474–5) would distance himself from Hegel by saying that the latter's struggle for recognition applied to the relation between two actors whereas modern relations are complex and multilateral. In this form of recognition Tully is appealing to naturalistic identity politics in order to avoid artificial consent theory. However, the conditions of political dialogue to which he refers include 'reasonable counter-proposals', democratic negotiations and shared principles which do not seem very complex or multilateral. In another recent account of recognition Tully suggests that political engagement is a kind of play aimed at generating self-respect and self-esteem ('The Challenge of Re-imagining Citizenship and Belonging in Multicultural and Multinational societies', in C. McKinnon and I. Hampsher-Monk, eds, *The Demands of Citizenship*, London: Continuum, 2000, p. 231). These more recent accounts stress the positive aspects of self-recognition rather than the harsh objective and economic aspects of Hegel's views on human relations.

45 See J. Z. Rubin and B. R. Brown, *The Social Psychology of Bargaining and Negotiation*, New York: Academic Press, 1975, pp. 93–4. Tully believes – apparently as an article of faith – that illocutionary games of reciprocal disclosure and acknowledgement prevent violence (see 'Struggles over Recognition', p. 479).

46 Tully, 'The Crisis of Identification', p. 78.

47 Ibid., p. 79.

48 Ibid., p. 91.

49 Tully, *Strange Multiplicity*, p. 198. M. Milde ('Critical Notice', *Canadian Journal of Philosophy*, 28, 1, March 1998, p. 142) has observed that Tully has failed to specify which criteria are required for a group to secure legitimate recognition or to say when a group can refuse to accommodate another group.

50 There is some evidence that indigenous Canadians regard increased democracy as the death of their own style of decision making (*Restructuring the Relationship*, p. 134).

51 G. Potts, 'Bushman and Dragonfly', *Journal of Canadian Studies*, 33, 2, Summer 1998, p. 192.

52 Barsch, 'Indigenous Peoples', p. 46.

53 W. P. Kinsella's collection of short stories, *Born Indian*, was published by Oberon Press (Ottawa) in 1981. While Kinsella has been criticized for reconstructing the life experience of a young indigenous man while he himself lacks First Nations ancestry, I cannot see why his insights into an individual should not be taken as seriously as those of Tully and Kymlicka when they imagine a community.

54 Potts, 'Bushman and Dragonfly', p. 189.

10 Identity, reflection and justification

Peri Roberts

Identity and community

In *Thick and Thin* Michael Walzer breaks off from his explorations of social criticism and international morality to tell us a little about how he regards the notion of identity or the self. He says,

> I am like a newly elected president. ... Though he is called commander-in-chief, his choices are in fact limited, his freedom qualified; the political world is full of *givens*. ... My inner world is full of *givens*, too, culturally bestowed or socially imposed – I maneuver among them insofar as their plurality allows for the maneuvering.[1]

I was struck here by the use of the term 'given' and Walzer's claim that identity, the inner world, has limits, and that those limits are bestowed by a culture, by the community of which the self is a member. In this chapter I am concerned not to examine closely the details of Walzer's particular position but, instead, to work through what it means to claim that identity is *given* by community and to ask what follows from such a claim. In working through this claim I will not identify it with any particular theorist but will highlight instances when this and related claims are made by a number of thinkers. This will involve initially what is, to some extent, a revisiting of the familiar ground occupied by communitarianism. This ground is also occupied by thinkers making claims under the heading 'multiculturalism'.[2]

The claim that identity, our conception of ourselves, is given by the community of which we are a part is a complex one that we find reflected in the work of a number of thinkers. Sandel, for instance, finds himself adopting the same language as Walzer. He claims that the identity of the self is 'constituted in the light of ends already before it'; ends provided by the community of which that self is a member. 'The relevant question [then] is not what ends to choose ... the answer to this question is already *given*.'[3] He goes on to claim that we cannot view ourselves removed from our community and our communal loyalties and convictions. '[L]iving by them is *inseparable* from understanding ourselves as the particular persons we are ....'; 'Allegiances such as these are ... enduring attachments and commitments that ... *define* the person I am.'[4] For members of a society, their community is 'a constituent of their identity' which brings with it unchosen attachments they must 'acknowledge' as their own.[5] This language is again reflected in MacIntyre. He claims that we

> approach our own circumstances as bearers of a particular social identity. ... I inherit from the past of my family, my city, my tribe, my nation, a variety of debts, inheritances, rightful expectations and obligations. *These constitute the given of my life*, my moral starting point.[6]

> We enter human society ... with ... roles into which we have been drafted ... [and] the individual is identified and constituted in and through certain of his or her roles, those roles which bind the individual to the communit[y]. ... There is no 'I' apart from these.[7]

Parekh slips into similar terminology. He argues that as members of cultural communities human beings acquire 'deep and powerful' 'tendencies and dispositions' which constitute a culturally specific nature.[8] As individuals these dispositions are '*inseparable and ineradicable* from their being ... and constitute ... *their* nature'.[9] Again, cultural sentiments 'strike deep roots and become an *inseparable* part of their personality'.[10] Margalit and Raz highlight a similar view of the relationship of the self to community when they claim that it is 'no more than a brute fact that people's sense of their own identity is bound up with their sense of belonging to encompassing groups' or communities.[11] '[A]t the most fundamental level our sense of our own identity depends on criteria of belonging.'[12] Finally Charles Taylor, in a celebrated essay on multiculturalism, asks us to '[c]onsider what we mean by *identity*. It is who we are, "where we're coming from." As such it is the background against which our tastes and desires and opinions and aspirations make sense.'[13] This is because 'we become full human agents, capable of understanding ourselves, and hence of defining our identity, through the acquisition of ... language in a broad sense'. This broad sense covers not only the local spoken language but also 'other modes of expression whereby we define ourselves'. That is, it is through our cultures and communities, through their art, music, morality and other modes of social interaction, that we become capable of 'self-definition'.[14]

We find in this variety of statements from a number of sources certain terminological and conceptual similarities. Identity, our conception of ourselves is *defined* by membership of particular communities. Our various communal ties and attachments inform our sentiments and *constitute* that identity. We are the sum of the roles we inhabit and inherit in a particular context. As a result we are *inseparable* from the cultural context in which we find we *belong*, to which we are *rooted*. Inhabiting such a particular context imbues us with a *given* and *ineradicable* identity.

If identity is a given and its particular features ineradicable, then this is indicative of a certain attitude towards the self and its cultural context. We will regard the self as somehow 'fixed' by that context. Both the boundaries and the content of that self are shaped or determined by a cultural background and the social understandings that background embodies. The range of attitudes, desires, attachments, commitments, dispositions, sentiments and ends that constitute our particular identity will necessarily find their source in the community of which we are a member. As a consequence, we must always understand our particular conceptions of the good for both us and our community as conditioned by the social understandings embodied in that community. As such, my conception of the good is, at least in its broad features, fixed by or determined by context. MacIntyre expresses this as the claim that 'the relationship between me, my social identity, and my good will preclude ... re-evaluation'.[15] We are indelibly marked by and shaped by our context.

In a later lecture MacIntyre develops these thoughts, arguing,

> The questions of *where* and *from whom* I learn my morality turn out to be crucial for both the content and the nature of moral commitment. ... it is an essential characteristic of the morality which each of us acquires that it is learned from, in and through the way of life of some particular community.[16]

He regards our morality as dependent upon our place in a community because this basic position ties our self-understandings so closely to particular communities that other communities become unintelligible to us. We have no resources to enable us to make sense of what those around us in a strange and unfamiliar context are doing or saying. '[W]hen we enter alien cultures or even alien structures within our own culture', the actions of participants in that culture are unintelligible to us. They are unintelligible because we are not embedded in their practices in the same way that they are, or that we are in our own.[17] As a consequence, we cannot escape and temporarily or permanently step outside our particular context. Nor are the features of that context, or the ways in which we are shaped by those features, available for negotiation or reassessment.

This understanding of the relationship between self and community focuses our ideas of moral context inwards onto particular communities, and onto the moral understandings that membership and belonging have endowed us with. It leads us to regard morality and justice as 'relative to social understandings' and to regard universal or cross-cultural moral claims with distrust. If, as Rorty claims, universal morality 'centers around the assumption that we must step outside our community long enough to examine it in the light of something that transcends it', then, if we accept all we have heard so far, we must challenge this assumption and regard a reasonable universal morality as beyond us.[18] The conception of the self and of identity as necessarily situated or embedded in social understandings and practices explicitly denies the claim that the self is detached from, and not reliant upon, particular contexts, which underpins this universalist assumption. There are simply boundaries to the intelligibility of moral values and of moral claims that match closely the boundaries of our

communities and of identity. Intelligible moral claims are herded inwards by these boundaries, enabling a rejection of universal morality on the basis of fundamental claims about identity and community. Because of these boundaries to intelligibilty, instead of attempting to construct or discover a universal moral conception, 'the most philosophy can hope to do is summarize our culturally influenced intuitions about the right thing to do'.[19]

A further consequence of regarding intelligibility as constrained within communal boundaries is to constrain reason within those boundaries too. If reasons are unintelligible beyond these boundaries, then reason itself is bounded and rational cross-cultural moral and political consensus is ruled out. Further than this, cross-cultural rational argument is also ruled out. Put starkly, reasons do not cross boundaries, reason does not travel. If we deny reason a visa, then rational justification is parochial too. A rejection of universal morality on the grounds that we have outlined means that moral justification, since based on local reasons, can be no more than local justification. Any attempt to justify beyond the limits of a realm of shared understandings quickly dissolves into unintelligibility.

To summarize the stark position outlined so far: we have stressed the tight fit between identity and community identifiable in some of the literature concerned with identity and justification. The claim appears to be that individuals' conceptions of their self and their good are given by a social context. The morality and values of a society also find their source in that cultural context. As a consequence, evaluative judgements are intelligible only within this context, and so justifying reasons must refer to that context. In effect, the boundaries of community equal the boundaries of intelligibility equal the boundaries of justification.

Individual and social understandings

We have spent some time highlighting features of a basic communitarian and multiculturalist position on identity and justification. I am of course aware that I have painted it fairly starkly and in rather a one-sided manner. This section will run through what is at issue between communitarians and their critics here and will take the form of an argument about the relationship between identity and community.

An initial response to this communitarian position was forcefully put by Caney in his forthright 1992 article in *Political Studies*.[20] Caney's initial portrayal of communitarianism is as uncompromising as the account I've just given. His response is to argue that the self, rather than being determined by the community of which it is a part, participates in its own creation. He argues that it is a more accurate reflection of our self-understandings if we regard the individual as capable of rational reflection on his or her ends or his or her conception of the good and, also, of their revision.[21] Caney argues that individuals, to a greater or lesser degree, construct their own identities. Consequently, communities are not authoritative when it comes to the identification of the self and its goods. He supports this conclusion by showing how the communitarians themselves admit

as much. He cites MacIntyre as denying that 'the self is or becomes nothing but the social roles it inherits', and Sandel claiming that 'the subject is empowered to participate in the constitution of its identity' and is only 'to some extent' defined by community.[22] Communitarians, argues Caney, cannot claim that individuals are 'wholly embedded' in their contexts. Parekh too allows that human beings might 'shape themselves' and that their identities, at least in part, are shaped by 'what they succeed in giving themselves as reflective individuals'.[23] The argument in Caney is that communities do not define or determine identity. Individuals, to some degree, make themselves. They are capable of 'stepping back' from at least some of the values or ends they have inherited from their community and subjecting them to reflective assessment. What is 'participating in the constitution of your identity' if it is not making choices about the sort of person you want to be and the sort of values or ends you want to hold? In making these identity-shaping choices, we will be subjecting ourselves and, at any one time, some of our 'given' ends to rational scrutiny. In doing so we can reaffirm those ends or we can reject or modify them. Whichever course we take, affirmation or rejection, we will take it for reasons, whether or not those reasons are transparent to us. The conclusion we draw from this might be that communities are not authoritative and, as such, communal boundaries need not be boundaries to either intelligibility or justification.

Perhaps this is a bit quick. 'OK', respond the communitarians, 'strict cultural determination looks to be a non-starter, but this was never the claim we made. Of course the self is creative to some degree. Of course individuals can shape their own identities.' The communitarians argue instead that admitting a degree of individual identity creation does not show that there is necessarily a significant disjuncture between the self and shared communal understandings. Whilst there may be no obvious one-to-one mapping of communal values and shared understandings onto individual identity, a fundamental relationship still exists between the two. In Sandel's words, individuals are still 'defined to some extent by the community of which they are a part'.[24] Self-creation doesn't go all the way down. Indeed, as MacIntyre claims, 'we are never more (and sometimes less) than the co-authors of our own narratives'.[25] Whilst we may choose and revise some aspects of our identity and conception of the good, a proper respect for and understanding of our relationship to our communities may involve placing 'our ties to our nation beyond rational criticism' and so beyond revision.[26]

So, rather than claim strict cultural determination of identity, the claim is instead that, as Parekh puts it, '[m]embership of a cultural community … *structures and shapes* the individual's personality in a certain way and gives it a content or identity'.[27] Instead of determining identity, community structures or constrains it. Individuals do participate in the formation of their own identities, but within a range of options. The range of available options is culturally bounded and so the choice posed to us between conceptions of the good or between sets of ends to be pursued is posed in, and bound by, a particular context. Context affects us deeply, so deeply that there are certain culturally bounded fundamental links between the self and its community, links that struc-

ture identity formation and are beyond revision. Whilst we participate in the formation of the superficial aspects of the self, the community is still fundamentally authoritative for individual identity. Identity (at the important levels) is properly regarded as *inseparable* from social understandings. As such, the boundaries of the community *do* equal the boundaries of intelligibility, which *do* equal the boundaries of justification. The basic communitarian point still stands.

So far we have rehearsed familiar arguments and gone over pretty familiar ground. However, there are important implications of the modification to the communitarian position that we have yet to explore. In denying the strict communal determination of identity and allowing that the individual is empowered to partake in a process of self shaping, more may be allowed by the communitarians than is often noticed. Because shared understandings inform or participate in individuals' conceptions of the good, they play a role in shaping the range of such conceptions: the range of ends and values endorsed by the individuals in the community. Therefore, as individuals rationally reflect on which ends they have reason to affirm or endorse and which they have reason to modify or reject, they are, at the same time, reflecting on the social understandings that present those ends and values as available options. If someone has reason to reject certain values, this may also give him or her reason to reject or modify the social understandings tied up with those values. Whilst an individual alone may not radically influence social understandings, it would appear that those understandings are at least under constant examination and may be subject to reasoned pressures to adapt or change. The relationship between social understandings and individual identity and understandings is not one of one-way determination but is a reciprocal relationship of mutual influence. Social understandings influence individual identity, but in reflecting on that identity, individuals influence social understandings.

That this is the case seems obvious but is under-appreciated by communitarians. Social understandings and values *must* bear some relation to individual understandings and conceptions of the good. Social understandings would not be social understandings if they did not form part of the individual views of a significant portion of the community. Conversely, if a value has been rejected by an overwhelming number of individual members of that community it would be odd to claim that it was still fundamental to social understandings within that community. Even if such social understandings do not consciously present themselves to the members of the community it is unlikely that they could persist in a central role if the values they entail were systematically rejected. Individual rational reflection can lead to rational reflection at the level of social understandings. The relationship is not one-way but is one of mutual influence between social and individual conceptions. Influence, and therefore change, may flow in both directions. Note that such changes at the individual level are the result of *rational* reflection, of having *reasons* to adopt, affirm, modify or reject ends. If influence is reciprocal, then reflection on social understandings is also a rational process. Social understandings are capable of being adopted, affirmed, modified or rejected for reasons also.

So, if the relationship between social and individual understandings is recip-rocal, then the community is not authoritative for identity, as communitarians claim. If this is the case, then a vital support appears to have been removed for their claims that community boundaries necessarily equal boundaries for intelli-gibility and justification. If individual identity is not determined by community, then there is no reason to think that cross-cultural rational argument, justifica-tion and consensus are ruled out. Through the process of rationally reflecting on ends and values, the members of the community might be able to reflect on ideas and values from a broader range of sources than the communitarians admit, perhaps from a community of which they are not at present a member. In doing so, they may import ideas and values, modify their own in favour of novel ideas, or merely glance at them curiously; we cannot know in advance what the outcome will be. However, we have removed a basic communitarian reason for claiming that boundaries are impermeable.

Or have we? All we have established so far is that individuals are capable of rational reflection and that such reflection may result in the evaluation and revi-sion of social understandings. Communitarians may respond that nothing so far necessarily undermines the claim that the boundaries of community are also boundaries to intelligibility and justification. Whilst noting re-evaluation of social understandings as a possibility, communitarians may insist that such re-evaluation is limited. This is not a claim that it doesn't happen often. As we have seen, any significant revision of individual understandings is always at the same time a revision to some degree of social understandings. Accepting this, the claim might be instead that social revision may be limited to less significant aspects of social understandings or that revision might be limited to within a certain range. This range may be limited by the history of that community and the evolution of its understandings. Will social understandings always and unavoidably bear the indelible scars of the past?

This is the position of MacIntyre who, whilst recognizing that membership in communities may still allow for an individual to reflect on his or her moral inher-itance, notes that 'particularity can never be simply left behind or obliterated'.[28] In any ongoing process of revision at least some of the community's 'projects and practices will be ... treated uncritically ... some at least must be perma-nently exempted from criticism'.[29] Central elements of my identity and of the social understandings of my community are beyond revision. 'What I am, there-fore, is in key part what I inherit ... whether I like it or not, whether I recognize it or not.' 'The story of my life is *always* embedded in the story of those commu-nities from which I *derive* my identity.'[30] Sandel agrees. He argues that '[w]hile the contours of my identity will in some ways be open and subject to revision, they are not wholly without shape'. I have only 'limited scope for self-reflection' within limits set by the community of which I am a member. 'As a self-inter-preting being I am able to reflect on my history and in this sense distance myself from it, but the distance is always precarious and provisional, the point of refer-ence never finally secured outside the history itself.'[31]

The argument is that even if the evaluation and revision of social understandings is a corollary of individual introspection, this evaluation is secured within limits. Again, as with individual reflection, our communities present us with a range of available options, possibilities for revision. However, as with individual reflection, such revision is structured, and that structure is provided by communal horizons and the deepest level of given social understandings. Once again we may be forced to conclude that the community is authoritative, but instead of authoritative determination we experience authoritative structures or limits.[32] The boundaries of community are again reinforced as boundaries of intelligibilty and justification. These communitarian conclusions seem strong. However, they only stand if there are these 'givens' at some level of social understandings that are not just difficult to place before the reflective mind but are impossible to subject to rational reflection. A lot is going to turn here on whether in the process of reflective identity formation the term 'given' should be taken to mean 'immune from revision' or instead to mean 'starting point'. This is a question that has a more general relevance. This dichotomy in attitude towards our undoubted cultural baggage is mirrored in the literature concerning reflection and justification. More specifically, it is paralleled in the discussion that surrounds the notion of reflective assessment of values and the search for reflective equilibrium. The communitarian position can only be strengthened by association with the equivalent position in this discussion.

There is no room here to spend much time running over the basics of Rawls's notion of reflective equilibrium, and so I will go ahead and assume a basic familiarity.[33] Whilst the idea of a search for a reflective equilibrium is not intended to apply directly to the process of identity formation, it *is* a sophisticated attempt to understand how we might best hold up to the light of rational examination the various assumptions, presuppositions and intuitions we presently endorse. This reflective approach insists that we assess our given individual understandings and try to make sense of the ways in which they may or may not fit together. In this process of rational scrutiny, Rawls insists that we may endorse, revise, modify or reject the individual understandings we possessed initially. He specifically utilizes this approach in the public realm, in an attempted justification of principles of justice for the basic structure of a well-ordered society. In doing so, he makes explicit his understanding that individual reflection can in turn lead to reflection on social meanings.

What is at issue in the literature on reflective equilibrium is the relationship between the principles, ends or values that our reflection settles upon and the convictions and intuitions with which we started. In this literature we find two positions on this question that parallel the positions in the identity argument. On one interpretation of reflective equilibrium we have a given starting point, our set of considered convictions about justice. This is our set of basic assumptions, shorn of those that we are least certain about or those that we hold only in abnormal situations (such as when we are angry or drunk). In this interpretation the considered convictions must be recognized as 'a sub-class of initial opinions which are to be seen as fixed points around which all else must be accommodated ... fixed points which perform the same function as basic statements do in scientific enquiry'.[34] On this 'fixed-point' interpretation, reflective equilibrium is akin to a caricatured account of the reasoning of the natural sciences, where deliberation can lead to only one-way adjustment of theory to match starting points, empirical data. Support for this interpretation comes from Peter Singer, who writes that 'Rawls's view is that a normative moral theory is like a scientific theory ... the aim of the theory is to explain all the data'.[35] The data themselves, the starting point, are at no time up for revision. They are the given upon which reflection reflects.

If this 'fixed-point' interpretation is correct, then this sophisticated under-standing of individual reflection functions within specific limits. Reflection is limited in that it is tied to a fixed point or points which are beyond revision. As such, Little claims that reflective equilibrium is no more than a 'technique for systematizing ... antecedent moral convictions'.[36] As it holds these antecedent convictions together, then, as well as being 'given' to us by our community, they themselves fulfil the role of 'given' in the reflective process. They are the background assumptions against which all our reflection takes place. Any reflective 'justification offered here is relative to ... [this] set of background assumptions, with the result that if they are not satisfied then the argument has no grip'.[37] We have seen (and not disputed) that the source of our background assumptions, our ideas about morality and justice, is likely to be found in the community of which we are members and its 'given' social understandings. We might also regard, as the communitarians appear to, the term 'given' as synonymous with 'beyond revision' and not simply as 'basic starting point'. Basic social understandings shape our moral convictions and are in turn 'beyond revision'.

The point is also made that any justification of principles of justice or value that is identified as a result of reflection only has purchase where the argument 'has grip'. That is, it is only as far as we have background assumptions that we have in common with others that justification has purchase. If background assumptions are not shared, then neither are any reasons based on such assumptions. The communitarian understanding is that these background assumptions are those that we receive from our communities and so it seems that any justification that 'grips' only does so between the members of a community that share common assumptions at some level. If we inhabit different communities, we will have different background assumptions, and so will hold different things to be given. If we don't share the assumptions, if we have different sets of givens, then the reasoning process will be unintelligible to us and cannot justify. This interpretation of reflection and the fixed, one-way relationship between individual and social understandings and the principles and values we reflectively endorse, parallels the one-way limiting relationship we saw between community and identity in the multicultural and communitarian literature. It highlights that in both accounts of reflection, and justification we function within limitations set by our membership of communities. For Singer, Brown and Little, as well as for the communitarians, the boundaries of community do equal the boundaries of reflective justification.

Crossing the boundaries

How can we address this claim that boundaries are impermeable? The question that we must focus on is whether reflective evaluation of both individual and social understandings is necessarily contained within the same boundaries as is the cultural community. This is the claim of a basic communitarianism. We have seen that the self participates in the formation of its own identity and also in the shaping and reshaping of social and cultural understandings. What we must accept from the communitarians, though, is that these social and cultural understandings *do* have an influence on identity, but no one will dispute this.[38] This amounts to the claim that in justification we must start from where we find ourselves. But the key issue is whether, in reflective assessment, we are necessarily constrained by these starting points. Communitarianism, with the support of Singer, Brown and Little, contends that we are. Singer argues that, '[i]f I live in one society and accept one set of considered moral judgements, while you live in another society and hold a quite different set, very different moral theories may be "valid" for each of us'.[39]

This is challenged by the second interpretation of reflective equilibrium. On this interpretation, the reflective evaluation that characterizes the search for reflective equilibrium *does* start from where we find ourselves. It does so in order that our reflection bear some relation to the person we are and to what we might believe. For example, Rawls starts with our common convictions about justice, with things that we do accept.[40] Indeed, Rawls, Scanlon and Milo each point out that we might need to identify some of our convictions as provisional 'fixed points' in the reflective process. These constitute paradigmatic instances of our moral understandings such as slavery is wrong, as is torturing for amusement and the unnecessary suffering of children.[41] Given this, are Singer, Brown and Little right to characterize reflective equilibrium as fixed-point reflection, making only one-way revision possible? Can we only revise principles and ends if they do not fit with our convictions and not vice versa? The key word describing these paradigmatic moral understandings, above, however, is *provisional*. While we need to assume something in order to get the reflective process started, these starting points have no privileged epistemic status. In the attempt to match principles and theories to individual convictions that the search for reflective equilibrium consists in we expect to undertake potentially extensive revisions of both our convictions and our principles. In fitting one to the other, we can imagine an adjustment process that moves back-and-forth from convictions to principles to background theories, adjusting each in turn until a satisfactory equilibrium is attained. Whilst we may not yet be able to imagine revising our convictions that slavery is wrong and so is torturing infants, what is important, Rawls claims, is that this process could 'lead … us to revise and extrapolate our judgements' at whatever level they are made.[42] Rational reflection need not regard itself as chained to its starting points. Concerning the paradigmatic moral understandings, 'however much they may be treated as starting points … at every point we are forced to assess their acceptability'.[43] On this interpretation the search for reflective equilibrium gets off the ground by utilizing our intuitions but does not place them on a pedestal. It does not 'assign a privileged status to 'what we are already inclined to think'.[44] Reflection is a process of 'open-ended questioning' in the construction of a 'recursive justification'.[45]

This brief characterization of reflective assessment and its attitudes towards its starting points highlights its contrasts with Brown and Singer, who understand the search for reflective equilibrium to be akin to the search for a scientific theory to explain a set of data. It seems they may well be mistaken in their understanding of the reflective method. It need not be constrained by its starting points at all: 'not even the firmest considered judgements ... are taken to be immune from the possibility of revision'.[46] This reflective attitude towards our culturally acquired moral inheritance is a constructivist one and involves regarding every aspect of that inheritance as a candidate for reassessment.[47] Obviously we would not expect to reassess our entire inheritance at once; it is not often an entire way of life that is in question. Here we get Neurath's boat sailing into view. On this leaky vessel we make running repairs, removing some planks for repair if necessary but unable to repair all planks at once without sinking. We caulk our leaks in a gradual manner, holding firm to one part of the structure in order to fix another, one part at a time. Sooner or later, however, we may have replaced every plank in the boat. We must always stand somewhere, but we can always later stand somewhere else to look more closely at our initial footing. As Kai Nielsen puts it, we start

> from traditions and return to them. There can be no simple stepping out of our societies and traditions. ....We will never be without our more or less local identities, though they need not ethnocentrically hobble us. ... we are not imprisoned by our traditions. ... No belief is in principle immune to criticism and rejection and whole traditions, plank by plank, can be trans-formed as we repair and even rebuild the ship at sea.[48]

Our communal and traditional backgrounds are not to be regarded as unalter-able limits on identity, forever constraining our understanding of who we are and who we might like to be. We can regard ourselves as empowered to properly shape those limits ourselves and so shape our identities.

This reflective process also enables us to take on board the resources of other cultures and traditions. In reflecting on our individual and social understandings, there is no reason to think that our reflection is unable to consider a wide range of alternatives. In assessing and testing our understandings, we are naturally confronted by alien understandings, the understandings of other individuals and communities. Indeed, Parekh allows that we may turn our critical faculties inwards on our own cultures when contact with alternative cultures alerts us 'to the fact that human life can be understood and organized in several different ways and that their own is contingent and changeable'. He goes on to say that when people reflect, 'other cultures ... enable them to view their own from the outside'.[49] Rather than contact with alternative cultures necessarily being portrayed as clash or confrontation and leading to retrenchment, it may also be possible that such contact might lead to mutual understanding and critical reflection.[50] It seems that we may be linked in the reflective process to the past but that there need be no indelible scars of history, no inevitable limitations set by the boundaries of communal understandings.

Conclusion

The dispute we have had with the communitarians in this chapter has taken the form of two distinct understandings of reasoning. The communitarians have described the process of reasoning and reflection we probably undertake most of the time. When we cruise through our lives day by day we are able to take for granted almost everything about our cultural and normative environment. Our lives are content, we are happy with who we are, the things that we believe and the judgements we make. We regard many of these things as settled, and, doing so, take our places alongside the many others in our community who regard themselves and their lives as equally settled. As a community and as individuals we inhabit a settled cultural and normative environment and so across a wide range of issues, questions and concerns there is likely to be little to disagree about. The identity and concerns of individuals will be informed and reinforced by those around them and by the ideals embodied in their public culture. The settled set of institutions, individual and social understandings and conceptions of the good that make up this public culture can be seen as the joint construction of the members of the community. It has been jointly constructed over time by the working through of that reciprocal formative relationship between individual and social understandings, and would be characterized by the development and evolution of traditional (local) ways of doing things. I would like provisionally to call such a construction a secondary construction. It is secondary because of the way in which it takes basic questions to be settled, beyond reflective examination and revision. Whilst basic understandings are not felt either by the individual or socially to be under threat they are regarded as immutable, perhaps as an indelible national character or an indispensable individual identity. Certain basic materials in a secondary construction go unexamined and therefore unrevised. Secondary constructivism regards certain individual or social understandings as foundations, fundamental starting points, that cannot be brought before the reflective gaze. As such, these firm foundations outline the limits of reason and justification. When called to account for a principle or action, we can justify ourselves by showing how that principle or action is recommended/supported by our shared understandings. Neither reasons nor justification will have purchase where these foundational assumptions are not shared. This identification of a secondary construction ties together the concerns of Singer, Brown, Seung and the communitarians in an understanding of the ordinary ways we interact with each other and our community.

On the other hand, what I will term provisionally primary constructivism draws attention to the open-ended critically reflective process that, we have claimed, need regard no starting point as an unrevisable or immutable foundation.

Anything that primary constructivism provides reason to support has been subjected to a critical and comprehensive examination. We are likely to feel the need for such a constructivism, feel pushed to the primary level when, as an individual or as a culture, we become aware of the contingent nature of our commitments, or when we become aware of alternative methods of social organization, cultural practices or individual self-understandings. Encountering novel ideas and institutions unsettles us (or inspires us) and pushes us to turn the critical gaze inwards upon our own assumptions in the search for a better-justified and more objective understanding. Indeed, as we become aware of alternatives to our current understandings, these alternatives demand our attention. For our understandings to be critically justified, we must do more than bury our heads in the sand. We must either satisfy ourselves that we have good reasons not to be troubled by these alternatives or accept that we have good reasons to modify our understandings. If we do neither, then we have stepped outside the project of justification and into the realm of faith. It is the possibility of this level of primary constructivism that the communitarians miss, by and large. In doing so, then, they understandably regard secondary constructivism as the best characterization of our reasoning and methods of justification. This does not mean, however, that they are justified in so doing.

Rather than attempt a detailed analysis of the nature of constructivism and the relationship between its primary and secondary variants – tasks to be undertaken elsewhere – here, the idea of a constructivism has arisen naturally in an examination of the ways in which individual understandings of the self and morality may be related to social understandings. Whilst we have only glanced at the possible constructivist attitude towards those understandings, we have found our way to a basic distinction between primary and secondary constructivism. Secondary constructivism is the result of the reciprocal interaction of communal social understandings and individual reflective practices bounded, as they ordinarily are, by the boundaries of the community. This secondary constructivism *is* the set of social, political and moral practices that constitute the cultural community, and we can ordinarily refer to it if we need to justify our actions or principles. However, we cannot always refer to only this secondary level. There will be times when individually, or as a community, we find ourselves faced by problems, questions (posed possibly by developments within our own culture, possibly by encounters with the ideas and practices of other communities), that require us to think beyond the boundaries of our current practice. Faced by the problem of having to justify ourselves either when we are unsure of our cultural inheritance, or to people who don't carry our cultural baggage, we are pushed towards primary constructivism.

It has been important here to outline these two different forms of constructivist justification and different levels of reflective assessment. This is so because it reminds us that we cannot simply accept that the boundaries of community are necessarily the boundaries of justification. We should not accept that reasons are tied to a particular context that is authoritative for us. We may not here have demonstrated that cross-cultural, perhaps universal, moral justification can be achieved. What we have done is to remind ourselves that such justification appears to be possible and so prevent ourselves from accepting a too premature foreclosure on the potential for cross-cultural rational discussion and argument. Indeed, since our political existence has a habit of reminding us that not everyone thinks as we do, cross-cultural reflection will be a necessary part of successful political justification. The communitarians and their multiculturalist allies have not won the day and so they need not be allowed to declare victory.

What must be established, what is at stake fundamentally, is whether a recognition of the basic pluralism that characterizes the world is the end point of an argument or the starting point of one. For the communitarians, the identification of communal pluralism is the end of an argument. From this they draw out the implications that we have been considering in this chapter. For a primary constructivism, such pluralism is the starting point for a possible discussion, argument or justification. The notion of a primary constructivism holds out the possibility of going beyond the recognition of pluralism as such to the achievement of a *principled pluralism,* where we justify at the primary level substantive minimal universal principles.

Notes

1   M. Walzer, *Thick and Thin: Moral Arguments at Home and Abroad*, Notre Dame, Ind.: Notre Dame University Press, 1994, p. 99, emphasis added.
2   In examining this claim, I will set aside several basic questions that are often asked of communitarians and multiculturalists. These include 'What is a community?', 'How do we identify a community's boundaries?' and 'Are communities internally homogeneous?' These are obviously central questions, the answers to which may reinforce the conclusions of this chapter, but I set them aside in order to focus on the issue of identity and the self.
3   M. J. Sandel, *Liberalism and the Limits of Justice*, Cambridge: Cambridge University Press, 1982, p. 59, emphasis added.
4   Ibid., p. 179, emphasis added.
5   Ibid., pp.150 and 153.
6   A. MacIntyre, *After Virtue: A Study in Moral Theory*, 2nd edn, London: Duckworth, 1985 (1st edn, 1981), p. 220, emphasis added.
7   Ibid., pp. 216 and 172.
8   B. Parekh, *Rethinking Multiculturalism: Cultural Diversity and Political Theory*, London: Macmillan, 2000, p. 122.
9   Ibid., p. 122, first emphasis added.
10 Ibid., p. 156, emphasis added.
11 A. Margalit and J. Raz, 'National Self-Determination', in W. Kymlicka, ed., *The Rights of Minority Cultures*, Oxford: Oxford University Press, 1995, p. 87.
12 Ibid., p. 85.
13 C. Taylor, 'The Politics of Recognition', in A. Gutmann, ed., *Multiculturalism: Examining the Politics of Recognition*, 2nd edn, Princeton: Princeton University Press, 1994, pp. 33–4.
14 Ibid., p. 32.
15 A. MacIntyre, 'Intelligibility, Goods, and Rules', *Journal of Philosophy*, 79, 1982, pp. 663–5; p. 664.
16 A. MacIntyre, 'Is Patriotism a Virtue?', reprinted in M. Rosen and J. Wolff, eds, *Political Thought*, Oxford: Oxford University Press, 1999, pp. 269–84; p.274.
17 MacIntyre, *After Virtue*, pp. 209–10.

18 R. Rorty, 'Solidarity or Objectivity?', in his *Objectivity, Relativism, and Truth: Philosophical Papers, Vol. 1*, Cambridge: Cambridge University Press, 1991, pp. 21–34; p. 22.

19 R. Rorty, 'Human Rights, Rationality and Sentimentality', in S. Shute and S. Hurley, eds, *On Human Rights*, New York: Basic Books, 1993, pp. 112–34; p. 117.

20 S. Caney, 'Liberalism and Communitarianism: A Misconceived Debate', *Political Studies*, 40, 1992, pp. 273–89.

21 See, for example, ibid., p. 287, where he claims that '[i]t is one of our deepest intuitions that morality is not *simply* a mirror of our shared values'.

22 Ibid., p. 276.

23 Parekh, *Rethinking Multiculturalism*, pp. 122 and 123.

24 Sandel, *Liberalism and the Limits of Justice*, p. 150.

25 MacIntyre, *After Virtue*, p. 213.

26 MacIntyre, 'Is Patriotism a Virtue?', p. 282.

27 Parekh, *Rethinking Multiculturalism*, p. 156, emphasis added.

28 MacIntyre, *After Virtue*, p. 221.

29 MacIntyre, 'Is Patriotism a Virtue?', p. 278.

30 MacIntyre, *After Virtue*, p. 221, emphasis added.

31 Sandel, *Liberalism and the Limits of Justice*, pp. 180, 181 and 179.

32 If they don't hold at least this, then what is at dispute here?

33 See J. Rawls, *A Theory of Justice*, Oxford: Oxford University Press, 1972, section 9.

34 A. Brown, *Modern Political Philosophy: Theories of the Just Society*, Harmondsworth: Penguin, 1986, pp. 75–6.

35 P. Singer, 'Sidgwick and Reflective Equilibrium', *The Monist*, 58, 1974, pp. 490–517; p. 493.

36 D. Little, 'Reflective Equilibrium and Justification', *The Southern Journal of Philosophy*, 22, 1984, pp. 373–87; p. 373.

37 Ibid., p.383.

38 See Caney, 'Liberalism and Communitarianism'.

39 Singer, 'Sidgwick and Reflective Equilibrium', p. 494.

40 Rawls, *A Theory of Justice*, p. 21.

41 See ibid., pp. 579 and 19; R. Milo, 'Contractarian Constructivism', *Journal of Philosophy*, 92, 1995, pp. 181–204; p. 203; and T. M. Scanlon, 'Moral Theory: Understanding and Disagreement', *Philosophy and Phenomenological Research*, 55, 1995, pp. 343–56; p. 346.

42 Rawls, *A Theory of Justice*, p. 580.

43 N. Daniels, 'Wide Reflective Equilibrium and Theory Acceptance in Ethics', *Journal of Philosophy*, 76, 1979, 256–82; p. 267.

44 T.M. Scanlon, 'The Aims and Authority of Moral Theory', *Oxford Journal of Legal Studies*, 12, 1992, pp. 1–23; p. 14.

45 O. O'Neill, *Constructions of Reason: Explorations of Kant's Practical Philosophy*, Cambridge: Cambridge University Press, 1989, p. 21.

46 K. Nielsen, 'Grounding Rights and a Method of Reflective Equilibrium', *Inquiry*, 25, 1982, pp. 277–306; p. 292.

47 By referring to such an attitude as 'constructivist', I mean to draw on the notion found in, for example, Rawls's *A Theory of Justice* and *Political Liberalism* (New York: Columbia University Press, 1993); O. O'Neill's *Towards Justice and Virtue: A Constructive Account of Practical Reasoning* (Cambridge: Cambridge University Press, 1996); T. M. Scanlon's 'Contractualism and Utilitarianism' (in A. Sen and B. Williams, eds, *Utilitarianism and Beyond*, Cambridge: Cambridge University Press, 1982); and Milo's 'Contractarian Constructivism'.

48 K. Nielsen, 'Relativism and Wide Reflective Equilibrium', *The Monist*, 76, 1993, pp. 316–32; p. 320.

49 Parekh, *Rethinking Multiculturalism*, pp. 158 and 167.

50 See F. D'Agostino's 'Relativism and Reflective Equilibrium' *(The Monist*, 71, 1988, pp. 420–36) for an argument as to how such understanding might result from mutual critical reflection.

11 Brian Barry's egalitarian critique of multiculturalism

A liberal nationalist defence

Margaret Moore

This chapter argues, from a perspective sympathetic to minority nationalism, that Brian Barry's critique of multiculturalism in his book *Culture and Equality* misunderstands the issues involved in minority nationalism. Although the book makes many good points against various kinds of group-specific rights and policies based on culture, I argue that it inappropriately places self-government claims under the general rubric of 'cultural argument'. The resulting critique that is developed either does not apply to minority nationalism at all, or applies in a very limited way but still fails to address the legitimate grievances and concerns of minority nationalists.

The first part of this chapter will describe briefly the thrust of Barry's argument, his conception of culture, and the treatment of both majority and minority nationalism. The second part is divided into three sections. It argues (1) that Barry incorrectly characterizes minority nationalism as a cultural phenomenon and that this impacts (2) on his argument from neutrality and (3) on his differential treatment of minority and majority nationalism. A sub-theme of all these sections is that the mis-categorization of minority nationalism leaves Barry bereft of institutional or constitutional proposals to deal with nationalist aspirations or national conflict.

Overview of Barry's argument

The stated aim of *Culture and Equality* is to offer a critique, from a theoretically sophisticated egalitarian liberal perspective, of recent works known under the rubric 'the politics of difference' or 'multiculturalism', which politicize group identities based on culture. Barry's attack is wide-ranging, spanning a number of authors and works which disagree with each other in profound ways,[1] but which, Barry says, all share the same basic assumption that reference to a common identity based on a common culture can legitimately be used as part of an argument to criticize liberal equal treatment and equal opportunity norms. There are a number of problems with this type of argument, Barry argues.

(1) One strand of argument in the book, which operates at the level of Grand Theory, or at the meta-theoretical level, is the claim that multicultural policies and rights presuppose some kind of cultural relativism. Advocates of multicul-

turalism, Barry charges, assume that there is no common standard by which cultures and the practices embedded in them can be evaluated and that, in the absence of a common standard, different cultures should be presumed to be of equal value.[2] In this discussion, Barry is certainly effective in demonstrating the problems attached to James Tully's, Charles Taylor's and John Gray's move from the idea (a) that all cultures have equal value (itself disputed by Barry) to the stronger claim (b) that cultures must be publicly affirmed to be of equal value.[3] The stronger demand for public affirmation, implicit in multicultural politics, is probably both psychologically and logically unattainable (especially when many cultures disagree in their substantive claims). It is also probably undesirable, at least for cultures which endorse some pretty nasty ideas.

In laying out this argument, and throughout the book, Barry has a very expansive view of 'culture': sometimes he means ethnic identity, sometimes he means religious identity, sometimes he means political or national forms of identity.[4] Relatedly, he lumps together different kinds of laws and claims as similar in that they involve some kind of cultural argument: he discusses demands for religious exemptions, language protection, cultural autonomy rights and aspirations for jurisdictional authority over territory by minority national groups as all examples of 'cultural rights'. These are all different kinds of claims and, on the face of it anyway, different kinds of identities, and it is not clear, as I will go on to argue below, that the argument that he develops is appropriate to all of them.

(2) A second strand of argument in *Culture and Equality*, which proceeds more on the level of common-sense theorizing about the bases of state decisions, is the claim that multiculturalists rely on a gross caricature of what is involved in liberal neutrality. Many theorists in the multicultural camp reiterate the mantra that 'liberalism cannot be neutral', and Barry says that this misunderstands what is involved in liberal neutrality. Liberal neutrality cannot possibly mean that there are no existing (or possible) world views with which it is incompatible. Liberalism is incompatible with most versions of organized Christianity as they have existed during most of their history, and many forms, too, of Islam. Still, liberalism can be described as neutral, not in the impossible sense of being neutral in its effects, but in the sense that it defines a notion of equal treatment. What matters from an egalitarian liberal standpoint are equal opportunities in the sense that people make choices from identical choice sets.

In deploying this argument, Barry makes use of an elaborate analogy between the privatization of culture and the privatization of religion. Liberalism arose, he emphasizes, not as an assimilationist method of enforcing uniformity, but in order to *protect* religious minorities. Liberalism represented a strategy to cope with religious pluralism in the state after the clear failure of the doctrine of *cuius regio, eius religio*, and ensuing religious strife. It did so by resisting demands for special treatment by some religious groups, and by treating religion as a purely *private* matter, beyond the appropriate jurisdiction of political authorities. In an analogous way, culture should be treated as a private matter: the state should resist all calls for special exemptions or rights based on cultural grounds. This privatization strategy will allow the greatest scope for pluralism and tolerance.

Barry concedes that this strategy cannot guarantee that all policy decisions by the state are completely neutral in their effects, by which he means the distribution of benefits and burdens. Some decisions will impose greater burdens on some groups than on others, but if the decision is a good one – if there is a good justificatory rationale for the decision – then this unequal burden will have to be accepted as an inevitable corollary of the exercise of political authority. It is not easy to be a Rastafarian in a country where marijuana smoking (or possession) is illegal. Perhaps marijuana should be legalized. But *if* the law is justified (a big 'if' in this case), then the burdens it imposes are justified – and these burdens are felt not only by Rastafarians but also by artists and musicians who rely on the weed for inspiration, by stressed-out executives whose recreational preferences are being curtailed, and by many others.

(3) A third argument which runs throughout *Culture and Equality* is that, in many cases, multiculturalism is destructive of liberal egalitarian policies and polities. The policies endorsed under the banner of multiculturalism often harm those they were designed to benefit. Explicitly egalitarian policies, which are designed to benefit the economically marginalized and least well-off among us, would do much more for members of these targeted minorities. This argument takes a number of different forms. One part of it is suggested by the previous argument, namely that the only kind of neutrality that can be expected is neutrality in the distribution of political rights and freedom. It is only as citizens that we can stand in an equal relation to each other, and multiculturalism places this principle in jeopardy on the grounds of 'correcting' the distribution of benefits and burdens, and so represents a misguided attempt to get rid of the only achievable kind of equality.

In other places, Barry suggests that the emphasis on culture is problematic, in the more mundane sense that it diverts attention away from crucial issues of income differentials and distributive injustice. And, in relation to specific policy programmes – such as Spanish language-retention classes for Hispanic students in the United States – he suggests that the actual policies endorsed under the banner of multiculturalism often do not work in the best interests of those they are intended to serve. In the case of Spanish language education for Hispanic students, Barry argues that students' interests would be served better by ensuring that they are able to join the English-speaking mainstream; the practice, however, is that bureaucratic elites endeavour to retain them in Spanish language schools in order to fulfil the elite-driven goal of transforming America into a bilingual (English–Spanish) country.[5]

Another line of argument supporting uniform citizenship rights is the contention that civic forms of integration are functional for the (liberal democratic) state and that they are undermined by demands for exemptions or special treatment on the part of minority groups in the state. This argument begins by noting that liberal democracy is a relatively rare, and fragile, form of government in the world, and that there are certain conditions that must obtain for it to flourish. He identifies three such conditions. First, general acceptance of a conception of political and moral equality of persons is essential to a flourishing liberal democracy. Barry writes: 'It must be accepted on all hands that the interests of everyone must count equally, and that there are no groups whose members' views are to be automatically discounted.'[6] Second, it is important (because instrumental to the fostering of a common identity, which Barry regards as essential) that there should be a narrow spread of income in society, or, to be more precise,

> a spread of income narrow enough to prevent people from believing – and with some reason – that they can escape from the common lot by buying their way out of the system of education, health care, policing and other public services that their less fortunate fellow citizens are forced to depend upon.[7]

Finally, and most significantly for the purposes of this chapter, Barry argues that the citizens of a just liberal democracy must share ties or bonds of solidarity towards one another and sentiments of attachment or patriotism towards the polity that is their common political project. He writes:

> we cannot expect the outcomes of democratic politics to be just in a society that contains large numbers of people who feel no sense of empathy with their fellow citizens and who do not have any identification with their lot. ... [It is] important [that there be] a willingness on the part of citizens to make sacrifices for the common good – which, of course, presupposes that they are capable of recognizing a common good. Moreover, citizens do not just as a matter of fact have to be willing to make sacrifices; it is also necessary that citizens should have firm expectations of one another to the effect that they will be prepared to give up money, leisure and perhaps even life itself if the occasion arises. What shall we call this cluster of attitudes towards fellow citizens? I propose to define it as a sense of common nationality, distinguishing the appropriate concept of nationality from both the formal one embodied in a passport and also the ethnic interpretation of nationality. In contrast with either of these, I shall describe the relevant sense of nationality as 'civic nationality'.[8]

This is an argument for the instrumental value of shared civic nationality, on all fours with the liberal nationalist arguments advanced by Jean Jacques Rousseau, John Stuart Mill and David Miller, to the effect that we need a sense of belonging to a polity and a sense of solidarity with other members for the good functioning of a just liberal democratic state.[9] In this part of his book, then, Barry is relying on a well-established line of argument, ostensibly showing the need for a common civic political identity, which encourages trust and facilitates co-operation and sacrifice. It is this identity, and the uniform citizenship rights that embody this political status, that is jeopardized by the divisive calls for special political rights or separate political institutions for cultural groups. Barry attempts to distinguish his conception from the more standard liberal nationalist claim about the instrumental value of national identity by stressing the thinness of the identity – by which he means that it is compatible with various ethnic/regional/sexual identities.[10] This capacity for additive identities is related to the human capacity to learn and use more than one language, acquire new cultural habits, and transform many aspects of the self, which means that identity formation is not a constant sum-game where the acquisition of a new identity necessarily occurs at the expense of the original one. Rather, a thin political identity can be compatible with a number of religious and ethnic identities. Barry does concede, however, that certain cultural traits must be shared in a given political association, and immigrants, for example, would have to adopt these in order to participate fully in the new polity. However, this is contrasted with the demands of minority nationalists, which typically involve aspirations for political rights in order to impose or extend a certain culture in the area in which the nationalist gains jurisdictional authority.

Why minority nationalism doesn't fit Barry's analysis

There are three problematic elements in Barry's analysis which bear on its applicability (or lack thereof) to minority nationalism: (1) the description of minority nationalism as primarily about the protection of culture; (2) the description of liberal neutrality as it relates to the concerns of minority nationalism and his analogy with religion, so prominent in this argument; and (3) related to the above two, the treatment of minority nationalism *vis-à-vis* majority nationalism in Barry's civic integrationist or liberal nationalist argument.

Why minority national groups are not cultural groups

Barry's classification of minority nationalists (the Scots, Basques, Quebecois, and so on) as an example of a cultural group, and minority nationalist aspirations to political self-government as an example of demanding a cultural right, presupposes a close identification of nation with cultural community. It assumes a 'snooker ball' view of nationality, according to which nationality is a knock-on effect from culture and language.[11] In this section, I will argue that this conception misunderstands the relationship between nationality and 'objective' characteristics such as culture and language. National identities are primarily political identities, and national groups are fundamentally about self-government. The aspirations of nationalists are importantly bound up with the structure and boundaries of the state. In contrast to Barry's assumption, there may be only a very tenuous (by which I mean historical and contingent) relationship between nationality and thick cultural characteristics. For example, it is often remarked by anthropologists, sociologists and political scientists who study national conflicts that national (and ethnic) identities require some 'cultural marker', some mechanism for mutual recognition of members (and so implicitly a method for recognizing outsiders), but that these do not necessarily correlate with sharp linguistic or cultural differences.[12] Of course, in some cases, national identities do correspond to cultural differences but, even in this case, it is not clear that the identities are *based* on the different cultures. Rather, the political or institutional structures that correspond to national identities, or the various mechanisms of boundary-maintenance that groups employ, can be used to *reinforce* cultural homogeneity and so increase the extent to which the members of the group are different from outsiders. Whatever the precise relationship, the important point is that linguistic and cultural differences are not central to national identities, because national identities can be mobilized along other lines.

This insight is confirmed when we think about some of the most violent conflicts between competing national (or ethnic) groups. If we compare Northern Ireland, Burundi/Rwanda and the former Yugoslavia with Canada, Switzerland, Belgium, what is striking is that, in the first group, (a) the level of violence involved in the conflicts tends to be greater and (b) the members of the antagonistic communities speak the same language and have broadly similar cultural values; whereas, in the latter group, (a) relations between the communities are generally peaceful and (b) the members of the communities speak different languages and exhibit deeper cultural differences. In other words, cultural differences do not correspond to the violence or intensity of the conflict.

This cultural similarity is often recognized by members of the antagonistic groups themselves. For example, in Northern Ireland, where there are two distinct and mutually antagonistic national communities on the same territory, the conflict between the two groups is not about some objective cultural difference. Despite a common misconception, it is not religious in nature. The groups are not arguing over the details of doctrinal interpretation. Religious leaders – priests, nuns, ministers – are not targets for violence, as they were in the Reformation period, when conflict was genuinely religious.[13]

Nor is the argument about sharp *cultural* differences. In fact, a 1968 survey of cultural similarity in Northern Ireland revealed that 67 per cent of Protestants thought Northern Irish men and women of the opposite religion were about the 'same as themselves', while only 29 per cent thought the same about the English. Similarly, 81 per cent of Catholics regarded Ulster Protestants as about the 'same as themselves' but only 44 per cent thought this about Southern Catholics.[14] Similar results have been found by Rosemary Harris, an anthropologist studying a rural community in Northern Ireland, who argued that, despite social segregation, there was a 'considerable area within which Catholics and Protestants shared a common culture'.[15]

Analysts of the conflicts in the former Yugoslavia, especially those who adhere to the elite-manipulation school of conflict analysis, almost universally emphasize the cultural similarities between the different groups.[16] Analysts begin the puzzle of explaining what happened in the former Yugoslavia by noting that, prior to the conflict, Serbs, Croats and Muslims shared a common life, language, physical appearance, a lot of history. The Muslims were among the most secularized Muslims anywhere in the world. One of the primary divisions was between urban and rural communities, which meant, in effect, that an urban Serb would have more in common with her or his urban Croat neighbour than with rural

Serbs. In short, the groups themselves were culturally very similar; and cultural variation was as great *across* groups as within them.

Of course, the initial formation or construction of the political identity can often be explained in terms of historical, cultural, linguistic or institutional differences between groups. In an important study, *Britons: Forging the Nation 1707–1837*, Linda Colley asks why the Welsh, the English and the Scots could feel that being English, Scottish and Welsh was consistent with *also* being British, and the Irish could not. Her answer is that the Irish were effectively excluded from developing a British national identity because Protestantism was absolutely central to Britishness, particularly in the eighteenth and nineteenth centuries. On this analysis, the Irish national identity was a relational one, defined, at least in part, in opposition to a British identity.[17]

The explanation for why (English-speaking) Canadians and Americans have different political identities, and see themselves as forming different political communities, is not in terms of great cultural differences between the two, but in terms of their different historical development and institutional differentiation. This does not mean that the national identity is not authentic or genuine – Canadians do see themselves as forming a separate political community, and do not want to become Americans (at least not collectively, as a group) – even though the cultural differences between the two are quite minor. It would be a mistake to subsume this different political aspiration under the rubric of 'culture', for that would render the term 'culture' vacuously broad, incorporating not only the habits, traditions and customs normally associated with 'thick culture' but, in addition, the institutional identification and aspirations felt by the different peoples.

The case of Scotland and England is similar in the sense that, while there are some cultural differences between the English and the Scots, there is also cultural variation within Scotland (between Highlanders and Lowlanders, say) and within England (both in class and regional terms). Nevertheless, the historical rights and distinct institutional development of Scotland, preserved in the 1707 Act(s) of Union, help to explain why (many) Scots see themselves as forming a distinct political community, and aspire to political self-government, within either a British or a European context.[18]

Minority nationalism, then, is not necessarily characterized by an aspiration to protect or promote a particular culture, and so it is problematic to classify it as a cultural right, or to treat minority national groups simply as distinct cultural groups. Of course, the jurisdictional authority that minority nationalists seek means that they will have the institutional capacity to make decisions on cultural matters (as well as other matters). It is, however, a majoritarian prejudice to assume that minority nationalists will use this jurisdictional authority to oppress minorities and impose cultural uniformity on them (whereas majority nationalists are so tolerant and respectful of diversity). Many minority nationalists in Quebec and Western Europe (Catalonia, Flanders, Scotland) are liberal democrats: they support traditional liberal rights, democratic governance and the rule of law, as well as access to a global economy.[19] There is a cultural element in the exercise of the jurisdictional authority, just as there is in any exercise of jurisdictional authority, but this is something which Barry approves of as functional to the creation of a unified body politic.

In summary, then, Barry's description of minority nationalism as primarily about the protection of culture seems to miss the mark. Nationalism is primarily characterized by the aspiration to political self-government (either through institutional structures within the state in which they live – thereby transforming it into a genuine multi-national state – or through secession), and the desire to be collectively self-governing is not necessarily connected to the issue of the protection of a particular culture.

Why Barry's neutrality argument doesn't work

An important line of argument in Barry's book is connected to his clarification of what's involved in liberal neutrality. One aspect of this argument is to point out that critics of liberalism wrongly characterize neutrality in unrealistic and even silly terms, which make it easy to shoot down. A more positive argument concerns Barry's own description of the way in which liberalism can be described as neutral, and here he means that it is neutral in the sense that it offers identical sets of choices to all. Uniform sets of political rights and principles are conducive to pluralism; indeed, they were developed precisely in the context of conflict over religious division. In an elaborate analogy between divisive religious and cultural matters, Barry argues that the solution to the two kinds of conflict is the same: liberalism involves neutral sets of public choices, and the privatization of both religious and cultural matters. In this section, I will argue that there is a problem with this general, positive line of argument, as it applies to a whole range of groups in the state, and then a particular problem connected to its applicability to minority nationalism.

The general problem concerns the description of choice sets, and the related analogy with religion. It is not clear that the state can privatize culture in the same way that it can privatize religion. As Kymlicka has argued effectively, and as Barry concedes, although obliquely, in his discussion of liberal integration, the state cannot completely ignore or avoid cultural matters. As Kymlicka has written, in direct response to what he calls a policy of 'benign neglect' of ethnic and national differences (but which is the same as Barry's policy of neutrality and privatization):

> The idea of responding to cultural differences with 'benign neglect' makes no sense. Government decisions on languages, internal boundaries, public holidays and state symbols unavoidably involve recognizing, accommodating, and supporting the needs and identities of particular ethnic and national groups. The state unavoidably promotes certain cultural identities, and thereby disadvantages others.[20]

Once this point is recognized, it is clear that culture is inevitably politicized, because, in a heterogeneous modern society, the state has to make some decisions on the languages spoken in the courts, the bureaucracy, the legislature, the schools, the symbols with which the state will be associated, the internal borders for devolved decision making in the state, or the public holidays recognized within the state. These decisions inevitability serve to privilege certain linguistic or cultural or religious groups in the state, and not others, and this will mean that there is always the possibility of disagreement and political wrangling over the actual content of that decision. It is hard to see how there could be agreement, in advance, on treating these neutrally, since that is exactly what is at issue.

If by 'neutral' treatment, Barry means that the majority decision should prevail, at least in terms of public holidays and language issues, on administrative convenience and/or instrumental grounds, then, at the very least, it should be recognized that this may be very costly for minorities. Moreover, in practice, this general policy is not easy to implement, especially if the minorities are territorially concentrated in a particular region, for then the question might revolve around the level of jurisdiction in which the decision is made – for a minority in the state as a whole may well constitute a majority in a particular region, and the administrative efficiency argument (combined with some views about the value of decentralization of decision making) may well favour the minority position. At the very least, it is hard to see how this can be taken completely out of the political realm.

There are two issues, then, which seem to make Barry's proposed solution to cultural conflict very problematic. The first is connected to the meaning of neutrality, and the almost inevitable politicization of cultural issues. The second issue is that privatization, even if it were possible, is obviously more costly for minorities than Barry is willing to admit. Majorities, because they are majorities, are naturally privileged in the democratic arena, where majoritarian decision-making rules generally prevail, and minorities are out-numbered. Of course, in some democratic societies and on some issues, this is not a serious cause for concern, because who is in the minority and who is in the majority on each particular issue will change, and everyone can expect to win some decisions and lose some. But, in some divided societies, and especially on issues that have a cultural component, the majorities and minorities may be known in advance. We might expect, for example, that Romanian speakers in Romania would resist efforts to publicly fund Hungarian language schools and universities; whereas we might expect the Hungarian minority to mobilize in favour of this. In this context, privatization of cultural matters (combined with ordinary democratic decision making) will mean that the minority will be consistently out-numbered and out-voted.

One way to look at this problem is to consider it a problem connected to the choice sets available to people. Barry describes neutrality as involving identical sets of choices (principles and rights) for everyone. On the face of it, this seems fair. However, if the choice set is only attractive for one group of people in the state, or reflects only one particular identity in the state, then, surely, as a matter of fairness, there should be some opportunity to reconsider the choice sets themselves. Is it really fair that the only choices on the menu are pork chops, bacon and glazed ham, and the Jews and Muslims in the state, for whom eating pork is forbidden, are not allowed to introduce some vegetarian or beef or chicken or lamb alternative? Barry asks rhetorically: who ever said that it should be easy to keep your faith? Perhaps it is not supposed to be easy, but the question at issue should be that, if his policy involves real hardship on minorities because of the actual choice sets that are available, then, surely, this bears on whether they can plausibly be described as 'neutral'.[21]

This problem is particularly acute for *national* minorities in the state. These are minorities who seek some political or institutional recognition of their identity, and their identity is closely bound up with the desire to be collectively self-governing. In the case of the multicultural identity groups just discussed – religious, ethnic, sexual orientation groups – the state cannot be neutral, and cannot be entirely fair (because there has to be some common public space and have to be some standardized cultural practices), but the state can attempt to be as inclusive of these various identity groups as possible (and this is not the same as ignoring ethnic or cultural or religious issues). The structural injustices that ethnic, religious, sexual orientation and other kinds of minority groups face can be partially remedied by ensuring that the state adopts policies of fairness, tolerance and accommodation, and thereby tries to ensure that these various ethnic or sexual orientation identities are compatible with the over-arching political identity in the state. The main limit to this policy of accommodation is the need to maintain a common public life, which is itself also morally justified.National groups, by contrast, are situated in a different context. First, they have the capacity to act as the carrier of the values of modernity, to be democratically self-governing, to dispense justice and create a common, public life in which people can participate. Second, and related to the first point, they are generally sufficiently territorially concentrated that the exercise of self-government is possible, and they typically aspire to this as a remedy to the minority disadvantage that they experience. Indeed, national communities are defined by the presence of aspirations to be politically self-governing. In cases where political self-government is at least conceivable, and denial of this aspiration is not connected to natural causes – it is not demographic or territorial – questions of fair treatment arise. In such cases, whether the minority national identity is recognized or denied, their aspirations are fulfilled or unfulfilled, is inextricably bound up with the institutional structure of the state and majority willingness or unwillingness to countenance changes to the state structure. It is the state, controlled by the majority national community, which either functions to facilitate this political self-government through devolved power, or some other institutional expression of this aspiration, or serves to deny it. In these cases, the only way to be fair to minority national identities – as distinct from gay identities or ethnic identities or other kinds of identities – is through creating the institutional or political space in which members of the nation can be collectively self-governing. If the state attempts to deal with this issue as Barry suggests – by ignoring it, and wrongly treating the identity as a purely private matter (when it is, as I have been arguing, essentially political) – this in effect privileges the majority national community which seeks to deny the minority the same kinds of mechanisms for collective self-government that it enjoys, and this is a political decision.

The unfair treatment of minority nations vis-à-vis *majority nations*

We have seen that Barry classifies minority national groups in the state under the rubric of 'cultural group' and treats them as essentially the same as other cultural identity groups, by which he means various religious and ethnic groups. This conception does not allow him to develop a comparative framework for analysing the similarities between majority and minority national groups. Rather, they are seen as fundamentally different: majority national groups are viewed as functional to the state in the sense that they are instrumental to the creation of a common public life, and thereby facilitate the dispensing of liberal justice and democratic conversation, whereas minority national groups, along with other cultural groups, who are demanding particular recognition of their own identity, are destructive of this.

It is implicit in the argument developed thus far in this chapter that this is (a) an inaccurate reflection of minority national groups' aspirations and identity, and (b) unfair because it serves to privilege the status quo. Once it is acknowledged that national groups (majority and minority) are primarily characterized by their desire to be collectively self-governing – that they are essentially political identities – then it becomes clear that the central comparison is not between minority nations and religious or ethnic groups in the state but between minority and majority national groups. The central question raised by the analysis developed here is: why should majority national groups in the state receive institutional recognition of their desire to be self-governing, and not the minority nations in their midst? Why should Canada be given full institutional recognition of its national identity, and not Quebec? And why should Quebec be allowed, under the terms of the Canadian constitution and especially the 1998 reference case, to be collectively self-governing and not the First Nations people, such as the Cree, who are also minority national communities? This is an argument not for secession, but for the idea that multinational arrangements – in which different political communities are accommodated – are more fair than Barry's proposed 'solution' of ignoring the desire to be collectively self-governing. In this section, I will argue that Barry's misconstrual of minority national identities infects his book at various places, and means that some of its central arguments simply don't apply to minority nations. If Barry had recognized that the relevant comparative framework was one of national groups, rather than seeing minority nationalists as relevantly similar to leaders of other cultural groups, he would not have fallen into these sorts of errors.

As we saw in the first part of this chapter, it is central to Barry's argument in *Culture and Equality* that any kind of group-targeted or group-specific policy will undermine egalitarian policies enacted by the state. Barry identifies two different ways in which this could happen. First, he makes the general point that group-specific rights and policies are generally divisive and so can undermine the trust and solidarity that are functional for a redistributive, liberal democratic state. Second, the political recognition that minority national groups seek typically involves asymmetry, which means that citizens are treated unequally, and so these arrangements represent a violation of political equality. I will examine each of these claims in turn.

It is not clear that the first argument – about the conditions that support trust and indirectly a redistributive practice – even if true,[22] actually points to the civic integrationist/equal citizenship policies that Barry supports. This conclusion only follows if we also assume that the national divisions are *created* by the national elites who demand special political rights for their group. It may be, however, that the direction of causation is the opposite, namely that, as a result of a history of domination of one group over another, or conquest or oppression, a group has become nationally mobilized in the sense that its members share the view that they constitute a nation in their own right, and seek to be collectively self-governing, and they tend to elect or be responsive to leaders who share this view. In that case, the demand for political rights is an expression of, or evidence of, the mobilization that has occurred over time. If that is true, the relevant question is not, as Barry thought, whether the political rights will create divisions, for the society is already divided along national lines. The question is: what is the best institutional solution to deal with the fact that there is more than one political community in the state? When that question is posed, it becomes clear that Barry's proposed civic integrationist solution is extremely problematic. It is likely to be viewed by the minority as assimilationist in intent, and to be more divisive than giving the group some political autonomy within the state, which would at least have the merits of (a) being desired by the groups themselves,[23] and (b) helping to consolidate stability within the political unit by ensuring that each group has a stake (but not an all-or-nothing stake) in the institutions of state. Further, granting political autonomy or some jurisdictional authority in the state through a federal or quasi-federal arrangement is consistent with Barry's analysis of identity formation, in which he notes that identities are not constant-sum games, but additive. The idea is that it is possible to be both Catalan and Spanish, Quebecois and Canadian, Scottish and British, Corsican and French.

The second argument – concerning asymmetry – is essentially a standard argument against any form of asymmetrical federalism or territorial autonomy arrangement that is targeted at a specific group which seeks additional political autonomy. The problem with giving a group specific or targeted group rights, such as devolved political authority to manage its own affairs, is that this will create political inequality in the state. Of course, most states have some political inequality: individuals are not counted equally in any state, and particularly federal ones, even ones that have symmetrical areas of jurisdictional authority. The voters in Vermont and Maine 'count' for more than voters in California (they have the same number of senators, and same veto rights over constitutional amendments, but only a fraction of California's population). But in asymmetrical arrangements, the problem is more severe and qualitatively different. As Barry explains, in his description of the West Lothian question (named after the Scottish MP for West Lothia – not East Lothia, as Barry says), granting political autonomy to Scotland, but not to England, would mean that Scottish MPs would have a voice in matters concerning England, but English voters would not have a say in matters devolved to Scotland.[24] This raises questions not only of democratic accountability but also of political equality: it is said to be simply unfair that Scotland has powers that England lacks, and that Scottish voters have a say in matters concerning England, whereas the reverse is not true of English voters.

On the face of it that seems like a decisive objection to asymmetrical territorial autonomy designed to accommodate national minorities in the state. This objection has been raised in Canada with respect to asymmetrical federalism proposals for Quebec, and in Spain with respect to demands for increased political autonomy on the part of Catalonia, the Basque country and Galicia. However, I think that this argument not only is over-stated, but also operates with an inadequate conception of political equality. To see this, it is necessary to examine both the usual dynamic of majoritarian decision making in unitary states and the historical rights that typically attach to minority national groups. In the example of Scotland and England, it is true that, in areas of political authority devolved to the Scottish parliament, there is some asymmetry in powers between the two, which is justified by the fact that Scots seek increased autonomy, whereas the English have evinced no desire for their separate political legislature. But, in most areas, and certainly for most of the history of the union between Scotland and England, Scottish voters were consistently out-voted by an English majority. In many cases, governmental policy could be made and unmade, and the rules and principles under which Scottish people lived could be decided, by people living in England, who had no knowledge of Scottish affairs. This fact is obscured from view by the doctrine of popular sovereignty, which does not acknowledge any divisions within the body politic. But it is manifestly apparent to most national minorities, who have a keen sense of the vulnerability attached to their minority status. It seems only fair, in view of this, that we depart from the standard conception of individual equality which, in ordinary democratic politics, favours majority groups, to a conception that acknowledges the group-based divisions in the society, and the more vulnerable minority status of the Scots. This is small compensation indeed for throwing in their lot with England and permitting, in a whole range of decisions and powers, an English majority to make crucial decisions over Scottish life and affairs. Indeed, it is evidence of how blind the majority are to their own privileged position that they fail to see that English decision making over affairs Scottish is the typical result of majoritarian decision making in which everyone counts equally, and they only notice which group is making the decisions when it is the case that English public affairs could be determined by Scottish MPs!

Further, Barry's conception of strictly equal treatment and proportional (to population) representation fails to take into account the historical compromises and rights which often accompanied the development of the (multi-national) state, at least in cases where the state could be described as a product of compromise (even if that compromise was against the backdrop of unequal majority–minority power relations), not a blatant product of conquest. In the case of Scotland, the Act(s) or Articles of Union, which created the new British state, allowed for the continuing survival of a separate Scottish identity, through civic institutions, such as the church, as well as the common law and the courts. Scottish public and private law could continue, except where inconsistent with the union,[25] and out of this developed other special dispensations for Scotland – a Secretary of State for Scotland, a separate Scottish education system and distinctively Scottish local government. These are all subject to Barry's egalitarianism critique, as special rights which create divisions among the body politic, but they are the result not of multicultural theory, but of a practice of recognition of the minority nation's more vulnerable position within a larger state. Getting rid of these would be in violation of the historical rights and compromises worked out over centuries, and would be unjust, not only because there are now settled expectations on the part of people who have grown up under these institutions but because, in any society that respects the rule of law, historical rights should be respected, especially when these involve the basic terms of the original foundation of the state.[26]

On the precise issue of representation, which Barry discusses at length, a more historically nuanced view of the matter would reveal that, when Scotland originally entered the union with England, albeit somewhat under coercion, its representatives, such as they were, recognized that in this much larger body they were likely to be out-voted and overpowered,[27] and so worked out, as part of the compromise (in addition to preserving some distinct Scottish institutions), the assurance that the minority nation would be granted representation in the central government at a level higher than strict proportionality would require.[28] This precedent dates back to 1707, and can be justified as a reasonable assurance of input or voice in the central institutions of the state for the minority national community, who would clearly be very much the junior partner in the new state. (There is a modern-day equivalent to this: smaller states in the European Union also seek similar guarantees – a departure from strict population voting rules – whenever the issue of 'greater European Union' is discussed.) Barry criticizes such things as anti-egalitarian, as a violation of political equality, but his own egalitarianism seems to involve the denial of these historical rights, and a strictly proportional (to population) conception of representation. His proposal ignores the vulnerable status of minority national groups, who have eked out these concessions from majorities, and seems oblivious to the fact that majorities should be willing to pay them as part of the price of the common venture in which they are very much the more powerful partner. Indeed, his understanding of the requirements of political equality makes sense only if we ignore the unequal power and status of the two national groups, the Scottish and

the English, which is a clear case of doing what Aristotle warned us against –
treating unalikes alike.

Conclusion

In this chapter, I have argued that Barry's conception of a cultural group and a
cultural right is over-inclusive, and that minority nationalist groups should be
characterized by their *political* identity, by their aspirations to be collectively self-
governing, but not necessarily by a desire to institutionalize a thick culture in
the public sphere. Instead of viewing minority nations as analogous to religious
or ethnic groups in the state, they should be viewed in a comparative analysis
with majority nations, who enjoy the institutional recognition of their political
aspirations. This mis-categorization of minority nations as cultural groups has
implications for Barry's argument in favour of liberal neutrality and his argument that there is a serious tension between egalitarianism and various
group-specific rights, including accommodations for minority nationalism.

It is a fundamental premise of this chapter that minority national communities are relevantly similar to majority national communities except that, as a
result of historical failures of state building, or conquest or empire, they have
been on the losing side of the state-building game. They are equally able to be
the carriers of the values that Barry endorses – liberal rights, democratic governance, tolerance of diversity. I have not argued for that here, or explored the
conditions in which minority groups are likely to be liberal democratic, except
to employ examples of minority national groups that share this general political
culture. It has also been a sub-theme of this chapter that Barry's proposed solution – privatization – is a non-starter as far as national groups in the state are
concerned, and that the only way to resolve national conflicts is to consider
various institutional mechanisms to accommodate these political communities,
in ways consistent with democratic governance and liberal values.

Notes

1   Barry spends a lot of time criticizing I. M. Young, *Justice and the Politics of
    Difference*, Princeton: Princeton University Press, 1990; W. Kymlicka, *Multicultural
    Citizenship: A Liberal Theory of Minority Rights*, Oxford: Clarendon Press, 1995 –
    although almost everything written by Kymlicka is subject to critique; C. Taylor,
    'The Politics of Recognition', in A. Gutmann, ed., *Multiculturalism: Examining the
    Politics of Recognition*, Princeton: Princeton University Press, 1994, pp. 25–75;
    Tariq Modood, especially 'Anti-Essentialism, Multiculturalism and the
    "Recognition" of Religious Groups', *Journal of Political Philosophy*, 6, 1998, pp.
    378–99; various works by Bhikhu Parekh, many of which are now incorporated
    into his book *Rethinking Multiculturalism: Cultural Diversity and Political Theory*,
    Basingstoke: Macmillan, 2000 (although 'Equality in a Multiracial Society', in J.
    Franklin, ed., *Equality*, London: Institute for Public Policy Research, 1997, pp.
    123–55, is singled out for a particularly vitriolic attack); C. Kukathas, 'Cultural
    Toleration', in I. Shapiro and W. Kymlicka, eds, *NOMOS 39: Ethnicity and Group
    Rights*, New York: New York University Press, 1997, pp. 69–105; and J. Tully,

Strange Multiplicity: Constitutionalism in an Age of Diversity, Cambridge: Cambridge University Press, 1995. Many of these authors have internal disagreements with one another.

2   Barry also points out that the incompatibility of values argument is inconsistent with the idea that they are of equal value. B. Barry, *Culture and Equality: An Egalitarian Critique of Multiculturalism*, Cambridge, Mass.: Harvard University Press, 2001, pp. 278–84.

3   Ibid.

4   Culture refers to ethnic identity at pp. 73–5, 314–15, 325–6; to religious exemptions and religious claims at pp. 166–7, 170–3, 182–7, 306–7; to language policy at pp. 103–4, 106–7, 226–8; and to minority nationalism at pp. 77, 82–3, 217–20, 260–1, 326–7.

5   Ibid., pp. 297–9.

6   Ibid., p. 80.

7   Ibid., p. 79.

8   Ibid., pp. 79–80.

9   In his *Discourses on Political Economy* and *The Government of Poland*, Rousseau confronted the political problem of how to achieve and maintain unity and stability (which was thought to be especially difficult for a democratic regime). His solution was for the state to embark on a nation-building project to ensure that members share a common identity, for this, he thought, would facilitate the mutual trust necessary to undergird consent and secure sacrifice. Another version of this argument is found in J. S. Mill's famous discussion 'Of Nationality' in *Considerations on Representative Government*, where he argues that democracy can only flourish where 'the boundaries of government coincide in the main with those of nationality'. His argument in support of this contention is based on an analysis of the necessary conditions for a flourishing democracy: 'Among a people without fellow-feeling, especially if they read and speak different languages, the united public opinion necessary to the workings of representative institutions cannot exist.' (J. S. Mill, *Considerations on Representative Government*, ed. Currin V. Shields, Indianapolis: Liberal Arts Press, 1958, p. 230.) More recently, David Miller and Yael Tamir have developed this argument to suggest that national identification is instrumental to achieving the good of liberal citizenship which, in turn, is supportive of liberal political principles of redistributive justice and respect for diversity. Miller's argument that a shared national identity engenders trust among members, which in turn helps to support a redistributive practice, is a variation of the communitarian insight that, unless people feel bonds of membership to the recipients, then redistribution by the liberal state will be experienced by the individual (who is taxed) as coerced and therefore as incompatible with individual freedom.

10 It is doubtful, however, whether this constitutes a difference between this part of Barry's argument and that of *liberal* nationalism. Miller, for example, is at pains to argue that nationality should be sharply distinguished from ethnicity, and uses the example of hyphenated identities and nested identities. This presupposes a thin political identity of the kind discussed by Barry. See D. Miller, *On Nationality*, Oxford: Clarendon Press, 1995, pp. 20–1.

11 I have made this argument about a number of different academic works in M. Moore, *Ethics of Nationalism*, Oxford: Oxford University Press, 2001, and in 'Beyond the Cultural Argument for Liberal Nationalism', *Critical Review of International Social and Political Philosophy*, 2, 3, Autumn 1999, pp. 26–47.

12 W. Connor, *Ethnonationalism: The Quest for Understanding*, Princeton: Princeton University Press, 1994, pp. 32–6; D. L. Horowitz, *Ethnic Groups in Conflict*, Berkeley: University of California Press, 1985, pp.36–54; T. H. Eriksen, *Ethnicity*

and Nationalism: Anthropological Perspectives, London: Pluto Press, 1993, pp. 38–46.

13 J. McGarry and B. O'Leary, *Explaining Northern Ireland*, Oxford: Blackwell, 1995, pp. 171–213.

14 R. Rose, *Governing without Consensus: An Irish Perspective*, London: Faber, 1971, p. 218.

15 R. Harris, *Prejudice and Tolerance in Ulster*, Manchester: Manchester University Press, 1972, p. 131.

16 M. Ignatieff, 'Nationalism and the Narcissism of Minor Differences', *Queen's Quarterly*, 102, 1, 1995, pp. 13–25: P. Mojzes, *Yugoslavian Inferno*, New York: Continuum Press,1995, p. xvi; N. Malcolm, *Bosnia: A Short History*, New York: New York University Press, 1994, p. 282; C. Bennett, *Yugoslavia's Sudden Collapse: Causes, Course, and Consequences*, New York: New York University Press, 1995, p. 247.

17 L. Colley, *Britons: Forging the Nation, 1707–1837*, London: Pimlico, 1992, pp. 11–54, 322–3.

18 On this, see M. Keating, *Nations against the State: The New Politics of Nationalism in Quebec, Catalonia and Scotland*, London: Macmillan, 1996, pp. 163–76; M. Keating, *Plurinational Democracy: Stateless Nations in a Post-Sovereignty Era*, Oxford: Oxford University Press, 2001, pp. 33–40, 102–33; and N. MacCormick, *Questioning Sovereignty: Law, State, and Practical Reason*, Oxford: Oxford University Press, 1999, pp. 49–95.

19 In countries that have no liberal democratic traditions or history, minority nationalists, not surprisingly, have a weaker commitment to liberalism and democracy. But this does not seem to be related to their status as a minority national group.

20 W. Kymlicka, *Multicultural Citizenship: A Liberal Theory of Minority Rights*, Oxford: Oxford University Press, 1995, p. 108.

21 Barry also argues that the rules or principles themselves have to be justified by a good argument. It is easy to amend the pork case to take into account this requirement: we might imagine that vegetables are out of season and very expensive, and that all other meat alternatives were also much more expensive.

22 There are many critiques of the empirical claims being made by arguments of this kind. See D. Weinstock, 'Is There a Moral Case for Nationalism?', *Journal of Applied Philosophy*, 13, 1, 1996, pp. 87–100.

23 I am assuming that it is possible to 'test' this desire in standard democratic terms, through free and fair elections or referendums on clear questions.

24 This discussion is in Barry, *Culture and Equality*, pp. 310–13.

25 MacCormick, *Questioning Sovereignty*, pp. 51–2.

26 It is worth noting that the question of historical rights and compromises is central to Basque nationalism. Basques demand the restoration of these historical rights, which were abolished under Franco and not included in the 1978 Spanish constitution, although, since then, they have been (partially) recognized in an annexe, the First Additional Disposition. See Keating, *Plurinational Democracy*, p. 140.

27 The Scots Commissioners' opening gambit was for what is known in constitutional jargon as a 'federal union', in which they would be equal partners, but this was rejected by the English Commissioners, who favoured an 'incorporating union' in which the larger partner would be a continuing entity. Nevertheless, within the terms of an 'incorporating union', it was possible to work out some compensatory concessions to the minority nation. It is worth noting that the negotiating position of Scotland at the time (1703–5) was very weak indeed. See MacCormick, *Questioning Sovereignty*, p. 57.

28 Ibid., p. 51.

12 Rights and human rights

Rex Martin

Civil rights are at the core of basic rights (including those enshrined in constitutional bills of rights) and, I would argue, of human rights as well. This thesis, simply stated, is likely to be controversial. I want to lay out the case for it systematically. In the section that follows I will examine the character of civil rights as a genus and then the kind of justification appropriate to them, generically. In the section after that I will try to show how basic rights (a special case of civil rights) can be understood in the context of democratic political institutions.

Civil rights

Active civil rights are political rights universal within a given society. They are ways of acting, or ways of being treated, that are specifically recognized and affirmed in law for each and all of the citizens there (or, in the limiting case, for all individual persons there) and are actively promoted.

All civil or political rights, simply in so far as they are truly universal within a society, are important matters there and all reflect a high level of social commitment. But not all can be justified as natural rights (as what we today call human rights). Nonetheless, all can be justified in a distinctive way – in accordance with one and the same pattern.

The background supposition here is that all rights (be they natural rights or simply civil ones) are, in some way, beneficial to the rightholder. Thus, all proper civil rights (all political rights universal within a given society) should identify specific ways of acting, or of being treated, that are of benefit to each and all of the citizens. The *same* way of acting or the *same* way of being treated is said to be beneficial for each and every one of the rightholders (that is, all citizens or all persons within a given body politic), beneficial in the sense that that way is, arguably, a reliable means to or a part of some good, some interest of the holders.

Here person a's having a right R benefits person a, and person b's having that same right R benefits person b, and so on. The idea here is *not* that person a's having a right R benefits both person a and all other persons. For nothing like this would follow, as to mutual and general benefit, simply from a's having a right that benefits *a*, or from *b*'s having a similar one. Rather, it's from the fact that *everyone* has the same right(s) that this mutual and general benefit arises.

Admittedly, we might never be in a position to say that literally all alleged civil rights policies – let alone all alleged constitutional rights – are in fact beneficial to every citizen, or to every resident person. But we do have adequate evidence for saying that many well-established civil rights, assuming here that a highly concurrent favourable social opinion exists in their case, are justifiable on the regulative standard of mutual perceived benefit. And these we can take to be the paradigm basic civil rights.

Where this requirement (of individual and general benefit) holds good in a given case, then what is, legally speaking, a civil right is a way of acting (or of being treated) that is correctly understood to be in everybody's interest, or would be so understood, upon reflection (and given time and experience). All active civil rights could be regarded as justified in so far as they actually do identify and sustain ways of acting, or ways of being acted toward, that satisfy the criterion of mutual and general benefit.

It is always germane to bring this criterion to bear on any politically universal legal right, regardless of what other standards (in particular, moral ones) might also have bearing in a given case. The standard of mutual and general benefit sets an appropriate and uniform justifying pattern for all civil rights.

Civil rights and democratic institutions

Though rights may arise in the social relations that persons have with one another, a certain over-arching political arrangement is typically required as well. Active civil rights require an agency to formulate, maintain and harmonize them. More specifically, they require an agency to identify and establish ways of acting, or ways of being treated, that can reasonably be supposed to be in everyone's interest.

It could plausibly be argued that democratic institutions – universal eligibility to vote (on a one-person, one-vote basis), regular and contested voting operating at two distinct levels (the level of parliament and the level of general elections) and majority rule – can, acting as a set (and on a majority electoral base), effectively perform this job and thus provide the setting required by civil rights. This could be claimed here because democratic procedures are a stable and relatively reliable way of identifying, and then implementing, laws and policies that serve interests common to the voters or to a large number of them, presumably at least a majority.

On reflection, though, we see that this argument (though true so far as it goes) is deeply ambiguous; it covers a number of quite distinct, even disparate, options. Thus, the answer could be read as covering and emphasizing (i) those policies and laws that are in the interest of each and all or, alternatively, (ii) those policies and laws concerned, for example, with national defence or the growth of GDP, that is, concerned with things that are in the corporate or collective interests of the group of which each is a member (though not necessarily in the interests of each person there) or, finally, (iii) those policies and laws that are in the interests of indeterminately many (presumably a majority) though not in the interests of some others (presumably a minority).

How should we proceed in order to avoid the impasse posed by these distinct and disparate options? Most likely, we do not want to eliminate any of them from the list altogether. But to stick with all of them in a completely unstructured way would, in effect, amount to buying into unrestricted majority rule.

The best solution, then, would be to try to rank these options in some definite order. This ranking, if it could successfully be achieved, would thereby become *part* of the very justification for having and relying on democratic institutions. But if we cannot establish a plausible ranking, then we (as democrats or as citizens of a well-ordered democratic state) are stuck with unrestricted majority rule. This is the problem the disparate options force us to face.

I think that an ordering would, in fact, emerge as we reflected on these options (while keeping in mind that further one, of unrestricted majority rule). Here it would be decided, I am suggesting, that policies or laws should conform to a definite schedule of priorities. In sum, the ordering of permissible options, put in terms of the interests involved, would be (i) over (ii) and (i) or (ii) over (iii). And (iii) would have to be understood in a very definite way – as limited to (iiia) those policies and laws that help or hurt interests in a way that is *not* incompatible with serving interests under (i) or (ii).

It follows, on this account, that packages of interest-favouring policies (where the interests, say, of group A and of group B are supported by a majority coalition of A and B) are allowable if they conform to (iiia), even though the interests of others (a minority) were not helped here or were even harmed. But some policies – (iiib) policies that help or hurt interests and do so in such a way as to be *in*compatible with serving interests under the first two options – would be ranked last and ruled impermissible.

My main claim, in short, is that a people, accepting the basic rationale for democratic government, would probably refine that rationale by making laws and policies that are in the interest of each and all the principal political objects in their democratic society. They would thereby commit themselves to according a certain priority to civil rights over other legitimate political concerns.

Of course, democratic institutions won't always achieve the object identified. But if democratic institutions stay in line with that which justifies them in the first place, they will in fact *tend* to produce civil rights laws (among other things) and they will not act so as to supersede or otherwise impair such rights.[1]

Now, I grant, an argument would be required to show that democratic institutions have a special affinity for the interests of each and all and thus would accord such interests (and, as a special case, basic civil rights) priority over other eligible options. But such an argument could, I think, be set out.[2]

The upshot, then, would be that our two key notions (accredited basic rights – of individual persons – and a suitably justified set of democratic institutions) are mutually supportive of one another. Thus, they can form the central undergirding of a distinctive political system, one in which basic civil rights are accorded priority over other concerns of policy.

This priority does not arise from the idea of universal rights or from their presumed grounding in certain moral principles or other transcendental norms, as one might have initially supposed. Rather, it arises from the idea of democratic institutions, as suitably justified.

What conclusions can we draw here as to the ideal of political community and of citizenship in a democratic system of rights (of the sort I've just sketched)? We turn to that question now.

Sometimes a particular way of acting or of being treated – identically the same way in each case – can be a beneficial thing for a wide number of people. It would be likely, then (where this was so), that when someone perceived that it was a good for him or her, he or she would also perceive that it was a good for others as well. Now, such ways have to be sustained in practice; they don't just happen. They have to be accomplished and maintained through some sort of effort and choice. Typically, they are sustained through joint effort, in the case at hand *democratic* joint effort.

Here citizens or lifelong members of a given system of civil rights have pooled their efforts, through the democratic institutions mentioned earlier, to achieve a common set of values or norms for conduct in their society, as given (especially) in the civil rights laws that constitute or are among the main rules in this particular system of rights. The texture of any such body politic is spelled out not only in the specific list of civil rights that all enjoy but also in the normative directives imposed on the conduct of every person – but variously – by those rights. Thus, persons who are citizens or lifelong members of that particular society are rightholders there and have made their contribution to that society and to its system of rights when they've acted in character as typical citizens, through their conduct, in supporting civil rights and in conforming to rights laws.

It is *their* system, for they have contributed to it in this way. Its flourishing is the work of their hands and of others like them.

In sum, the model theory we have been examining appeals directly to the idea that some ways of acting or of being treated are mutually beneficial when engaged in by everyone. The theory then deepens this account, in the ways I have indicated, by showing that reciprocity is required to make that idea work. Recognition of this fact in turn generates an abiding and reflective commitment, presumably a widespread one, existing on many sides, to a sense of one's own good as a *social* good, in significant respects: a good fully realizable in a certain kind of society.

The key notion here is that of a set of *institutionally* justified rights of each and all, among which would be a set of basic civil rights. Because this focal set of rights is not individualistic in the unattractive way deplored by communitarianism, and because it is democratic and because it depends on reciprocity and engenders allegiance to a particular kind of body politic (and, within that kind, to particular ongoing societies), it can avail itself of the resources of a robust sense of political community and of citizenship.

What I have in mind with basic civil rights, sometimes called fundamental constitutional rights, is simply this. They are, paradigmatically, those civil rights (such as freedom of political speech or liberty of conscience) that have passed the double test of being enacted by legislative majorities and of being affirmed and, then, supported over the years by checking devices (such as judicial review). And they are rights that have survived the scrutiny of time and experience and public discussion; they have been winnowed (focused, revised, affirmed) by the self-correcting character of the democratic process, and now continue to enjoy a very high level of social consensus support.[3]

These are the basic rights in a democratic system of rights. They have a peculiar title for being regarded as constitutional essentials there. Indeed, this particular conception of basic rights may be the only one fully compatible with the idea of justified democratic majority rule and, hence, the only kind of basic right we can reasonably expect to flourish in a democratic system of civil rights.

The model account we have been developing does not ignore the fact that civil rights, including the basic ones, are themselves political constructions and involve certain express undertakings. Quite properly, then, this account politicizes the notion of basic constitutional rights. It recognizes that decisions must be taken here, and lived with. It recognizes that such rights must be formulated (subject to revision) and maintained and harmonized, like all rights, in political give and take.

Not all constitutional rights (for example, uninhibited freedom of contract or, to cite another, the right of persons to own and carry guns) will meet the standard set by the notion of basic civil rights, and some rights not thought to be constitutional rights (like the right to a primary and secondary education) will in fact meet it. The standard set by basic civil rights is a normative, not a descriptive, theory of constitutional rights in a democratic system.

Conceptions of human rights: two main camps

In the remainder of the present chapter I want to extend key elements of this analysis of basic rights to include human rights. Let us begin with an observation.

The vocabulary of rights, in particular, of human rights, may actually be used at any of several steps: that of mere claim, that of entitlement (where only the claim-to element is really settled), that of fully validated claim (where we have the idea both of a justified claim *to* something and of a justified claim *against* some specific person[s] for it) and, finally, that of satisfied or enforced claim (where the appropriate measures required to support or to fulfil the claim have been given effective embodiment as well). The presence of these possible stages has introduced a degree of ambiguity into assertions that a right – in particular, a human right – exists.

Accordingly, we find a significant variety of contemporary opinion as to the point at which such assertions can most plausibly be thought to take hold. While some have said simply that rights are *claims* (Mayo[4]), others say they are *entitlements* (McCloskey[5]), and yet others (most notably Feinberg[6]) say they are *valid claims*. Ranged against them have been those (such as Sumner[7]) who emphasize that rights, even human rights, are basically established ways of acting or being treated. And, last of all, some (for example, Rawls or Melden[8]) have treated rights as legitimate expectations and, hence, have landed more or less in the middle.

For simplicity we could divide these contrasting views into two main camps: the view that rights are justified claims and the view that they are socially recognized practices. I want to lay out the main case for each view rather briefly. But ultimately, as you will see, I come down on the side of social recognition.

The main starting point to the view that rights are (valid) claims is, I think, the common opinion that to have a right is to have a justification for acting in a certain way, or a justification for being treated in a certain way. Now, suppose that a candidate for rights status had all the rights-making features but one. Though accredited (in the sense of justified), it was not established; it lacked the *social* acceptance or the official recognition which it ought to have.

Why should the lack of such recognition deprive it of rights status? Clearly, a morally justified claim can be valid as a claim even though it has not been 'answered', so to speak, by governmental or by individual action; for the validity of the claim is in no way infirmed by the fact that the called-for responses have not been forthcoming. A morally valid claim can be purely a claim, for it is possible to conceive any such claim as one which holds in the absence of practices of acknowledgement and promotion, and yet is fully valid as a claim.

The thesis that human rights are universal, morally valid claims is understood by its proponents to be a way of asserting that human rights (simply in so far as they are justified or valid claims to ways of acting or of being treated, applicable to all people) are rights, whether responded to or not. The proposed thesis stands or falls on the point that morally justified claims, simply in virtue of being morally valid, are rights, and that human rights owe their status as rights solely to the element of justified claim.

Human rights can be conceived, without loss, as morally justified or valid claims and nothing more. Thus, if we modelled the rights-making features on what was justified (what was accredited in *that* sense), the thing was already a right even before it was recognized, even before it became a practice. And when it was recognized, it would be recognized *as a right* (as something that was fully justified) and would not simply *become* a right in being recognized.

Human rights are moral rights that are 'held to exist prior to, or independently of, any legal or institutional rules': that is, they are rights which are 'independent of *any* institutional rules, legal or nonlegal'.[9] The word 'moral' seems to be doing much of the same work in this context that the word 'natural' used to do. Describing rights as natural implied that they were not conventional or artificial in the sense that legal rights are, and the same is implied here by describing human rights as morally valid claims. This way of looking at such rights is widely thought to be one of the great virtues of the idea that human rights are justified or valid moral claims.

The opposing view is that rights are socially recognized practices, and I would argue that a number of important figures in the history of political thought (for example, Jeremy Bentham and T. H. Green) as well as political thinkers working today belong in this camp. The social recognition view rests on three main contentions.

The first of these is the contention that the notions of authoritative recognition (if not explicit, then at least implicit, as evidenced by conduct) and of governmental promotion and maintenance (usually on a wide variety of occasions) are themselves part of the standard notion of a *legal* right, that is, when we are concerned with rights that are more than merely nominal ones.

Thus, on the social recognition view, the fatal flaw in the theory of rights as justified or valid claims (in any of its formulations) is the suggestion that practices of governmental recognition and enforcement in law can be dispensed with in the case of *legal* rights. Indeed, this is the very point at which both Dworkin and Raz, who might otherwise be taken to be sympathetic to some form of the valid claims thesis, desert that thesis for one that emphasizes the necessity of institutionally establishing ways of acting or being treated, if these are to count as *legal* rights.[10]

The second point put forward by the social recognition view is that it is desirable to have, if possible, a single, unequivocal sense of 'rights': one that is capable of capturing both basic civil rights (as a special case of legal rights), on the one hand, and human (and other moral) rights, on the other, under a single generic heading.

Now, if the argument just sketched is to be credited, then the view of rights as justified or valid claims does not provide an adequate generalized notion of rights, one that can comfortably include both legal and human rights. For we have already seen that legal rights cannot be satisfactorily accounted for under the heading of mere justified or valid claims. Thus, we must consider the contention that the notions of social recognition (of some appropriate sort) and of promotion and maintenance (usually on a wide variety of occasions) are themselves internal to the notion of *any* active right.

This brings us to the third point urged by the social recognition view. Here the argument is that *all* moral rights, as accredited moral rights, can themselves be construed as involving established practices of recognition and maintenance. The question is: why *should* we so regard them?

In order to answer this question, we need to put a certain amount of logical pressure on the notion of a legitimate expectation or, if you will, of a justified or valid claim. When we regard rights (identifiable ways of acting or of being treated) as morally justified, we expect this standard to provide significant normative direction to the conduct of people, as regards a given right. Otherwise, were this not so, rightholders would be deprived of the very substance of what individual rights are rights *to*: deprived of the benefits that can reasonably be expected to accrue to the various ways of acting or being treated that have been designated as the core of the rights they held.

Imagine now a rather extreme case. Imagine an ideal foundational morality that no one was aware of. In all likelihood it was not even reflectively available to persons in the society in question. Such a morality could not be normatively effective in that place and time. It could not normatively direct conduct there, and the grounds of good conduct and of good judgement in moral matters, whatever these grounds were in that society, could not be connected to this ideal morality.

This is a matter about which one should not be dogmatic or too assured. But it does not seem implausible to believe that something like Nozick's libertarian individualism was not merely not known but was simply not reflectively available to our Neanderthal ancestors (human though they were and, indeed, living in the state of nature). So the case I've asked us to imagine is not an impossible one and may even be a likely one.

This being so, no one would think such an ideal morality could justify rights (could justify ways of acting or ways of being treated) there. I mean it could not provide effective moral justification in such a case. It could not effectively underwrite claims and entitlements to given ways of acting or ways of being treated there, claims that could figure in the self-understanding of people. And, of course, it could not provide effective normative direction to the conduct of people in that society. It could not normatively justify duties to act in an appropriate manner toward these ways, duties that could figure in the self-understanding of people there. Our hypothetical ideal morality would be wholly normatively ineffective.

This example suggests, then, that there is an inexpugnable element of 'social' acceptance (of social recognition) – and behind that, of normative soundness in the justifying standards – in the idea of *moral* rights. It is built into them, if we regard these justified ways of acting or ways of being treated as entities in a real social world, regard them as more than the conclusions demanded, or the practices enjoined, in an ideal critical morality.

Let me put this basic point slightly differently now. Substantial or at least adequate moral justification is justification that is not blocked by competing normative considerations.[11] And it is not justification that exists only in Plato's heaven. It is moral justification that is reflectively available to the people involved. But more than this is required for rights (be they moral rights or legal rights) to gain a grip. The people must take that justification on board, internalize it. Where it is a right they *all* have or involves duties that all (or many) of them have, this business of 'taking on board' must be widespread. It must affect the self-understanding of the people involved (a whole lot of people) in the appropriate ways.

Now let us take this analysis one step further, from mere social recognition to maintenance. I would argue that any right would be vitiated *as a right* if it were not protected or promoted at all. In such a case the right would be a merely nominal one, a right that existed in name only but not in fact. Such rights do not, as some have suggested,[12] constitute a special class of full-fledged rights. Rather, they constitute a defective way of exemplifying any justified and recognized right; merely nominal rights are rights only on paper and nowhere else.

Now, to be sure, nominal rights are rights. The point is, though, that we regard the complete and continuing absence of promotion and maintenance as infirming a right, as rendering it totally (or almost totally) ineffective. Nominal rights are rights *in one sense only* (that of formal acceptance or recognition and, presumably, of sound moral justification), and they fail to function as rights. A merely nominal right gives no normative direction to the conduct of other persons in fact; such persons act as if the right did not exist even on paper. None of them takes the nominal existence of the right as a reason for doing, or not doing, as the right directs. The right here has in actual practice no directive force. Where normative justification and social recognition effectively count for so little, the rightholder is without any effective guarantee respecting that which has been recognized and formulated as a moral right. Any such a right – when merely nominal – has failed in a crucial respect. It represents at best a marginal and precarious example of a moral right.

Here we have, then, the main arguments for the social recognition view that opposes the contention that rights are essentially justified or valid claims. And we reach the conclusion that the notions of acceptance or recognition (of some appropriate sort) and of promotion and maintenance (usually on a wide variety of occasions) are themselves internal to the notion of *any* active right, be it a legal right or a moral right or a social right.

The role of government in human rights

We are concerned in this chapter with human rights. On the assumption that any right under serious discussion is not merely nominal, then, for any particular moral right (a human right included), there would have to be certain appropriate practices of identification, promotion, protection, enforcement and so forth, in place on the part of society, and at least forbearance by (other) private persons. The determination of what is appropriate for a moral right – and here I have particularly in mind human rights (sometimes called natural rights) – then becomes the exact point at issue.

The great natural- and human-rights manifestos were intended to impose restraints upon governments. Individuals were involved as beneficiaries of these restraints but, for the most part, were not the parties to whom the manifestos were addressed. Or, at least, the class of all living individuals, taken one by one, was never the sole addressee of such manifestos, nor was it the primary one. The right to a fair trial, which is often given as an example of a human right,[13] is a right that one has against governments in particular, especially one's own.

The example is by no means atypical. The right to travel (found in the UN's Universal Declaration of Human Rights, 1948, article 13) certainly contemplates the absence of restraints imposed by governments; indeed, in so far as the issue is the liberty to travel, as distinct from the wherewithal to do so, it is primarily government that is addressed. And the right to freedom from the injury of torture is peculiarly held against governments; this is clear from the context – court proceedings and, in particular, punishment – in which the right is set (article 5). The same pattern holds with rights to the provision of a service. The duty of providing social security is explicitly enjoined on governments (articles 22, 25), and the duty to provide for elementary education, which 'shall be compulsory' (article 26), is clearly addressed, in this crucial detail at least, to states in particular.

It seems, then, that government's being an intended addressee of human rights norms is too deeply embedded to be erased. Whether we look at details of specific rights, as we find them in the great declarations of rights, or at the theory of human rights/natural rights (including its actual history), we find that government is in fact an addressee, often the principal addressee.[14] So a consideration of the relevant governmental practices is never a dispensable or even a negligible matter as regards the human rights status of these moral norms. This is not to deny, of course, that individuals are often addressed as well (the crucial prohibition invoked in the right not to be killed is addressed *both* to governments and to individual persons, for example).

It may be, though, I would add, that for *some* universal moral rights the role of government is incidental or even non-existent. These rights hold strictly between persons. Examples are the moral right to be told the truth (or at least not to be lied to), the moral right to gratitude for benefits provided and, perhaps, the moral right to have promises kept. Such rights differ from, say, the right not to be killed – even when we're talking about the latter right as held against individuals – in being rights maintained *exclusively*, or almost exclusively, by conscience. They are moral rights merely and in no way claims against the government. Interestingly, though, it is often in these very cases that, while we are willing to call such rights moral rights, we would tend to withhold from them the name of human (or natural) right.

There is a sound basis for saying, then, that human rights norms (that is, morally justifiable claims) are addressed to governments in particular, often to governments primarily. And natural or human rights can be distinguished from other universal moral rights in this very circumstance.

There is an important reason, which needs bringing out, for precisely this emphasis on governments. In talk of specifically human or natural rights, it is assumed that human beings live in societies. The goods that are identified in claims-to are here conceived as goods obtained and enjoyed in a social setting. That is, such goods are conceived as provided peculiarly or especially through life in a society. They are not, in short, thought to be attained principally, if at all, on a mere individual-person-to-all-others basis. Here then, where the social context is emphasized, claims against others are for the most part addressed not to individuals as such but, rather, to individuals in so far as they exercise the powers of some assigned agency in that particular social setting. Such claims-against hold not against everyone individually, but against an organized society; and it is of the institutions – or agencies – of that society that satisfaction is expected.

In cases of this sort, individual persons play only a derivative and sometimes incidental role. And since individuals *per se* are not addressed in *these* claims-against, it follows that the class of all persons – the class of all individuals considered simply as individuals – is not the principal intended addressee either. There is a definite sense in which the universality of human rights is not defined by the (universal) class of all persons; it is not when we have regard to the class of those who are primarily addressed in such claims (that is, the class of those who have relevant duties, responsibilities, and so on, toward the rightholder).

Moreover, though the benefit involved in a particular way of acting or of being treated is properly understood to be claimed for all human beings, the group of claimants is actually – for any given society – considerably smaller than that. It is not humanity *per se* but, rather, those who live in that society or who are significantly involved with it. They are the specific group to whom is due, or due primarily, that which is normatively required of the society in question. These important points, though little noted, set a powerful constraint on the sense in which human rights can be regarded as universal.

The role and character of government in human rights claims follows from these facts. Admittedly, it is not so much governments as it is organized societies that are selected out by human or natural rights claims. The point, though, is that the basic structures of such societies are correctly regarded as being *politically* organized; and it is governments that typically play, and have played, a major role in such organization.

Even if an organized society happened to be big enough and complex enough and over-arching enough to be so addressed, but did not have over it a government in the conventional sense (lacking certain coercive mechanisms or, perhaps, a territory of operation), it would still in some sense be a politically organized society. And there would still be significant analogues to government as we understand it (so long, that is, as it is – relatively speaking – an organized society and not a disorganized one).

What I have argued, then, is that those political institutions and agencies which are central to organized society are necessarily relevant to the status of human rights claims in all societies. In any given society it is these institutions (in the form they have there) that count.

Government, then, enters the human rights picture as the organizer, and as one of the major agencies, of the kind of society against which a human rights claim is characteristically lodged. Where human rights (as a special case of moral rights) are thought to be addressed to governments in particular (though not exclusively), we must regard practices of *governmental* recognition and promotion as being the main form for such recognition and maintenance to take for these rights.

A conception of human rights: summary and application

Let me conclude this chapter by first applying my overall analysis to the case of human rights as that notion is understood today (as exhibited, for example, by those rights found in the UN's Universal Declaration of Human Rights, 1948, or in the European Convention on Human Rights, 1954). Here I want not so much to expand on the model analysis as to reflect on and to appraise it. Then I want to say a brief, final word about international human rights.

In the account I've been giving, an active human right, understood simply as a moral right, is morally justified by accredited standards.

More particularly, I'd like to suggest that in this account a human right is justified by the standard of mutual and general benefit (the benefit of each and all). There may be other standards of justification that are useful and that would be normatively sound; but the standard of mutual and general benefit is, nonetheless, perhaps worth singling out. It would be hard to say, convincingly, that something was a justified human right if it quite clearly failed to meet the standard of mutual and general benefit. It would be hard, that is, if we continued to adhere to the supposition that all rights are beneficial, in some way, to the rightholder.

Where the right in question is a human right, then the specific way of acting or way of being treated it identifies should (at a *minimum*) be a matter of benefit to each and all of a vast number of human beings alive now (and for the foreseeable future). A specific way of acting or way of being treated that did not meet even this somewhat relaxed standard could not be justified as a human right.[15]

Let me enlarge upon the point just made. Sound moral justification is a necessary condition of any right's counting as a human right. I have argued that unless the standard of the benefit of each and all (*perceived* benefit) is satisfied (or can reasonably be expected to be satisfied), then we do not have an adequate moral justification in the case at hand.

How is this standard to be met? I have something fairly simple in mind. Each person is presumed to be able to reflect and to think reasonably carefully, within normal human limits, about important matters. Each is then presumed to focus and to reflect on a single consideration: whether (a) this particular way of acting or this particular way of being treated (if it were in effect for all) would on the whole be beneficial for the person so reflecting (as beneficial in itself or as a reliable means to some other good thing) and (b) that person can see how it would be beneficial to others as well, now and in the foreseeable future. If everyone could say, upon reflection, that this is so in their view, then the standard is satisfied. The standard is both minimal and abstract; it is very similar in these respects to W. D. Ross's idea of a prima facie duty (or, in the case at hand, a prima facie right).

The test probably cannot be satisfied for literally all people. Some people simply cannot or will not think straight. And others don't seem able to get the hang of engaging in moral reasoning, at any level. This is why I specified that the test could be satisfied if (arguably) the matter under consideration could be regarded as a benefit not only to but also by each and all of a *vast number* of human beings alive now (or in the foreseeable future).

Also, there's some question whether the standard in question is a *moral* standard. Now, it clearly is a moral standard of conventional morality – or, at least, is a standard compatible with many different conventional moralities. Accordingly, I am satisfied that, even in the relaxed form I have just provided, it is a moral standard of sorts. And this is enough said, for now at least. But this may not be enough for some normative moral theorists. They may want to enlarge the scope of those who can be regarded as perceiving the matter as beneficial so as to make it truly universal and to connect that perception with some accredited critical moral principle or with some accredited standard of practical moral reasoning.

Thus, a utilitarian, assuming certain conditions and certain matters of fact as background, might come up with some ideal moral rule (embracing all people, now and in the foreseeable future) which could itself be justified by the utilitarian general happiness principle. Or a contractarian (or 'contractualist') theorist might specify that no reasonable person could deny or *reject* the prima facie standard in question (Scanlon[16]) or specify that all reasonable people would accept or *endorse* it (Rawls[17]). My formulation requires neither of these two lines of attack (the utilitarian or the contractarian) to complete it. But it is compatible with both, while being neutral between them.

In sum, then, the notion of a justified human right (understood as a kind of moral right) has three main features:

1   It is a way of acting or way of being treated that is justified, for all human beings, by the standard of benefit for each and all, and perhaps by other moral standards as well.
2   That accredited way of acting or of being treated has some sort of authoritative political recognition (in the typical case, through recognition in law and in the action of courts).
3   It is maintained by conforming conduct and, where need be, enforced by governments.

It could fail at some of these points and still have substance as a human right; though if it failed on the point of justification (by the standard of the benefit of each and all), it would, I think, have reached a vanishing point. But a robust and fully functioning human right (understood as a moral right) satisfies all these points.

Let me fill in behind this contention a bit. Rights can be understood as having three distinct capacities. And we can take human rights to provide an illustration of each.

•   The first capacity is that of sound normative justification. The norms involved in the case of human rights must either include some norms that are themselves moral norms or be such as could be shown and understood to follow from accredited moral principles or practices.

- The second capacity is that of authoritative acceptance or acknowledgement. Without widespread acceptance, persons would not be able to conceive themselves as holders of human rights (or to act accordingly), nor could people see themselves as having duties toward these rightholders (nor could the bearers act according to those duties). Without *authoritative* acceptance, people could not be sure that they were all accepting the *same* way of acting or the *same* way of being treated as the one they all had a right to. And without authoritative acceptance, people could not effectively identify the scope of rights (let alone the main content of various rights), or assess the weight of particular rights when they were in competition with other rights or other normative considerations.
- The final capacity is that of delivering the substance of what a given right is *to* (be it a particular way of acting or a particular way of being treated). Without conforming conduct by those involved (involved either as rightholders or duty bearers) and enforcement of duties, as need be, by social or governmental action, the particular ways of acting or of being treated picked out by effective normative justification and by authoritative acceptance and acknowledgement could not be enjoyed on the wide scale one expects of things said to be human rights.

The fulfilment or realization, at a suitable level, of these three capacities is essential to any robust and non-defective human right (understood as a moral right). Their realization allows human rights to be, as they've always been thought to be, both practical and critical in character. The three features identified – sound justification, effective recognition, maintenance – are all linked elements in a effective procedure for constructing or constituting morally accredited human rights, functioning at full capacity.

The UN's Universal Declaration of Human Rights

The norms of the Universal Declaration, in order to be active human rights – active as constitutional rights or as international basic rights – and to be morally justifiable as human rights, must satisfy these three points. And, beyond that, we would require of them, as of any given right, some specification of content, some setting of scope (with provision for making scope adjustments), some competitive weightings in cases of conflict, some institutional devices for the on-site resolution of conflicts, and so on. For, otherwise, such rights will conflict with one another and collapse into an incoherent set.

Some may find extremely unattractive the notion that moral rights can be tinkered with – that new ones can be added to the list, existing ones revised, some even overturned. It is perhaps worth adding, then, that we are here principally concerned with the *implementation* of such rights and not their abstract formulation. Nonetheless, we should face up to the fact that changes such as these can occur even in our normative justifications. For one thing, many people believe (or hope) that by thinking more carefully about moral matters, bringing in new paradigms and perspectives, we can thereby improve our own formulations and understandings. In any event, moral norms gain or lose social support, so that they take on radically differing formulations at widely separated times in history (witness the sharply differing idea of the cardinal virtues held by the ancient Greeks in contrast to that of, say, medieval Christian culture). And blocking by competing normative considerations can be added or removed over time, or in different places on the cultural map coexisting at the same time. Such changes in effective normative justifications and their formulation can happen and, I think, do happen.

If all this is so, we cannot think adequately about human rights (where they are thought to be active rights, as distinct from mere norms) by dispensing with the institutional arrangements – scope adjustment, competitive weighting, promotion and maintenance – just emphasized. Features such as these are part of the mechanism of normative change (of helping it along or registering it) and, more to the point, are necessary to making moral norms into active human rights, functioning at full capacity.

The proper focus here, I am suggesting, should not be on the 'manifesto' element of the UN's Declaration but, rather, on the embodiment of those norms as active civil rights within states, where such rights (presumably appropriately justified morally) could be and were authoritatively recognized, harmonized and maintained.[18]

Some might argue that I've focused too often in my argument on the great rights manifestos and have ignored another tradition in human rights discourse – the tradition that sees moral rights as justified claims and standards for criticizing existing political or social arrangements, whether or not these claims are recognized and enforced at all. Though it's hardly fair to say that I've ignored this tradition (since I criticized it at length earlier), let us leave that caveat aside for now.

I readily grant that others would regard such justified claims as human rights, and I see no problem in their doing so. It is not part of my project to deny human rights status to such claims or to legislate how people should be talking about human rights. So long as the three-element procedure for constituting human rights is kept on the table as essential to the big picture, I have no quarrel with the view at hand.[19]

The essentials of the three-element procedure for constituting human rights are present in the UN Declaration. Thus, human rights are regarded there as constitutional rights within individual states. This is, in fact, the case primarily contemplated in the UN's Universal Declaration.[20] In so far as we emphasize this one type of case (the case of constitutional rights within individual states), the embodiment of human rights norms can be particularized (to a degree) to different cultural preferences and histories.

Let me illustrate this last point, about relativizing human rights to particular societies, with a brief example. The UN Declaration says that 'everyone has the right to freedom of thought, conscience, and religion' (article 19). The Bill of Rights of the US Constitution consists of ten amendments, proposed in 1789 and enacted in 1791. The first amendment says roughly the same thing as the article from the UN Declaration just cited, but what the first amendment says about religion in particular is worth pondering: it says, 'Congress shall make no law respecting an establishment of religion, or prohibiting the free exercise thereof.'

Now, as we know, many European states committed to human rights have established churches. The Scandinavian countries, for example, have. And some European states have more than one – Finland has two and so does Britain (in the latter case, the Church of England and the Kirk of Scotland). One might say that the fact that this is so shows that 'establishment of religion' is not a matter of any great import nowadays. But I would deny this. It is not simply a 'dead letter' issue.

The way the 'no establishment of religion' clause is interpreted in the United States, on the one hand, and the way acceptance of established churches functions in contemporary Europe, on the other hand, has led to important differences between the United States and Europe in such matters as the content of education at the primary and secondary levels, the place of religious education in state-supported schools, the degree and kind of budgetary support given by government to private religious schools, and so on.

These are not trivial examples. They exhibit how the embodiment of human rights norms can be and has been particularized to different cultural understandings and histories. And these examples could be multiplied.

International human rights

Let me hasten to add that a focus on constitutional rights within individual states is not the only option available to the resources of the present account. We are not – or need not be – limited exclusively to what might be called 'nation states' and their particular arrangements.

Some, of course, using arguments like the ones I have employed, have alleged otherwise. Michael Walzer, for instance, is one.[21] To the contrary, I would want to claim that the account I have presented could allow for the notion of basic rights in an emerging supranational entity or, better, a fairly unified confederation of states (like the nascent European Union, and within it the European Convention of Human Rights). And it could allow for such rights in a somewhat looser confederation of states such as we find in the UN, and within it the UN Declaration, the two main Covenants on Human Rights, and various other relevant international treaties (such as the treaty outlawing genocide).

Indeed, to think clearly about human rights in the present day, one would have to allow for such cases. If this is so, then, we must in the end add an international dimension to the account I have been giving.[22]

Notes

In the writing of the present chapter I have drawn on my paper on 'Basic Rights' (*Rechtstheorie, Beiheft* 15, 1993, pp. 191–201) and on my article on rights in the *Routledge Encyclopedia of Philosophy*, vol. 8 (London: Routledge, 1998, pp. 325–31); and also on two of my books, *Rawls and Rights*, Lawrence: University Press of Kansas, 1985, and *A System of Rights*, Oxford: Clarendon Press, 1993. Perhaps the simplest way to view and then extend the present chapter is to see it as an attempt to improve upon – to clarify and correct – *System of Rights*, ch. 4, wherein my main account (before now) of human rights can be found. Earlier versions of this chapter were presented at the University of Tennessee and at conferences in Pittsburgh and Cardiff. For their helpful comments, I am indebted to Will Aiken, John Arthur, Richard Brook, Mark Evans, Bruce Haddock, John Haldane, Mikael Karlsson, David Reidy, Peri Roberts, Peter Sutch and Anton Tupa.

1   Nonetheless, it would not be inappropriate, given this justification, to install further institutions (such as a written bill of rights, judicial review, whether understood in the American way or the British, executive veto, and so on) to help achieve the intended effect, or at least the effect of not superseding or otherwise impairing fundamental constitutional rights.

2   For the justification of democracy (and of the relative priority of the various options involved), see my *System of Rights*, chs 6 and 7 (summarized at pp. 127–8 and pp. 167–8). For the point (just made) about the fundamental compatibility of basic rights with justified democratic majority rule, see ibid., chs 7 and 12, in particular; for the idea that well-accredited rights are not to be superseded, in central cases, by other normative concerns, see ibid., ch. 5, § 4, also pp. 159–65; for an account of basic (or fundamental constitutional) rights, in particular, see ibid., ch. 12, § 2. And, for a convenient summary of the main argument I have been giving here, see the short paper 'Basic Rights'.

3   For the point about the role of checking devices (in particular, judicial review) as fundamentally democratic in character, see my co-authored paper with S. M. Griffin, 'Constitutional Rights and Democracy in the USA: The Issue of Judicial Review', *Ratio Juris*, 8, 2, July 1995, pp. 180–98. Roughly this same point is made in J. Waldron, 'Rights and Majorities: Rousseau Revisited', in J. W. Chapman and A. Wertheimer, eds, *Majorities and Minorities, Nomos xxxiii*, New York: New York University Press, 1990, pp. 44–75, and in S. Freeman, 'Constitutional Democracy and the Legitimacy of Judicial Review', *Law and Philosophy*, 9, 1990/1, pp. 327–79; also S. Freeman, 'Original Meaning, Democratic Interpretation, and the Constitution', *Philosophy and Public Affairs*, 21, 1992, pp. 3–42; and S. Freeman, 'Political Liberalism and the Possibility of a Just Democratic Constitution', *Chicago Kent Law Review*, 69, 1994, pp. 619–88. Finally, for the point about the self-correcting character of democratic procedures, see my *System of Rights*, ch. 7. This idea is taken from T. L. Thorson, *The Logic of Democracy*, New York: Holt, Rinehart and Winston, 1962, esp. ch. 8; also pp. 120–4.

4   B. Mayo, 'Symposium on Human Rights', II, *Proceedings of the Aristotelian Society Supplementary Volume*, 39, 1965, pp. 219–36.

5   H. J. McCloskey, 'Rights', *Philosophical Quarterly*, 15, 1965, pp. 115–27. See also H. J. McCloskey, 'Rights – Some Conceptual Issues', *Australasian Journal of Philosophy*, 54, 1976, pp. 99–115.

6   J. Feinberg, *Social Philosophy*, Foundations of Philosophy Series, Englewood Cliffs, NJ: Prentice Hall, 1973. J. Feinberg, *Rights, Justice and the Bounds of Liberty*, Princeton: Princeton University Press, 1980.

7   L. W. Sumner, *The Moral Foundation of Rights*, Oxford: Oxford University Press, 1987.

8   J. Rawls, *A Theory of Justice*, Cambridge, Mass.: Harvard University Press, 1971 (2nd edn, 1999); A. I. Melden, *Rights in Moral Lives: A Historical-Philosophical Essay*, Berkeley: University of California Press, 1988.

9 See Feinberg, *Social Philosophy*, p. 84, for the first quote, and Feinberg, *Doing and Deserving: Essays in the Theory of Responsibility*, Princeton: Princeton University Press, 1970, p. 85 n. 27, for the second.

10 See here R. Dworkin, *Taking Rights Seriously*, Cambridge, Mass.: Harvard University Press, 1978, ch. 4; R. Dworkin, *Law's Empire*, Cambridge, Mass.: Harvard University Press, 1986, ch. 11, also pp. 65–8; and J. Raz, 'Legal Rights', *Oxford Journal of Legal Studies*, 4, 1984, pp. 10–21.

11 We should not think that we in 'modern times' are exempt from the blocking phenomenon I've just mentioned. Most people in the secular West today would give precedence to the normative claims of logic, mathematics, natural science (and, perhaps, even social science and history) – precedence in the sense that moral claims must be compatible with the claims of logic, science and so on, and would be blocked (set aside, revised, discounted) where they are not. And in some parts of our contemporary world the claims of particular religions or of world-shaping ideologies (like those of communism or capitalism) would have similar precedence and blocking power.

12 For example, M. Cranston, 'Human Rights, Real and Supposed', in D. D. Raphael, ed., *Political Theory and the Rights of Man*, Bloomington: Indiana University Press, 1967, pp43-53, esp. p. 48.

13 By Cranston, ibid., p. 43, among other writers.

14 The US Declaration of Independence (1776) begins its famous second paragraph with the words: "We hold these truths to be self-evident, that all men are created equal, that they are endowed by their Creator with certain unalienable rights, that among these are Life, Liberty, and the pursuit of happiness. That to secure these rights, Governments are instituted among Men …".

15 For the point made about rights as beneficial, see my *System of Rights*, chs 2, 5 and 10. The point about such rights being mutually and generally beneficial for all or almost all living human beings follows from our characterization of the rights in question as *human* rights. Just as civil rights are rights of all citizens, so human rights are rights of all human beings.

   Here we need to take care. It is important to distinguish between conditions of constitution or existence for moral rights and criteria for their possession (a distinction I did *not* observe in the previous paragraph). *Two* ideas are involved here:

   (i)   Moral rights are not conclusively justified by mere physical or psychological facts (in other words, such physical or psychological facts are not sufficient grounds for saying that a particular moral right *exists*). Rather, moral rights are justified or constituted on other grounds, specifically on *normative* grounds.

   (ii) Physical or psychological facts bear not on what justifies rights, but on who might be a candidate for possessing any such justified right, once it has been justificatorily established.

   In the account I have been giving, that which justifies something as a right (be it a right to a way of acting or to a way of being treated) is that it is beneficial to the rightholder and can be understood as beneficial. If other moral standards are brought to bear, and typically (in the case of a human right) many kinds of moral standards will be, then they too are a part of the justification. Putting the point crudely, then, what justifies a moral right is that it can be understood as following from or being compatible with accredited moral principles or practices (or with accredited forms of practical moral reasoning).

   Most of the things in the UN's Universal Declaration of Human Rights could be regarded as justifiable in these ways. Interestingly, many of them would be beneficial *only* to adult human beings, within a certain range of capabilities and interests: freedom of political speech, the right to vote, liberty of conscience, right to a fair trial or to a job, and so on. The point is that since all or almost all adult human beings are within this range, all are eligible to possess the rights in question; no such adult should be excluded.

16 See T. M. Scanlon, *What We Owe to Each Other*, Cambridge, Mass.: Harvard University Press, 1998, p. 4 (and throughout his book), for this formulation and for elaborations on it.

17 See J. Rawls, *Political Liberalism*, New York: Columbia University Press, 1993, pp. 217 – also pp. 1, 137, 226, 241, 393. Later Rawls adds yet another possible line of formulating the contractarian rubric when he says that those proposing a principle of co-operation or of mutual relations 'must think not only that it is reasonable for them to propose it, but also that it is reasonable for [others] to accept it'. See J. Rawls, *The Law of Peoples with 'The Idea of Public Reason Revisited'*, Cambridge, Mass.: Harvard University Press, 1999, p. 57; also pp. 14 and 69.

18 The Universal Declaration avowedly has a 'manifesto' element: it speaks in its preamble of 'proclaiming' a 'common standard' and calls itself a 'declaration'. Clearly, then, it lays out a set of aspirations; but it does not stop there. Repeatedly, the idea of the recognition of the rights proclaimed and their observation is invoked.

19 I am often asked what I would call a human right that had only the one element, the element of morally valid claim (that and nothing else). I would tend to call it a *human rights norm*. This seems apt because the italicized phrase recognizes that we don't have a fully constituted right here (don't have a right functioning at full capacity) while at the same time affirming that a mere morally valid claim does have status as a human right even when only the first of the constituting conditions, the condition of sound normative justification, is fully satisfied.

A good example of the alternative way of talking, with which I find no problem, is provided by Henry Shue. In his book *Basic Rights: Subsistence, Affluence and US Foreign Policy* (2nd edn, Princeton: Princeton University Press, 1996), he begins by characterizing human rights as morally justified demands (pp. 13–15), but he immediately goes on to emphasize the importance of such rights being 'socially guaranteed' (pp. 15–18). In later chapters this particular feature is emphasized and it becomes clear that such guarantees necessarily involve the elements of social recognition and maintenance, by both private persons and governments (see esp. chs 2 and 5 and the Afterword). For a good summary of his views, in which all the components just identified figure, see his essay 'Solidarity among Strangers and the Right to Food', in W. Aiken and H. LaFollette, eds, *World Hunger and Morality*, 2nd edn, Upper Saddle River, NJ: Prentice Hall, 1996, pp. 113–32.

20 The preamble to the UN Declaration begins with the assertion that the 'Member States' are intent on achieving not only the 'promotion of universal respect' for human rights and 'fundamental freedoms' but also their 'observance'. The preamble ends with a commitment to secure for these rights and liberties 'their universal and effective recognition and observance, both among the peoples of the Member States themselves and among the peoples or territories under their jurisdiction'.

21 'Individual rights may well derive, as I am inclined to think, from our ideas about personality and moral agency, without reference to political processes and social circumstances. But the enforcement of rights is another matter ... . Rights are only enforceable within political communities where they have been collectively recognized, and the process by which they come to be recognized is a political process which requires a political community. The globe is not, or not yet, such an arena.' M. Walzer, 'The Moral Standing of States: A Response to Four Critics', *Philosophy and Public Affairs*, 9, 1980, p. 226; see also pp. 227–8.

22 I have not, in this chapter, developed the international dimension of human rights any further. I have attempted to do so elsewhere, in my paper 'Human Rights:

Constitutional and International' in M. N. S. Sellers and David Reidy, eds, *Universal Human Rights: Moral Order in a Divided World*. Nor have I, in the present chapter, attempted to lay out my characterization of rights in contrast to alternative accounts and to show the grounds on which I think mine is to be preferred. I have, however, done this in *System of Rights*, chs 2–5.

13 The transition from natural rights to the culture of human rights

David Boucher

In his autobiography R. G. Collingwood presented his now famous argument against perennial problems in philosophy.[1] He argued that Plato's conception of the state, or *polis*, formulated against the backdrop of ancient Greece, was very different from that of the seventeenth-century Englishman Thomas Hobbes. There was therefore little point in discussing them as if they were talking about the same thing. One might say that their ideas of the state were answers to different questions, and belonged to different question-and-answer complexes. This does not mean, however, that the two concepts of the state were unrelated. They are related in so far as they are both part of the historical process by which one becomes transformed into the other. In this chapter I want to suggest that even though natural rights and human rights are often associated, in so far as it is claimed that we have them independently of governments and by the mere fact that we are human, they are in fact quite different. They are nevertheless related in that they are part of the same historical process by which the one turns into the other. It is that process which I want to explore here by first looking at natural rights, the human rights culture, the link between the two, and finally to show how modern justifications are related to that link.

When the modern conception of human rights, generated by some version of constructivism or conventionalism, is juxtaposed with the various versions of natural rights, there appears to be a discontinuity between the two. In other words, there appears to be no process by which the one turns into the other, because of a fundamental discontinuity. The aim of the chapter is to show that there is a continuity and that the British Idealists constitute the missing link. Despite the denial of natural rights in their traditional form, namely as resting upon some conception of human nature, universal principles, or as having some religious foundation, the Idealists suggested that the term was better used in the sense that there are certain rights that are absolutely imperative for the social relations of a community at any one time, and that these rights, despite the fact that they are conventional and justified on the principle of their contribution to the common good, could with justification be described as 'natural'. The Idealists, nevertheless, ultimately relied upon a metaphysic and a conception of the person that was difficult to reconcile with the conventionalism posited in their accounts of natural rights. Modern philosophers have retained the conventionalism, or communitarianism, and jettisoned the metaphysics. The Idealists, then, stand in an intermediary position between natural rights and the modern human rights culture, and have contributed significantly to modern ideas on the moral community and how conceptions of human rights have to be conceived in terms different from the natural rights tradition.

Just as there is hardly any country that does not describe itself as a democracy, Jeremy Waldron contends that 'there is now scarcely a nation on earth which is not sensitive to or embarrassed by the charge that it is guilty of rights-violations'.[2] Richard Rorty, following Eduardo Rabbossi, has suggested that we live in a human rights culture, and Michael Ignatieff goes as far as to say that 'there is now a single human rights culture in the world'.[3] The presumption is, then, that we have human rights. How we come to have them, who ought to have them, and what human rights we should have are quite different questions.

It is not surprising that the modern obsession with rights should lead to a revival of interest in the natural rights tradition, and a preoccupation among theorists with the importance of human rights attaching to the individual independently of society. Robert Nozick gives one of the strongest reiterations of this individualist conception of rights: 'Individuals have rights, and there are things no person or group may do to them (without violating their rights).'[4]

Peter Jones has suggested that the modern doctrine of human rights is a direct descendant from liberal theories of natural rights. He argues that

> [t]he idea of a human right remains that of a right which is 'natural' in that it is conceived as a moral entitlement which human beings possess in their natural capacity as humans, and not in virtue of any special arrangement into which they have entered or any particular system of law under whose jurisdiction they fall.[5]

And elsewhere, in criticism of Rawls, he suggests that 'human rights have generally been conceived as rights possessed by human beings as such and as rights that must therefore be respected in all the various contexts and circumstances in which human beings find themselves'.[6] H. L. A. Hart reinforces this view when he suggests that people are conceived to have human rights 'by virtue of their humanity and not by virtue of human fiat, law or convention'.[7] What I want to suggest is that, contrary to these views, there is a disjuncture between the modern human rights culture and the natural rights tradition that is often assumed to underpin it.

The natural rights tradition

At the outset we need to distinguish between two very different usages of the term 'natural rights'. The one meaning is naturalistic, the other moral – that is, the descriptive and prescriptive versions of the doctrine. On the first, the fact that we have certain powers or liberties in nature is justification for their use. To have a faculty and the right to use it are one and the same thing. These are the rights that Hobbes talks of in his state of nature. They are really nothing more than descriptions of what certain types of creature tend to do in certain circumstances when exercising their natural inclinations. The natural rights about which Locke talks are quite different, and many of which have attached to them obligations deriving from natural law, which is divinely instituted. To deprive me of property, which I have acquired by mixing my labour with it, is morally to violate my natural right. What is missing when traditional natural rights thinkers such as Locke, Priestley, Price, Paine, Hamilton and Wollstonecraft, are claimed as part of the heritage of the contemporary human rights culture is the extent to which their conclusions depend upon a shared belief in God, who is the Creator of the moral world and of the human beings who inhabit it. This belief is sometimes a full-blown Christian theology or merely contains lingering remnants of deism, lacking the elements of divine intent, command and purpose. Any element of Christianity or deism, of course, is not a terribly convenient fact in the post-1945 western world, which has become increasingly secular, multicultural and sensitive to non-Christian religions. The claim to the universality of human rights is not best served by highlighting the particularity of their Christian origin.

Let me take a few obvious and not so obvious examples. Take Locke, for instance: his whole theory of rights and obligations ultimately rests upon our duty to God of self-preservation and, in so far as others are the property of God, the preservation of those others. This is because we are the products of His workmanship and political obligation derives from this generic obligation to God (*Second Treatise*, § 6). The obligation we have to obey a *specific* government rests on consent. Locke says:

> If he finds that God has made him and other men in a state wherein they cannot subsist without society, can he but conclude that he is obliged and that God requires him to follow those rules which conduce to the preservation of society?[8]

The theory of natural rights, as we know, reached its high-water mark in the American and French Revolutions. Arendt, for example, argues that these declarations posited man as the measure of all things.[9] It is clear, however, from the words of one of the great architects of the American Constitution, Alexander Hamilton, that this was not the intention. He maintained that

> [t]he sacred rights of mankind are not to be rummaged for amongst old parchments or musty records. They are written, as with a sunbeam, in the whole volume of human nature by the hands of divinity itself, and can never be erased or obscured.[10]

Mary Wollstonecraft's *A Vindication of the Rights of Women*, to take another example, extends the arguments made by the rational dissenters Richard Price and Joseph Priestley that all men have equal rights to encompass women, on the grounds that all human beings have rational capacities which access to education would allow to develop. Her work was very much in the tradition of devotional literature associated with Richard Allestree and Mary Astell. Wollstonecraft's themes of rational equality, the corrupting influence of the bodily passions, the injunction to restrain the passions within marriage, and the necessity for knowledge to aid the development of virtue are all derived from the writers of devotional literature.[11] Her emphasis upon rights, however, derive, directly from the writings of the rational dissenters. Wollstonecraft is no less committed to fundamental Christian beliefs than are Price and Priestley. In other words, our natural, or human, rights come from God, and all human beings should have them because we are all in principle capable of exercising reason, subject to a rational education.

Even natural rights theorists who are said to have secularized the tradition, such as Hugo Grotius and Samuel von Pufendorf, retain a heavy residue of theological presuppositions without which their arguments collapse at crucial points. Take Pufendorf. He believes that all law has an author, and to qualify as law proper it must also be enforced. Both natural law and human positive law qualify in these respects. Natural law, from which our natural rights derive, is the creation of God who, should we transgress against it, punishes our actions. Pufendorf argues that 'the obligation of Natural Law is of God, the creator and final governor of mankind, who by His authority has bound men, His creatures, to observe it'.[12] Because our intelligence and reason are limited, and because the punishment may not always immediately follow the crime, we rarely make the connection between our actions and God's punishment of them. Rights and duties in the state of nature are 'imperfect' because they are not enforceable, whereas legal rights and duties are 'perfect' because they are enforceable. Often what was once compelled by conscience became enforceable in positive law. What is significant is that Pufendorf thinks that both are equally morally obligatory.[13]

What has proved contentious about such claims is not that humans have rights, but that rights inhering in the individual could be the starting point of a theory of political morality. The riposte has been that rights are only intelligible when set against a suitable background theory of political and social morality such as utilitarianism.[14] Jeremy Waldron argues that at the rhetorical level the shift from natural rights to human rights betrays a loss of faith in the possibility of justifying rights with reference to truths about human nature. The term 'human rights' now signifies the scope of the claims rather than hints at anything that might justify them.[15] Increasing scepticism about objective values and principles in moral philosophy has not terminated moral argument or justification. Moral justification may no longer be characterized by the search for ultimate truths irresistible to rational beings, but it is concerned to determine the shared foundations, sympathies and considerations that underpin claims about taking rights seriously.[16]

Idealism and natural rights

The British Idealists are usually assumed to have been hostile to the idea of natural rights, but this is only part of the story. Natural rights remained very much part of the political geography of the late nineteenth century, even if, philosophically, their credibility had been diminished. There must have be something in their continuing persistence because people do not reflect and act upon meaningless symbols.[17] The British Idealists were nothing if not astute political operators, and knew how to exploit a popular vocabulary to serve their own arguments. They did this, for example, in relation to the evolution debate, denying Darwin's naturalistic evolution, and Huxley's bifurcated discussion of the cosmic and ethical evolutionary processes, and instead came up with their own Hegelian version of evolution that stressed its spiritual aspect, and which insisted upon what came later as the explanation of what came before, instead of explaining what came later in terms of what went before. Similarly, they took the vocabulary of human rights and transformed it, hoping that in the transformation they could retain what was best in natural rights and in the criticisms of that doctrine.

Like Burke, Bentham and Marx, the British Idealists accused natural rights theories of being abstract and one-sided, that is, idealizations in Onora O'Neill's sense of the term. They rejected both the naturalistic and moral forms of natural rights being perpetrated, often indistinguishably, by their proponents. With advances of our understanding of society in terms of evolutionary theory, and by use of the historical method in exploring institutions and problems, it was now possible to think of the ideal associated with natural rights theories not as something fully formed and definitive, but as something whose revelation is gradual – what Peter Sutch calls developmental communitarianism.[18] Following Hegel, David Ritchie argued that, historically, slavery as an institution may be justified on the grounds that it contributed to mitigating the brutality of war. It was more profitable to take prisoners than to slaughter them.[19] In giving the free population the leisure to develop political liberty and a self-awareness of the worth of freedom, slavery gave rise to the ideas that eventually made slavery appear wrong. In other words, slavery was once useful and did not appear contrary to what would then be considered 'natural' but, when it ceased to be an institution of progressive societies, it became a violation of what people regarded as natural rights. Genuine appeals to the injustice of such an institution were not appeals to abstract principles incompatible with the continuance of organized society, but appeals to higher conceptions of society that should replace the lower. In this respect 'evolutionary ethics' teach us 'to face the problems of human society without exaggerated expectations'.[20] In Ritchie's view, the common good which acts as the criterion of appropriate conduct changes from age to age and depends upon what actions and virtues contribute to the realization of the well-being of society. What is presupposed in the general liberal account of the individual, and explicit in the natural rights tradition, is that human nature is universal. The constitutive theory of the British Idealists, on the other hand, holds that human nature is significantly contingent. Human nature is largely a product of the different social circumstances in which people find themselves. Membership in a society and the common good are correlative, and the self that is to be realized through moral activity is 'determined, characterised, made what it is by relation to others'.[21]

Social cohesiveness requires any society to adhere to certain ground rules or conditions and thereby creates rights and duties for its members.[22] As members of a community, individuals possess rights. As T. H. Green says, all rights are 'secured to an individual by the community, on the supposition that … [their] exercise contributes to the good of the community'.[23] Rights are justifiable claims recognized as rational and necessary for the common good of society. Natural rights are those fundamental rights that *ought* to be recognized by a society, and to be judged wholly from the point of view of society. They are an appeal to what is socially useful not merely for the present generation, but also for future generations and as far as possible for humanity as a whole.[24] It is because they are fundamental to the life of a society that they may be called natural. Against Bentham, the British Idealists argued that rights are not the product of legislation, but recognized as essential to the development of the common good.[25] A natural right for the British Idealists is justified by the extent to which it contributes to the common good.

Without social recognition, rights are something less than rights. Recognition is intrinsic to the concept of a right. Natural rights, then, are a socially useful concept when they have as part of their definition social recognition, and as part of their justification the idea of the common good.

What is important about the Idealist account is that it is capable of explaining how human rights emerge. It does not rely on the fiction of a social contract. Human rights are justified not by individual consent, but because they are collectively useful and necessary for the common good. This particularist element in British Idealism is counterbalanced by a universalism that is ultimately based upon a thick conception of the good. The metaphysical assumption of a universal reason manifesting itself in each individual striving for self-realization to attain the best self remains ultimately religious, Christian and Protestant. There is no presumption of a transcendental God as there was among many of the natural rights theorists. Instead, the Idealists posit an immanent God who lives and expresses Himself through each of His creations. It is an assumption that does not deny the divinity of Jesus, because it does not deny the divinity of anyone. In sum, then, even though Idealism provides a form of conventionalism in human rights, the Christian residue fits ill with the modern human rights culture.

The human rights culture

There is certainly a residue of the traditional ideas of natural rights that coexist with the modern. Some writers on human rights contend that, without a religious element or theological foundation to the doctrine sanctifying human dignity, human rights for the protection of the person have very little purchase.[26]

Indeed, the discussions surrounding the establishment of the Nuremberg Tribunal most immediately highlight the tension. After the Second World War the allies were faced with the dilemma of how to punish those war criminals who claimed to be obeying the laws and orders of the governments and commanders they served. Various international treatises were invoked to establish the idea of crimes against humanity. Such arguments as were presented often implicitly invoked the idea of a natural law, and associated human rights inhering in individuals, which stand above any particular state's power and therefore should act as a restraint upon, and as a standard by which to judge, their conduct. More recently, Martin Luther King in his campaign for civil rights in America, the Solidarity movement in Poland, the liberation theology of Roman Catholic priests in Central America, and Pope John Paul II, in emphasizing the dignity of humanity, have all appealed to notions of the natural law or a higher law to condemn the actions of those whom they believe to be acting inhumanely and unjustly. King, for example, exhorted his fellow Americans to emulate the spiritual dissenters of the revolutions: 'giving our ultimate allegiance to the empire of justice, we must be that colony of dissenters seeking to imbue our nation with the ideals of a higher and nobler order'.[27]

It was H. G. Wells and his associates, including J. B. Priestley and A. A. Milne, who revived the idea of natural rights in the public consciousness, suggesting that, since birth is an accidental occurrence, as a matter of justice everyone ought to have access to food, shelter, clothing, education, access to information and freedom of discussion as a minimum to the realization of his or her potential. In addition each person should enjoy security of person and property. In an immensely successful Penguin Special in 1939, translated into thirty languages and serialized in newspapers throughout the world, Wells launched devastating attacks on Stalin and Hitler, maintaining that only a reassertion of individual rights, protected by international law rather than diplomacy, can act as a safeguard against totalitarianism.[28] The preservation of human rights officially became a war aim in 1942.

The Roosevelts were immensely moved by Wells's arguments and it was the Americans who were responsible for giving human rights such a prominent place in the UN Charter. The Universal Declaration, as Eleanor Roosevelt made clear, was not meant to be a treaty or international agreement, and placed no legal obligations on states. It was the Convention on the Prevention and Punishment of Genocide, which came into force in 1951, which was to have that status.

Except at the level of rhetoric, the justification of the human rights we are said to hold today is not to be found in natural rights or in most modern cosmopolitan theories, which often have only a tenuous link with current realities. The legal and political practices which emphasize the conventional and contingent character of human rights cannot be dismissed or ignored in the name of moral purity.

It is, of course, testimony to the inadequacy of the UN to deliver an effective human rights culture that regional arrangements emerged and even provided alternative routes to the redress of grievances in Europe, America and Africa, but these, too, require governmental acceptance, without which their citizens simply do not have the rights. The most effective of the regional arrangements, the European Convention on Human Rights, which has now been incorporated into British law, was established by the Council of Europe, and streamlines into a two-stage judicial process the enforcement mechanisms of the Commission and European Court at Strasbourg. This, however, covers only signatories. Indeed, not only does the preamble to the Convention not even feign universalism – it is quite explicit that like-minded western European states sharing a common heritage involving 'political traditions, ideals, freedoms, and the rule of law' have agreed upon certain standards that must be maintained by those states who wish to subscribe to them[29] – but also the human rights promulgated in the Convention are not even universal within their European context because of the political sensitivities of different states. Freedom of speech, therefore, means different things in different countries when filtered through the principle of 'the margin of appreciation'. Nevertheless, the first article of the European Convention charges 'Contracting Parties' to secure the stated rights and freedoms to everyone within their jurisdiction, and it does have the treaty power to compel compliance with its rulings, which often means compelling a change in domestic law, unless a state formally 'derogates' from the Convention in preference to accepting an unpalatable ruling.

The human rights culture is one to which states subscribe, not without considerable pressure from governmental and non-governmental agents alike. It is based on the principle of opting in, and until such time as the various conventions are explicitly adopted by governments, their citizens are effectively excluded from having such rights. There is a nascent principle of humanitarian intervention, but only for the most serious crimes against humanity, and then only on a very selective basis. Almost thirty years after the Universal Declaration of Human Rights, the International Covenant on Civil and Political Rights came into force (1976), with little superpower support. The USA, for example, did not ratify the Covenant until 1992, and states such as Cuba, Singapore, Malaysia, Indonesia and Pakistan still have not done so. The all-important accompanying Optional Protocol, which gives individuals the right to complain of human rights violations to the Human Rights Committee, has attracted very few signatories. Even signing this Protocol does not signify a willingness to co-operate with the Human Rights Committee or implement its decisions. As Geoffrey Robertson remarks: 'There is no "universality" about this human rights system.'[30]

At the intergovernmental level the discourse of human rights is by and large conducted in the language of consensus, convention and quasi-legal agreement. The human rights culture is very much based upon the principle of the rule of law, and assumes no philosophical foundations. Legal discussions of human rights begin where philosophical discussions end. There has been, in Michael Ignatieff's words, a 'juridical revolution' in the international protection of individuals.[31] Peter R. Baehr, for example, contends that 'human rights are internationally agreed values, standards or rules regulating the conduct of states towards their own citizens and towards non-citizens'.[32] They are self-imposed rules, or international standards that are not absolute. They may come into conflict with each other and have to be weighed against each other in any relevant practical situation. The final declaration of the Vienna Conference of 1993 at first appeared to affirm the universality of human rights, but then severely qualified it by certain particularistic considerations. It stated: 'the significance of national and regional particularities and various historical, cultural and religious backgrounds must be borne in mind'.[33]

The international lawyer Owen M. Fiss argues that human rights are not derived from a common understanding of human nature, nor are they deduced philosophically from first principles. They are instead the articulation of aspirations immanent in a culture, a statement of what that society wants to become, and provide a standard by which to judge what is.[34] Ignatieff is suggesting something similar when he maintains that the principal function of human rights language is to highlight the gap between what we say and what we do. [35]

This, of course is the understanding we encountered in the Idealists. It is not an appeal to natural law or to legal positivism, but instead the recognition that moral rights – that is, the aspiration for what ought to be – which are immanent in society, precede their legal recognition. In one of the most widely read books on the international protection of human rights, the authors suggest that 'only when the process of law making has taken place can any "new human right" move from the realm of aspiration'.[36] This is not to deny that the aspiration may have moral force. As Amy Gutmann suggests, if we believe that human rights are important instruments for the protection of human beings against oppression, cruelty and degradation, that is all we need to believe in order to defend them.[37]

Nevertheless, at the level where human rights are being violated, the rhetorical survival of the natural rights tradition is deeply embedded in the everyday currency of the human rights culture, which to some extent accounts for the high expectations of those who buy into it. Typically we are said to possess human rights by the mere fact that we are human, and they are commonly described as absolute, imprescriptible and inalienable. They are independent of governments, and indeed our safeguard against them.

In sum, the modern human rights culture comprises historical populations of loosely cohering theories, conventions and practices, which at the practical level exhibit little coherence or logical connection, which is not to deny the political impact of such ideas. If the human rights embedded in this culture are not to be accused of being arbitrary, how are we to account for and justify them if they have become severed from the natural rights tradition?

Constitutive theory and human rights

Attempts to get around the difficulty of finding firm foundations for human rights have centred upon various forms of conventionalism or constructivism, some of which are explicitly indebted to the Hegelian tradition out of which the British Idealists emerged, and others of which rely upon constitutive theories which are neo-Hegelian and communitarian in their leanings. In the first group are such normative theorists of international relations as Terry Nardin, Mervyn Frost and Chris Brown, and the philosophers Alan Milne and Charles Taylor. In the latter group we find such international relations theorists as Janna Thompson, Andrew Linklater and Peter Sutch. Among the philosophers are David Miller, Rex Martin, John Charvet and Richard Rorty, and even the later Rawls. In other words, there is an attempt to get away from the suggestion that human rights are possessed by humans by the mere fact of being human, or that they in any way predate political society because they have some divine or natural origin. Instead, it is suggested that with human progress, standards of behaviour among individuals have become more civilized, and that these civilized standards have become extended to broader and broader communities. It is the sense of overlapping communities where standards employed within one become extended into others by a process of recognizing others to be the same as us. By this I mean that certain standards of civility within classes or communities become more generalized as a result of recognizing others. This effectively means that guarantees of the rights of citizens are taken to be the prerequisite for human rights, rather than human rights providing the guarantee of rights of citizenship. In their different ways, the thin universals of Michael Walzer, David Miller, John Rawls and even Richard Rorty arise out of and are embedded in the thick particulars of specific cultures possessing a moral integrity and status of their own. Charles Taylor, Amy Gutmann and Michael Ignatieff agree that a human rights regime ought to be compatible with value pluralism and therefore cannot be anchored to any one version of foundationalism. Gutmann is more insistent than the other two that human rights need not deny all foundations. It is preferable for pragmatic and moral reasons that human rights rely on a variety of foundational arguments. In other words, 'an overlapping consensus is more compatible with moral pluralism'.[38]

The propensity, then, is to take the human rights culture as it is and ask not what human rights there ought to be but, instead, in Rex Martin's terms: exactly what does it mean to have a human right in this context?[39] Ignatieff puts the question slightly differently: 'if human rights is a set of beliefs, what does it mean to believe in it?'[40] What I want to suggest is that modern constitutive theory – the type of theorizing that British Idealists engaged in, but without the metaphysics – is better grounded as the philosophical basis of the modern human rights culture and provides better justification for adherence to principles of universal human rights than do theories which construct aspirational ideals from outside of the practices they seek to regulate.

The arguments of Brian Barry and Peter Singer for a fairer redistribution of resources to less well-off nations is an approach which makes deductions from first principles, and such considerations as the feasibility of their attainment do not deter their authors from drawing the full logical implications of their arguments. These are what may be called aspirational theories, and a long way from what Rawls calls 'realistic utopias'. Often we are not as such offered ethical theories. Usually we are presented with something to which it is is said that everyone would agree, and if we agree to that, then we must also agree to something else which is said to rest on the same principle. To argue that such widespread redistribution as Singer and Barry suggest is unlikely to come about is considered irrelevant to the argument. 'Since justice has never been prominent in the relations between states in the past, or in the internal arrangements of the great majority of states for that matter, why should we expect it suddenly to begin to do so now?'[41] When such a cavalier attitude is taken to the actual practices of states and there is such disregard for practicalities such as getting people to accept the principle of large-scale redistribution, it is logic that is likely to be the casualty. If the logic of an argument leads us to such radical restructuring, the politician may argue, then let's forget about logic. In the case of devolution within the United Kingdom, for example, logic would dictate that all three regional assemblies ought to have the same powers on grounds of equity. It was clear, however, in the Welsh case, that Ron Davies, the Welsh Secretary, would not be able to deliver a yes vote in Wales if tax-raising powers were included in the devolution proposals formulated in consultation throughout the first Blair Labour government. To hold out for the same powers as Scotland would have meant no devolution for Wales.

In their different ways such political theorists as Richard Rorty, Michael Ignatieff, Rex Martin, Michael Walzer, John Rawls and Charles Taylor, and international relations theorists such as Chris Brown and Mervyn Frost, and even Hedley Bull, take as their starting points what it means in the current international context to possess a human right, and go on to show in what sense they can be universally applicable and more effective against international injustice. Let me illustrate this move towards constitutive theory, or conventionalism in the construction of human rights, by taking examples from both international relations theorists and political theorists of international relations.

Hedley Bull, in acknowledging that international order must be premised on some conception of international justice, which includes respect for human rights, was relying not upon foundational arguments based on an omnipotent Creator or on a universal human nature as the source of such conceptions, but instead upon the practical and pragmatic idea of consensus or moral constructivism. Order itself is considered a good, or norm, worth promoting and preserving because of its beneficial consequences. The achievement of order may be facilitated by incorporating justice and human rights into the scale of international values, but without a consensus on these norms the international order itself may be put in jeopardy. In other words, order, to use Dworkin's terminology, may trump justice and rights on the scale of values, and militate against humanitarian intervention in the absence of consensus. This is clearly acknowledged by Ignatieff,[42] and is implicit in the work of all commissions of reconciliation which seek to restore order without necessarily administering justice to the victims or their families.

Bull recognizes that the international society of which he speaks is not solidarist enough at present to overcome the tension between state sovereignty and non-intervention, on the one hand, and the principle of humanitarian intervention, on the other. There is an extreme reluctance at the international level even to entertain the possibility of conceding a right of humanitarian intervention to states, and little agreement on what human rights actually are.[43] The extension of the moral community, in the sense of its becoming more solidarist and being able to act in unity to promote justice and protect human rights, is a matter for Bull of attaining consensus, and is the basis of a gradual and progressive negotiation of terms of reference.

Again in the theory of international relations, John Vincent has identified three levels at which rights operate internationally: the individual, the state and non-state organizations. It is the state, however, which dominates in terms of being the repository of rights and the location of obligation. Individuals and non-state organizations are not free-floaters inhabiting a plane above communities and states. Individuals derive their identities from being members of communities which are themselves subsumed under the auspices of states. Citizenship is part of what it means to be human because there is no global *polis*. This is why the plight of refugees is taken so seriously because the loss of citizenship rights in one state, whether by fleeing its borders, or by being stripped of them by governments, is accompanied by no guarantee that other states will accept such 'displaced persons' and re-institute them into humanity.[44]

Mervyn Frost and Chris Brown, for example, employ a demythologized or secular Hegelianism in order to establish the point that, in order for rights to function, certain conditions have to pertain which together comprise an ethical community. What is presupposed in this general liberal account of the individual is that human nature is universal. Constitutive theory, on the other hand, thinks human nature circumstantial. Brown, for instance, suggests that '[h]uman beings live in different kinds of groups and these different types of group create different kinds of individuals'.[45] Human nature is a product of the different social formations in which people find themselves. The role of politics in this formative process is much more pronounced in constitutive theory than in liberalism. A political structure is part of the social fabric that shapes individuals. Thus republicanism as a political structure provides the conditions constitutive of republicans. In order to avoid the charge of conservativism, constitutive theory needs to show how development and change can be incorporated into the theory without presupposing an ahistorical pre-social individual as the reference point. What Frost and Brown retain of Hegelianism is the idea that the self is constituted by the relationships in which it stands to the family, civil society and the state. In other words, the self is nothing outside of the social relationships that have served to form it. Similarly, the settled norms – what Hegel called *Sittlichkeit* – or customary morality, both implicit and explicit, in the relations among states can, for Frost, be explained in terms of constitutive theory in a way that alternative background theories, such as the contractarian rights-based theories or utilitarianism, cannot because of their inability to reconcile norms of sovereignty with human rights norms, both of which are integral to modern international relations. The privileging of human rights over sovereignty in cosmopolitan theories simply does not square with the discourse or norms of the modern state system. Constitutive Hegelianism does not acknowledge a conflict between human rights and state sovereignty, because both are part of and arise from the social practice of international relations.[46] It seems to me that the basic point of what Frost is getting at is this. Irrespective of the reasons we may give for saying that morality cannot be grounded in any firm foundations, or that the realities of power and politics militate against the appropriateness of moral considerations in the behaviour of states, it is nevertheless the case that there are shared moral assumptions that are explicitly appealed to, and we do have moral expectations not only of ourselves and other individuals but also of politicians and states. Such shared values have to be accounted for rather than explained away. While the foundations of ethical reasoning may not be of the type for which philosophy once hoped – in other words there may be plenty of reason to be sceptical about the foundations of ethics – this does not provide conclusive argument for desisting from talking about ethics altogether. Reasoning about ethics can take place on the basis of identifying shared premises. These normative issues can only arise in a domain of discourse in which they have meaning and are recognized as important problems. To those who do not belong to the domain of discourse, or do not subscribe to it, the issues do not arise.

A constitutive theory does not start with the premise that individuals are rightholders independently of the state, and that the state is somehow, often by means of contract, the instrument to protect those rights. Instead, individuals are seen to be constituted by the relationships, social and political, into which they enter, and the rights they possess are the products of these institutions.[47] Like Hegel, and of course Fukuyama, Frost stresses the importance of the role of recognition in the development of individuality. Individuals recognize and value each other in the context of social practices which serve to constitute the individuality of the person. Frost tries to show how selves are constituted through a hierarchy of social institutions including the family, civil society and the state.

Brown contends that constitutive theory can share with many cosmopolitans a commitment to human rights. These human rights, they claim, have to be realized in a state. It needs to be emphasized that the source of these rights is seen to be the various communities which give them expression. In other words, the individual does not possess them independently of the community.

It is quite common among those who deny the ethical significance of a cosmopolitan community to argue that much closer ties of kinship or group solidarity generate the obligations we have to others. Frost believes that quite a thick conception of international morality is manifest in the settled norms of the modern states system, even to the extent of supplying answers to difficult ethical questions. Whereas Michael Walzer, David Miller and John Rawls, for example, argue that there is no consensus that the needs of other humans simply in their capacity as humans impose any obligations of justice upon us – indeed, there is insufficient consensus on what counts as a need – but there are principles which constitute a thin universalism, even if they are not determinate enough to offer guidance in specific situations. The universal principles that we recognize, such as those relating to human rights, have arisen in the course of our encounters with other peoples whom we acknowledge to be making similar claims to our own, this acknowledgement itself being a moral act. Moral minimalism depends upon 'the fact that we have moral expectations about the behavior not only of our fellows but of strangers too. And they have overlapping expectations about their own behavior and ours as well.'[48]

To include Rawls among the company of constitutive communitarians is by no means eccentric. Sibyl A. Schwarzenbach goes as far as to suggest that the early Rawls of *A Theory of Justice* employs much of the structure of Hegel's political theory while jettisoning the metaphysics.[49] Rawls argues that, within constitutional democracies, the aim of political philosophy is to achieve a political conception of justice through overlapping consensus which can be publicly justified and is stable over generations. There are three principal features: first, it is a moral conception in that it is concerned with how the main political institutions or basic structure coheres and contributes to social co-operation; second, it is not a comprehensive or perfectionist doctrine, in that its concern is with the basic structure of society, thus it is able to accommodate a variety of comprehensive doctrines and conceptions of the good; and, third a political conception of justice has recourse to those ideas which are immanent, or latent, in a democratic society's public political culture. The human rights endorsed by Rawls's political conception of justice operate on a different plane from those that arise from and are supported by comprehensive doctrines.

Charles Taylor has taken up Rawls's idea of an unforced overlapping consensus and applied it to the idea of human rights. What we need is not necessarily consensus on universal values, but consensus on norms of conduct which outlaw such things as genocide, slavery and torture. In order for there to be such a consensus there would have to be agreement on fundamental norms of behaviour, while at the same time acknowledging that the norms may be valued for very different and incompatible reasons from our own, which are anchored in quite different background views of theology, metaphysics and human nature.[50] The norms have to be enforceable on governments, have some philosophical justification and be enforced, that is, be articulated in the context of legal institutions. We cannot assume from the outset that a consensus is possible formulated in terms of rights, or some other universal value such as human dignity or well-being. Agreement at the level of norms of conduct is a useful first step but, unless there is mutual respect for what sustains them the agreement is liable to be fragile. This is because the agreement can never be complete, and when it comes to implementing norms, the different sustaining background ideas may have different practical effects on, for example, the ordering of such norms, and the attitudes we express. The place of indignation, anger, punishment and righteous condemnation is different with Thai Reform Buddhism and western humanism. This may involve coming to some compromise version of the interpretation of norms that requires mutual respect and understanding if they are to be acceptable to both sides. Second, disagreements may lead to a breakdown in the consensus, which may need to be renegotiated, which is impossible without mutual respect. We in the West have to reconcile ourselves to the fact that the route that we took which led to human rights is not the route that other societies will take. Taylor argues that 'world convergence will not come through a loss or denial of traditions all around, but rather by creative reimmersions of different groups, each in their own spiritual heritage, travelling different routes to the same goal'.[51]

This does not mean, of course, that human rights norms need be compatible with all value systems. There may be some that are abhorrent on any criteria, such as that of the Taliban in Afghanistan, which systematically deprived women of opportunities for self-realization, and irrevocably destroyed valued cultural artefacts incompatible with its beliefs. Amy Gutmann makes the sensible point that with proliferation of human rights the achievement of broader cultural assent becomes more difficult. In this respect they should not aspire to be guarantors of social justice or substitutes for comprehensive conceptions of the good.[52]

The thin universalism of which Walzer talks is the result of an historical process which has given rise to a moral minimum, far less specific than the norms that Frost detects, but settled norms nevertheless. When we act in ways which support this reiterative universalism, such as protesting in the name of justice against the human rights violations perpetrated by corrupt governments, we are affirming a '(partial) communality' which extends not to a full endorsement of the values of another culture, but merely to this thin shared communality.[53] Cultural pluralism is not a universal value or principle which has overlapping consensus; it is in fact the product of modern liberalism.

This minimum international morality amounts to the principles of self-determination (non-intervention), non-aggression and pluralism (the accommodation of tribalism within borders). Walzer's fundamental point is that the international community regards infringements of territorial and political sovereignty as self-evidently wrong. Sovereign integrity is ensured by the internationally accepted right of non-intervention, which is equivalent to the moral right of the individual to self-determination. Any infringements would therefore require extraordinary circumstances and special justifications. Given that the rationale of a state, in Walzer's view, is the protection of individual rights, particularly human rights, only gross infringements on a significant scale, for example genocide, would justify intervention if there are 'reasonable expectations of success'.[54] In such circumstances a state falls significantly below what the idea of statehood requires, and breaches the trust endowed upon it by its citizens in some form of social contract. Walzer concedes, however, that it is not always clear when a community is self-determining and thus entitled to claim the right of non-intervention.

Ignatieff wants to jettison foundational arguments based on such ideas as natural law, human dignity, equality of creation, and the like. Instead, the purpose of human rights, for him, is to sustain human agency. What is this if it is not a foundation? If the need for human rights to protect human agency is an indubitable reason, then that is all that is required for it to be a philosophical foundation. It is indeed the sort of foundation to which the Idealists appealed, but to it they added a developmental logic of reason which need not be part of any such justification. Ignatieff recognizes that human rights are not above politics, and that to imagine a globalized world that somehow supersedes state sovereignty is not only utopian but also dangerous. It is necessary to acknowledge the extent to which state sovereignty creates and sustains the international order within which national constitutional regimes provide the best guarantee of natural rights.[55] Rex Martin goes a step further in equating human rights with civil rights and making them dependent upon state recognition and enforcement.[56] The great human rights documents are addressed primarily not to individuals, although individuals are the beneficiaries, but to governments of states. In so far as this is the case, no account of human rights can ignore governmental practices of recognition and maintenance in characterizing them. Even rights *to* freedom from torture and injury claimed *against* individuals are also at once addressed to governments who are expected to protect and maintain these rights.

It is significant, then, at a time when many theorists such as John Hoffman, David Held and Andrew Linklater envisage a weakening of the state in favour of different and more internationally oriented configurations of authority, that the writers with whom I have been concerned and who have supported human rights with a form of constitutive theory seek to strengthen the constitutional state, as Hannah Arendt did, as the only hope of the salvation of humankind. Like the Idealists, they see the state as the sustainer of the moral community, and the most effective centre of authority to recognise, maintain and promote human rights and prosecute their violation.[57]

What is being suggested, then, is that modern constitutive theory is widely acknowledged and used to account better for the emergence of the human rights culture, and how we have the human rights we have, than either natural rights theories or the communitarian theories of the British Idealists. At the same time, it is recognized that these latter theories nevertheless forcefully put the case for understanding natural or human rights as those rights which are intelligible only in the context of a community that recognizes them as essential to social relations, and which are justified on the ground that they contribute to the common good.

Notes

This chapter is based upon the inaugural A. J. M. Milne Memorial lecture delivered at Durham University in November 2000. I would like to thank Julia Stapleton for inviting me to deliver the lecture and for giving me invaluable comments. I would also like to thank the Nuffield Foundation and the British Academy, who have generously supported my research on this project. I am also indebted to the editors for inviting me to contribute to this volume and for the conference at Cardiff that brought together the various contributors.

1   R. G. Collingwood, *An Autobiography*, with an introduction by S. Toulmin, Oxford: Oxford University Press, 1978, ch. VII.
2   J. Waldron, *Nonsense upon Stilts: Bentham, Burke and Marx on the Rights of Man*, London: Methuen, 1987, p. 155

3   R. Rorty, 'Human Rights, Rationality, and Sentimentality', in S. Shute and S. Hurley, eds, *On Human Rights*, New York: Basic Books, 1993, p. 115; M. Ignatieff, 'Human Rights', in C. Hesse and R. Post, eds, *Human Rights in Political Transitions: Gettysburg to Bosnia*, New York: Zone Books, 1999, p. 318.

4   R. Nozick, *Anarchy, State and Utopia*, Oxford: Blackwell, 1974, p. 5.

5   P. Jones, 'Human Rights', in D. Miller, J. Coleman, W. Connolly and A. Ryan, eds, *The Blackwell Encyclopaedia of Political Thought*, Oxford: Blackwell, 1991, p. 223.

6   P. Jones, 'International Human Rights: Philosophical or Political?', in S. Caney, D. George and P. Jones, eds, *National Rights, International Obligations*, Boulder, Colo.: Westview, 1996, p. 189.

7   H. L. A. Hart, 'Human Rights', in A. Bullock and S. Trombley, eds, *The New Fontana Dictionary of Modern Thought*, New York: HarperCollins, 1999, p. 405.

8   J. Dunn, *Locke*, Oxford: Oxford University Press, 1984, p. 31.

9   H. Arendt, *The Origins of Totalitarianism*, New York: Knopf, 1973.

10 Cited in J. A. Joyce, *The New Politics of Human Rights*, London: Macmillan, 1978, p. 7.

11 J. McCrystal, 'A Lady's Calling: Mary Astell's Notion of Women', *Political Theory Newsletter*, 1992, p. 4.

12 S. von Pufendorf, *On the Law of Nature and Nations* (1672, 1688 edn), trans. C. H. and W. A. Oldfellow, Oxford: Oxford University Press, 1934, book II, ch. iii, § 20.

13 S. von Pufendorf, *On the Duty of Man and Citizen*, trans. and ed. J. Tully, Cambridge: Cambridge University Press, 1991, book I, ch. 9, § 4.

14 J. Waldron, 'Introduction', in J. Waldron, ed., *Theories of Rights*, Oxford: Oxford University Press, 1984, p. 1.

15 Waldron, *Nonsense upon Stilts*, p. 63.

16 Ibid., p. 165.

17 M. Macdonald, 'Natural Rights', in Waldron, ed., *Theories of Rights*, p. 22.

18 P. Sutch, *Ethics, Justice and International Relations: Constructing an International Community*, London: Routledge, 2001.

19 D. Ritchie, 'Rationality of History', in *Collected Works*, vol. VI, *Miscellaneous Writings*, ed. P. Nicholson, Bristol: Thoemmes Press, 1998, p. 142.

20 D. Ritchie, 'Ethical Democracy: Evolution and Democracy', in D. Boucher, ed., *The British Idealists*, Cambridge: Cambridge University Press, 1997, p. 93.

21 F. H. Bradley, *Ethical Studies*, 2nd edn, Oxford: Oxford University Press, 1927, p. 116; T. H. Green, *Prolegomena to Ethics*, 4th edn, Oxford: Clarendon Press, 1899, §§ 183–4.

22 D. Ritchie, *The Principles of State Interference*, London: Swan Sonnenschein, 1891, p. 39.

23 T. H. Green, *Lectures on the Principles of Political Obligation*, London: Longmans Green, 1919, § 207.

24 D. Ritchie, *Natural Rights: A Criticism of Some Political and Ethical Conceptions*, London and New York: Sonnenschein, 1895, p. 103.

25 J. Watson, *The State in Peace and War*, Glasgow: Maclehose, 1919, pp. 222–3.

26 See, for example, M. Perry, *The Idea of Human Rights: Four Inquiries*, Oxford: Oxford University Press, pp. 11–41; and M. Stackhouse, 'Human Rights and Public Theology', in C. Gustafson and P. Juviler, eds, *Religion and Human Rights: Conflicting Claims*, Armonk, NY: Sharpe, 1999, p. 16.

27 Martin Luther King, *Where Do We Go From Here: Chaos or Community?*, New York: Harper and Row, 1967, pp. 157–8.

28 G. Robertson, *Crimes against Humanity*, Harmondsworth: Penguin, 2000, pp. 20–4.

29 A. J. M. Milne, *Human Rights and Human Diversity*, London: Allen and Unwin, 1986, p. 3.

30 Robertson, *Crimes against Humanity*, p. 53.

31 M. Ignatieff, *Human Rights as Political and Idolatory*, ed. A. Gutmann, Princeton: Princeton University Press, 2000, p. 5.

32 P. R. Baehr, *Human Rights: Universality in Practice*, London: Macmillan, 1999, p. 1.

33 Ibid., p. 10.

34 O. M. Fiss, 'Human Rights as Social Ideals', in Hesse and Post, eds, *Human Rights in Political Transitions*, pp. 273–4.

35 Ignatieff, 'Human Rights', in Hesse and Post, eds, *Human Rights in Political Transitions*, p. 323.

36 A. H. Robertson and J. G. Merrills, *Human Rights in the World*, Manchester: Manchester University Press, 1996, p. 296.

37 A. Gutmann, 'Introduction' to Ignatieff, *Human Rights*, p. xi.

38 Ibid., *Human Rights*, p. xix.

39 R. Martin, *A System of Rights*, Oxford: Clarendon Press, 1993, pp. 73–97. See also Rex Martin's chapter in the present volume.

40 Ignatieff, *Human Rights*, p. 53.

41 B. Barry, 'Spherical Justice and Global Injustice', in D. Miller and M. Walzer, eds, *Pluralism, Justice and Equality*, Oxford: Oxford University Press, p. 80.

42 Ignatieff, *Human Rights*.

43 H. Bull, 'The Universality of Human Rights', *Millennium*, 8, 1979, pp. 155–9; and T. Dunne, *Inventing International Society*, London: Macmillan, 1998, pp. 152–5.

44 J. Vincent, 'The Idea of Rights in International Ethics', in Terry Nardin and David Mapel, eds, *Traditions of International Ethics*, Cambridge: Cambridge University Press, 1992, p. 261. Also see J. Vincent, *Human Rights and International Relations*, Cambridge: Cambridge University Press, 1986. Of course, Hannah Arendt most famously addresses this problem in her *The Origins of Totalitarianism*.

45 C. Brown, 'The Ethics of Political Restructuring in Europe', in C. Brown, ed., *Political Restructuring in Europe*, London: Routledge, 1994, p. 168.

46 M. Frost, *Ethics in International Relations*, Cambridge: Cambridge University Press, 1996; and C. Brown, 'Universal Human Rights. A Critique', in T. Dunne and N. J. Wheeler, eds, *Human Rights in Global Politics*, Cambridge: Cambridge University Press, 1999, pp. 103–27. Cf Sutch, *Ethics, Justice and International Relations*, p. 126.

47 Frost, *Ethics in International Relations*, pp. 138–9; and C. Brown, *International Relations Theory: New Normative Approaches*, Hemel Hempstead: Harvester Wheatsheaf, 1992, p. 173.

48 M. Walzer, *Thick and Thin: Moral Arguments at Home and Abroad*, Notre Dame, Ind.: Notre Dame University Press, 1994, p. 17.

49 S. A. Schwarzenbach, 'Rawls, Hegel and Communitarianism', *Political Theory*, 19, 1991, p. 541.

50 C. Taylor, 'Conditions of an Unforced Consensus on Human Rights', in J. R. Bauer and D. A. Bell, eds, *The East Asian Challenge for Human Rights*, Cambridge: Cambridge University Press, 1999, p. 124.

51 Ibid., p. 144.

52 Gutmann, 'Introduction' to Ignatieff, *Human Rights*, pp. x–xi.

53 M. Walzer, *Just and Unjust Wars*, 2nd edn, New York: Basic Books, 1992, p. 17.

54 Ibid., p. 107.

55 Ignatieff, *Human Rights*, p. 35.

56 Martin, *A System of Rights*, and see his chapter in this volume.

57 J. Hoffman, *Beyond the State*, Cambridge: Polity, 1995; J. Hoffman, *Sovereignty*, Buckingham: Open University Press, 1998; A. Linklater, *Beyond Realism and Marxism*, London: Macmillan, 1990.

14 Reiterating rights

International society in transition

Peter Sutch

Politically and morally the problem of identifying the normative character of international politics is becoming more problematic, and more urgent, than ever before. The principle of sovereignty that we have used to shield international ethics from questions of cultural difference, or to deny transnational political responsibility, has changed and our normative frame of reference has changed with it. The constitution of international politics has not changed so much that issues of multiculturalism, identity and rights are the same in international political theory as they are in domestic political theory. But, with globalization, a growing refugee crisis and more calls for humanitarian intervention, the terms of these moral and political debates are beginning to overlap.

In this chapter I want to examine the most recent work of Michael Walzer. I turn to Walzer for a number of reasons. First, I admire the caution with which he treats both the politics of globalization and the ethical perspectives that we have come to group together under the label 'cosmopolitanism'. My main reason for this attitude is that Walzer's caution stems from a sensitivity towards the pace of moral and political change and an interesting grasp of the ways in which our moral and political lives are both separated and connected. Walzer offers a fascinating take on *how* and *why* the moral and political debates in domestic liberal political theory and international theory have come to overlap. Second, and more importantly, despite Walzer's trademark caution, I am not convinced by the arguments that his casuistical method is a way to do applied ethics without getting involved in political theory or that he is merely a conventionalist; that he is 'intrinsically conservative and that his just war theory, influential as it has been, merely serves as a kind of bandage over the real wound'.[1] Walzer's theory, and its range, is understated in his work. In this chapter I intend to restate it and argue that Walzer has the ability to offer a globalist theory that can accommodate cultural and political pluralism. Third, I want to explore how the tensions that are arising in our national-identity frameworks have contributed to what I hope to show is quite a remarkable transformation in Walzer's political theory.

Walzer on international justice: an unorthodox view

How can one present Walzer's theory of international justice? This question is at its most difficult when we are examining his political prescriptions, which appear to range from the consolidation of the nation state system to a radical reform of international society. Here I want to explore Walzer's more radical claims, such as his claim that the past injustices of world politics (the British empire or American or Soviet aggression) should be repaid, perhaps by 'far-reaching redistributions of wealth and resources'.[2] I want to examine these claims and see if there is one coherent theoretical underpinning that links them with his more conventionalist claims concerning the right to self-determination and inviolability of sovereignty, that is, with the established body of his work.[3] It is certainly the case that Walzer's pronouncements have grown more ambitious over the years. Indeed, the tension between his claim that '[a]ll in all, we cannot be happy with the current state of the world',[4] and the standard view of his work as strictly conventionalist seems too much to ignore. It is certainly true of the more radical aspect of Walzer's work, as Orend notes, that '[h]is most interesting and provocative contentions – like those concerning land transfers, international alimony payments and pacific unions – are only briefly mentioned, and then quickly set aside'.[5] Nevertheless there is enough consistency to his wish to reform international society to warrant a serious examination.

If we survey the range of Walzer's work, it seems that there is a tension between the claim that international justice hinges on the proliferation of nation states and the expansion of the nation state system, and his more recent claim that the best form of international society is characterized by what he terms 'the third degree of global pluralism', which, 'in its fully developed (ideal) version ... offers the largest number of opportunities for political action on behalf of peace, justice, cultural difference, and individual rights'.[6] This model incorporates national, regional and global political structures and places a heavy emphasis on the weakening of national sovereignty and the creation of 'alternative centres' capable of protecting and encouraging political and social identity, encouraging, as Walzer puts it, political possibility.[7]

I do not want to challenge the more conservative image of Walzer's political theory fully. The image of Walzer the advocate of sovereign independence and non-intervention in international affairs is correct (as far as it goes). Indeed, in the introduction to the third edition of *Just and Unjust Wars*, which was written nearly a quarter of a century after the work was first published, Walzer bemoans the fact that so little has changed in world politics. Nevertheless, there is another side to his theory, a more progressive side that has always sat uneasily with his conventionalist image. Without an adequate grasp of this side of Walzer's work we cannot understand the impact of his contribution to the most important debates of our time. My claim is that there is firm theoretical consistency between these sides of his work. The idea that I wish to examine is that the link between these contrasting views can be found in Walzer's distinctive approach to the issue of how universal political principles arise. The claim is that his understanding of what it is to have universal principles of justice has not changed but that the constitutive forces of international society have. All hinges, I think, on the nature and mode of international interconnectedness and on the creation and elaboration of identity in contemporary politics.

For a political theorist interested in world politics, Walzer's argument is immediately and intuitively engaging because it promises a universal theory that can explain the appeal of moral particularism[8] and the place of distinct (if not discrete) political communities. Such an approach offers to make sense of a world in which we are all keenly aware that political sovereignty is both a much cherished stalwart of world politics and the creaking hulk of the wreck of a political system that is leaking refugees. It is philosophically engaging because it promises to retell the story of universalism in a way that claims to avoid the pitfalls that beset much modern and virtually all cosmopolitan thinking.

At both of these points Walzer has been the object of much criticism. His emphasis on the necessity of particularist or communal 'thickness' to the everyday lives of the world's inhabitants and his subsequent defence of sovereignty and the principle of non-intervention has led to accusations of moral and political conservatism (for which read insensitivity) for over twenty-five years.[9] Similarly, the general view of liberal and cosmopolitan critics has been that there is a marked lack of substantive *theory* in Walzer's work; that he does not, and cannot, defend his conservatism or his occasional foray into universal (but very thin) human rights. Among his most strident critics are the cosmopolitan theorists Charles Beitz[10] and Thomas Pogge.[11] I think not only that their criticism of Walzer's justificatory theory is seriously misguided, but also that his general theory has brought him to a point at which he shares considerable political ground with cosmopolitans such as Pogge and Beitz. Walzer's theory is far more radical than a conventionalist defence of the status quo. His apparent communitarianism is to the cosmopolitan side of Rawls's *Law of Peoples*;[12] indeed, his theory is one step away from the ideal of a pacific federation found in the Kantian tradition.[13] Despite Walzer's own reticence in *Thick and Thin, The Company of Critics* or *Just and Unjust Wars*,[14] it is the logic of his theory of 'reiterative universalism' that has led him this way. In making these arguments, I want to begin to tease out the more radical side of Walzer's theory. I think his radicalism goes a long way beyond the moral minimum found in *Thick and Thin* or the amendments to the 'legalist paradigm' in *Just and Unjust Wars* that limit a state's right to self-determination. Ultimately I want to suggest that the force of Walzer's theory requires that we begin to rethink the dominant norms of international politics and ethics and the peremptory norms of international law (*Jus Cogens*). Far from being a statist with a 'sovereignty fixation', Walzer offers a vision of international society that has to change to become more politically effective and more tolerant towards lives 'without clear boundaries'.[15]

I am aware that this is an unusual reading of Walzer. It is part of an intellectual experiment that has two elements. First, I am trying to pull together under one conceptual framework the scattered parts of Walzer's theory of international justice and morality. This project is worthwhile in itself. I am convinced that Walzer is one of the most important and socially engaged political theorists writing today. I am also convinced that the standard view of his general theory does not tell the full story. This view can be summarized by drawing on Orend's recent book. He argues that,

> [w]hile Walzer does not ignore questions of international justice in general, it is clear that he does not devote much attention to them. Just war theory remains his overwhelming focus in international affairs. This is not, however, a mere difference in taste or relative expertise: it is rooted in his conviction that war remains the most significant interaction between states and so must be the main concern for theorists of international justice.[16]

I have no quarrel with Orend's analysis as far as it goes (in fact it is one of the few texts that explores the vital link between Walzer's just war theory and the moral theory laid out in *Thick and Thin*). However, Walzer has developed an important general theory of international justice. Just war is no longer his overwhelming focus in international affairs, as the legalist paradigm and the war convention (however amended) are no longer the most relevant or adequate tools in world politics. We use these tools to fight a rearguard action against the break-up of the old order of world politics, a break-up fostered by the actual mobility of people, businesses and their problems and the inability of the sovereign state system to deal adequately with this. Walzer acknowledges that war is still a big part of world politics, but war (at least the old-style national war) is no longer the most significant interaction between states. On the back of these arguments he has begun to focus his attention on the reform of the international system and the transcendence of the nation state system.

The second part of this intellectual experiment also serves as something of a safety net. If I am pulling Walzer's theory in directions that he does not want to fully explore (and I am reasonably confident that I am not), I am still convinced that this is the story about international politics that we should be telling. The problems we face in international affairs have changed and the principles and mechanisms we need to deal effectively with these new problems have to change, and are beginning to do so. The task of the social critic, it seems, is to tell the story of this transitional period in a way that helps us to manage it in the most effective and just manner.

Just and unjust wars: Walzer and the first degree of global pluralism

In his paper 'Governing the Globe: What Is the Best We Can Do?' Walzer presents us with the image of a continuum of ideal types or models of international society (see figure below). On this continuum our current situation is most accurately modelled by the first degree of global pluralism, one step in

from the right side and international anarchy. This is also where we find the
Walzer of *Just and Unjust Wars*, the defender of non-intervention. Caricatured
cosmopolitans favour a global state, but the more reasonable cosmopolitans,
such as Beitz and Pogge, tend to favour the federation model, as did Kant.[17]
Interestingly both Beitz and Pogge will, when pushed, accept something like
the third degree of global pluralism model which is Walzer's ideal (in the sense
of best).[18] These opposing forces arrive at the same position from different
sides of the continuum. This is not to say that any compromise is automatically
possible. While their political prescriptions may be similar, their disagreement
at the level of theory is total. The cosmopolitans rely upon the strong Kantian
idea that interdependence triggers our dormant obligations to the rest of
humanity,[19] a position that has philosophical difficulties and tends to push
them towards the stronger and, argues Walzer, more dangerous federative
ideal.[20] But my point is that Walzer can be seen to share political ground with
the cosmopolitans.

From the left side ———▶

UNITY: Global State/Multinational Empire/Federation\3rd degree\2nd degree\1st degree of global pluralism\Anarchy: DIVISION

◀——— From the right side

The Continuum

Source: Walzer, 'Governing the Globe', p. 50

    This, of course, is quite some claim. Walzer is more usually thought of as a
defender of national self-determination, non-intervention and, most recently, a
very thin but universal 'moral minimum' that serves principally to justify his
apparent communitarianism and statism. I have no quarrel with this as an interpretation of the main body of his work. However, if we explore the character of
his position here it becomes clear that the potential to move beyond the nation
state system was always present.
    The key to understanding the potential in Walzer's theory is the idea of
reiteration, which finds its fullest expression in *Thick and Thin*. The idea of reiteration, or reiterative universalism, is extremely important in Walzer's moral
theory as it is the vehicle by which we move (albeit temporarily in Walzer's first
instalment of his theory) from particularism to universalism and therefore from
international anarchy to the first degree of global pluralism. It is also the
concept that leads him in his most recent work to argue for what he calls the
third degree of global pluralism. Reiterative universalism can most readily be
understood if we contrast it with covering-law universalism (and here covering-
law universalism is what we usually refer to when we talk of universalism). The
reiterative way in which we arrive at the formulation of the universal law is

distinctly communitarian. We abstract from the particular to the universal through repeated experience of shared political problems. Walzer argues, 'perhaps the end product of this effort will be a set of standards to which all societies can be held – negative injunctions, most likely, rules against murder, deceit, torture, oppression, and tyranny'.[21] This all sounds very optimistic, but Walzer's initial position is not so upbeat. He argues that the very thing that allows us to form these minimalist positions necessarily prevents them from developing into maximalist ones.

> Reiterative universalism can always be given a covering-law form. ....But these are covering laws of a special sort: first, they are learned from experience, through a historical engagement with otherness ... second, because they are learned in this way they impose upon us a respect for particularity.[22]

Walzer does not believe that all agents make 'thick' or sustained assumptions, and so his conclusions are casuistical rather than transcendental. In essence he argues that we do make such globalist assumptions but only in the context of international political crises, and that we do not go on to incorporate these assumptions into the moral hierarchy of our everyday lives. The character of international society and the way we (as citizens of sovereign states) confront each other in the international sphere have historically limited the effectiveness of the reiterative process.

International society, writes Walzer, is the most tolerant of all forms of society.[23] This is not an expression of admiration but rather a consequence of the 'good fences make good neighbours' thesis.

> Sovereignty guarantees that no one on *that* side of the border can interfere with what is done on *this* side. The people over there might be resigned, indifferent, curious, or enthusiastic with regard to practices over here, and so may be disinclined to interfere. Or perhaps they accept the reciprocal logic of sovereignty: we won't worry about your practices if you don't worry about ours. Live and let live is a relatively easy maxim when the living is done on the opposite side of a clearly marked line. Or they may be actively hostile, eager to denounce their neighbor's culture and customs, but unprepared to pay the costs of interference. Given the nature of international society, the costs are likely to be high: They involve raising an army, crossing a border, killing and being killed.[24]

International justice is not a universalist ethic in the traditional sense. It is a product of a recognition of a multiplicity of claims to justice as a series of family resemblances, a distillation of what it means to have a claim to justice. It is a consensus on a minimalist position that is not sufficient to guide our lives but that recognizes each family resemblance for what it is, a glimpse of oneself in a totally separate 'other'.

We stand where we are and learn from our encounters with other people. What we learn is that we have no special standing; the claims that we make they make too ... . But it is a moral act to recognize otherness this way. If reiteration is, as I believe, a true story, then it carries in its telling the sorts of moral limits that are usually said only to come from covering-law universalism.[25]

Nevertheless it is important to note 'that what is recognized is just this (partial) commonality, not the full moral significance of the other cultures. Most people most of the time do not see the others, in context, as carriers of value; most people are not pluralists.'[26] For Walzer, cultural pluralism is a part of liberal maximalism, 'a thickly developed liberal politics'. Reiterative universalism in this first stage of the development of international society relies on something much weaker, on 'overlapping expectations' about the behaviour of others.[27]

Walzer argues that in the contemporary international system 'rights are only enforceable within political communities where they have been collectively recognized ... the globe is not, or is not yet, such an arena. Or rather the only global community is pluralist in character, a community of nations, not of humanity.'[28] Yet for Walzer the concept of individual rights is also central to the minimalist morality created in response to the problems of international relations. These values are not good in themselves. Walzer argues that 'the value of minimalism lies in the encounters it facilitates, of which it is also the product. But these encounters are not – not now, at least – sufficiently sustained to produce a thick morality.'[29] Nevertheless, Walzer believes that they both do important work in international politics. We develop a reiteratively universal standpoint to judge them from, a perspective from which a global ethics is a possibility and from where the right of sovereign powers to go to war or to act in certain ways towards their citizens in the name of *raison d'état* is limited. It is on this basis that Walzer develops the six propositions and five revisions that make up the legalist paradigm and, later, in *Thick and Thin*, states his case for the centrality of a 'thin' version of human rights.

These rules are constructed from within our social context, and while they may be framed as 'covering laws', they are historically conditioned and certainly not sufficient to mould a maximalist account of international ethics. The rights to life and liberty are, however, based on a commonly held perception (or a family of perceptions) of what it means to be a human being. Nations (domestically) and states (in the international sphere) are products of moral and political reasoning and producers of moral and political reason, the fount of our understandings of the moral reality of international politics. In an uncharacteristically optimistic moment, Walzer outlines the full range and derivation of his international theory, and it is worth quoting him at some length here.

These two arguments – first for what might be called the moral usefulness of the (nation-)state and the solidarity it generates, and second for the possible legitimacy of the citizenship/ethnicity or citizenship/culture connection – do not commit those who accept them to resign themselves to the 'drastic inequalities' of international society. They only require that the fight against those inequalities begin within existing political communities and that it aim at the progressive expansion, but not the abolition, of existing solidarities. ....They embody ... the admission of refugees to full citizenship; increased foreign aid, economic unification, and cooperation across borders; multilateral political and, if necessary, military interventions for humanitarian purposes; extensions of sovereignty to stateless persons; experiments in regional devolution and transnational agency. And the motive for all this can only be the hope of ordinary people in their diverse national, religious, and political communities for their own survival and well-being, and for that of their neighbours, under conditions of peace and justice.[30]

Walzer's method does not have the capacity to demand these reforms in world politics, but he is suggesting that these actions are already considered a part of the necessary framework for international survival and well-being. His reiterative universalism is intended to describe the basic reasons that can be given for this recognition, and his optimism grows in his most recent work.

Despite this optimism, Walzer is still firmly of the opinion that international society remains limited to this first degree of global pluralism. The nation state (or religious republic) is where and how most groups would prefer to be tolerated. Peoples, particularly those who are under threat, culturally or politically, aim for sovereignty 'with governments, armies, and borders, co-existing with other nation-states in mutual respect'.[31] For those seeking a kind of political sanctuary, this makes historical and political sense. But for those of us who seek international justice, the current organization of international society causes more problems than it solves. This tension is not just a tension in Walzer's theory; it is not Walzer the communitarian theorist versus Walzer the bleeding-heart academic. This tension characterizes our experience of world politics. What Walzer offers is a case for the development of international society beyond the nation state system (and beyond the UN system of international politics that is not so far removed from this model) that recognises the appeal of national sovereignty as well as its intrinsic dangers. The crux of the issue can be set out as follows. We have learned that we must respect the integrity of sovereign peoples, yet we have also learned, or at the very least are beginning to learn, that sovereignty necessarily establishes illegitimate moral and political boundaries. It is often the case that, by structurally encouraged act and omission, the intolerable is tolerated in international society.

Walzer recognized this problem early on in his career, and this is why the issues surrounding intervention have been so important to him. I do not want to explore Walzer's theory of legitimate intervention here. His views on this subject are well known and, in any case, such an exploration would take us away from our principal concern in this chapter. What I wish to examine is Walzer's understanding of the constitutive norms of international society, which once prioritized the principle of self-determination (as a matter of practical ethics) but now criticize such prioritization. The moral problem that seems to weigh heavily upon contemporary world politics is that, while

> [a]cts or practices that 'shock the conscience of mankind' are, in principle not tolerated ... [h]umanitarian intolerance is not usually sufficient to override the risks that intervention entails, and additional reasons for intervening – whether geopolitical, economic, or ideological – are only sometimes available.[32]

It is the weakness of international political structures in the face of reiteratively established norms or thin, minimalist principles that leads Walzer to advocate a renovated international society capable of supporting the third degree of global pluralism.

Reiterated norms and the case for the third degree of global pluralism

Characteristically, Walzer's reiterated moral minimum is very thin. Essentially this is because he is so wary of the intellectual hegemon that is liberal cosmopolitanism and the 'tyrannical potential' of powerful political regimes who offer aid in return for imitation. This concern is still a significant part of his thinking and the reason why he resists all pressure from the left side of his continuum of international societal models.[33] The key to Walzer's new theory, his argument in favour of finding political expression for a sustained moral minimum (a major move away from the typical Walzerian position), lies in the reiterated recognition that the nation state system simply cannot deal appropriately with the crises it faces. The system has come under sustained pressure from all sides. It is clear to us that the existing system of semi-impervious political boundaries is unhelpful. Border disputes, wars of secession, civil wars, ethnic cleansing – these are very familiar consequences of the current division of the world's territories. We might not know what to do about Rwanda, eastern Europe or Palestine, but we are aware that the nation-building projects that have forged these conflicts are part of the problem rather than part of the solution. From the opposite direction, the globalization of the world's economy and migration, in all its political and economic forms, is calling into question the utility and the justice of the nation state system. Again, the issues are huge but we can be sure that nation building (in both the territorial sense and the sense in which Kymlicka articulates the formation of national identity[34]) is unhelpful. That this is a position that can be ascribed to Walzer would undoubtedly come as a shock to many of his critics.

Let me unpack this last paragraph a little. The concept that is doing all the work here is still moral reiteration. The way that Walzer presented this idea in *Thick and Thin* stressed the temporary and casuistical nature of the moral minimum. We make urgent moral judgements in times of great crisis. Over time we develop a stock of reiterated judgements that we use to deal with each crisis as it arises. However, we do not incorporate such judgements into the thick moral fabric of our everyday lives. The reason we do not incorporate these judgements into our moral maximalisms stems from two interrelated roots. First, we are only called upon to make these universal moral judgements in unusual circumstances. The most sustained range of international judgements we make have related to the just cause and conduct of war. The relative thickness of the legalist paradigm and the war convention stand as testimony to this.[35] The decisions we make here are relevant only to an extreme situation and are therefore of limited use to us in the conduct of our everyday lives. Even the very thin universal moral principle of 'the rights to life and liberty' upon which the legalist paradigm is predicated find better expression in our separate moral maximalisms. 'The minimal demands we make on one another are, when denied, repeated with passionate insistence. In moral discourse, thinness and intensity go together, whereas with thickness comes qualification, compromise, complexity and disagreement.'[36]

The reason these principles find better expression in our thick everyday lives is related to the second point. The political context in which we make these decisions is very different from the context in which we live our everyday lives. Historically we have chosen to value our separate ways of life by privileging the principles of sovereignty and non-intervention, and the sorts of moral and political judgements we make in international politics are contorted to fit this model. Again we would make different and more effective decisions in our everyday lives, decisions that simply could not be entertained in international politics. But this is changing. Or at least this is what Walzer must be claiming if his new theory is to hold water. The sorts of crisis that we find intolerable and feel impelled to act upon are becoming (or have become) a fixture in our political lives, and the political constitution of international society has adapted to the point where the basic assumptions of sovereignty, non-intervention, self-determination and of the anarchical society do not make sense of our moral and political commitments. In short, we have reiterated and shared reasons for needing to change the shape of world politics.

An argument of this sort would not, I think, be a new departure for Walzer. Indeed, I think he underplayed the potential of the reiterative process in his earlier work. He did so because he wanted to highlight the fact that we need to let it happen in its own time. Forcing the issue corrupts the reiterative process. The image of the social critic in Walzer's earlier work is that of a person who is 'hanging in there'[37] waiting for the appropriate moment to steer international society towards a brighter future. For Walzer, this is the pattern that political morality takes.

If principles determine decisions, decisions in turn modify and refine principles: This is the way that both law and morality change over time. And
in this process it is not only the judgment of authoritative decisions that
count but [the judgment of all citizens].[38]

Walzer's claim must be that now the time is right to begin to steer international society towards a new political constitution. This claim is predicated on
a reading of international politics that claims that the way the peoples of the
world confront one another in this now politicized arena has changed significantly over time. Most importantly Walzer's argument is that neither the
nation state (the most intolerant of all societal structures[39]) nor international
society as currently constituted (the most tolerant) is practical or just enough
for our contemporary international political needs. This argument must be
predicated on the claim that our thin, reiteratively universal understanding of
human rights to life and liberty has thickened up in significant ways to become
a key part of our moral justificatory framework.

Statehood and toleration in a multicultural world

For Walzer, the modern project can be characterized as the search for 'collective toleration', which incorporates a struggle for boundaries.

> The crucial slogan of this struggle is 'self determination,' which implies
> the need for a piece of territory or, at least, a set of independent institu-
> tions – hence, decentralization, devolution, autonomy, partition,
> sovereignty. Getting the boundaries right, not only in geographic but also
> in functional terms, is enormously difficult, but it is necessary if the
> different groups are to exercise significant control over their own lives and
> to do so with some security.[40]

The key to this project, and the key to all of Walzer's political theory up until
his most recent work, is the need to recognize that membership in specific
groups is the basis of life in a differentiated world. In this model the nation
state is the core unit. The nation-building projects that fostered this development have given this, the most intolerant of political structures, the central role
in our domestic lives and have also given rise to the nation state system in
international politics, which Walzer characterizes as the most tolerant (indeed
as far too tolerant). As the key to Walzer's 'communitarianism' and as the key
to a description of how modern politics has developed, I find this position
compelling. However, just as compelling is Walzer's claim that both the intolerance of the nation state and the super-tolerance of the nation state system of
international politics have outlived their usefulness; that the modern project is
drawing, or should be drawing, to a close.

This argument rests on a strong claim about the ways in which we confront
others at a national, regional and international level. At the national level,

states are increasingly coming under pressure from within and pressure from without. From the inside, the disturbingly random way in which geopolitical boundaries have been drawn has led to secessionist movements and ethnic conflict. From the outside, immigrant pressure, from the fall-out from these conflicts and from the increased economic need for mobility has, Walzer suggests, led to the increasing recognition that the nation state has practical limitations. It seems that intolerance has become, in many vital ways, intolerable. Non-intervention makes no sense in light of our intolerance towards ethnic cleansing. Nation building (again in Kymlicka's sense, which Walzer adopts for his description[41]) makes no sense of, or rather cannot make full sense of, our experience of the world.

> In immigrant societies (and also now in nation-states under immigrant pressure), people experience what we might think of as a life without boundaries and without secure or singular identities. Difference is, as it were, dispersed, so that it is encountered everywhere, everyday. The hold of groups on their members is looser than it has ever been. And the result is a constant intermixing of individuals, intermarriage, and a literal multi-culturalism, instantiated not only in the society as a whole but in each and every individual. Now tolerance begins at home, where we often have to make ethnic, religious, and cultural peace with our spouses, in-laws, and children – and with our own ambiguous (hyphenated or divided) selves.[42]

This blurring of the basic principles of national membership has developed alongside repeated or reiterated encounters with a burgeoning international society. In dealing with refugee crises, or national catastrophes such as the Kosovo conflict, or a rapidly developing international civil society, we have developed 'a plurality of international political and financial organizations, with a kind of authority that limits but doesn't abolish sovereignty'.[43] An international society with nation states existing next to international organizations such as the UN, the World Bank, the IMF and the World Trade Organization is familiar to us all, as are its limitations. As Walzer notes,

> [T]he global organizations are weak; their decision mechanisms are uncertain and slow; their powers of enforcement are difficult to bring to bear and, at best, only partially effective. Warfare between or among states has been reduced, but overall violence has not been reduced. There are many weak, divided, and unstable states in the world today, and the global regime has not been successful in preventing civil wars, military interventions, savage repression of political enemies, massacres and 'ethnic cleansing' aimed at minority populations. Nor has global inequality been reduced … .[44]

The reiterated facts of international politics are that the globalist institutions of international society are too weak and that retreat into the nation state is not the solution. With these reiterations come others. The 'ultra-minimal' rights to life and liberty arose through repeated encounters with separate 'others' in world politics. We did not incorporate any 'thick' understanding of these rights in our moral maximalisms because of the way they arose. It seems that this minimalist universalism found its best expression in a very thin account of human rights in and, in a vast plurality of ways, in our separate moral maximalisms. But the logic of the reiterative process does not stop here. Once established in the moral consciousness of international society, these principles become more than the recognition of some 'partial commonality' in a totally separate 'other'; they become a critical tool. The consequence of this is that we come to recognize that our thin, but intensely important, moral minimum no longer finds adequate expression in membership of a sovereign nation state in a loose international society.

Walzer's theoretical and political shift to globalism and universalism is extraordinary. But we must not over-egg the pudding. It must be noted that this reiterative process is not simply a matter of unilinear progress. What Walzer calls, somewhat guardedly, his post-modern project has not superseded the modern project. Rather,

> [t]he one is superimposed on the other, without in any way obliterating it. There are still boundaries but they are blurred by all the crossings. We still know ourselves to be this or that, but the knowledge is uncertain, for we are also this *and* that. Strong identity groups exist and assert themselves politically, but the allegiance of their members is measured by degrees, along a broad continuum, with larger and larger numbers clustered at the farther end (which is why the militants at the near end are so strident these days).[45]

The argument is not that we have abandoned the categories of *inter*national relations, or that we universally acknowledge that the values of membership, sovereignty and non-intervention are now defunct: while the 'solid lines on the old cultural and political maps are turned into dotted lines … coexistence along and across those lines is still a problem'.[46] But Walzer's universal morality does, he insists, offer arguments that underwrite an international society that 'would bring many of the advantages of a global federation but with greatly reduced risk of tyranny from the center'.[47] To appreciate the monumental shift in Walzer's political argument, consider the following description of his ideal form of international society.

> So the third degree of global pluralism requires a United Nations with a military force of its own capable of humanitarian interventions and a strong version of peacekeeping – but still a force that can only be used with the approval of the Security Council or a very large majority of the General Assembly. Then it requires a World Bank and IMF strong enough to regulate the flow of capital and the forms of international investment

and a World Trade Organization able to enforce labor and environmental standards – all these, however, independently governed, not tightly coordinated with the UN. It requires a World Court with power to make arrests on its own, but needing to seek UN support in the face of opposition from any of the (semi-sovereign) states of international society. Add to these organizations a very large number of civic associations operating internationally, including political parties that run candidates in different countries' elections and labor unions that begin to realize their long-standing goal of international solidarity, as well as single-issue movements aiming to influence simultaneously the UN and its agencies and the different states. The larger the membership of these associations and the wider their extension across state boundaries, the more they would knit together the politics of the global society. But they would never constitute a single center; they would always represent multiple sources of political energy; they would always be diversely focused.

Now add a new layer of governmental organization – the regional federation, of which the European Community is only one possible model. We can imagine both tighter and looser structures (but tighter is probably better for the control of global markets and multinational corporations), distributed across the globe, perhaps even with overlapping memberships: differently constituted federal unions in different parts of the world.[48]

The key, for Walzer, is to 'create a set of alternative centers and an increasingly dense web of social ties that cross state boundaries'.[49]

This argument is, in terms of policy prescription, very similar to the cosmopolitanism of those, such as Pogge, who begin from the left side of Walzer's continuum. Indeed, if you take Pogge's excellent paper 'Cosmopolitanism and Sovereignty' as the basic expression of a workable cosmopolitanism, the similarities are startling. In this article Pogge makes a case for what he calls a broadly consequentialist institutional (rather than interactional) cosmopolitanism.[50] This theory argues that the current constitution of international society 'has been overtaken by the historical facts of the last two hundred years or so'[51] and calls for a vertical dispersal of sovereignty.

What we need is both centralization and decentralization, a kind of second order decentralization away from the now dominant level of the state. Thus persons … political allegiances and loyalties should be widely dispersed over these units: neighborhood, town, county, province, state, region and world at large. People should be politically at home in all of them, without converging on any one of them as the lodestar of their political identity.[52]

Pogge defends a decentred institutional cosmopolitanism rather than the global state model because centralization poses 'significant risk of oppression'. The institutional model of cosmopolitanism that he proposes both ensures that 'social and cultural diversity are better protected' and, he argues, is a political goal that we can reach without any revolution or global catastrophe that would annihilate existing states.[53] He realizes that group identity is empirically significant, but his reason for advocating cosmopolitanism more generally is because it gives effective expression to the human right to political participation.[54]

The argument that world politics should be so ordered that it gives individuals the opportunity to participate fully is one that is shared by both Pogge and Walzer.[55] The image of international society that they create is differently nuanced but focuses in both cases on the dispersal of sovereignty across a variety of diverse political units. There are still significant differences in the work of both thinkers, but they are not as diametrically opposed as the cosmopolitan/communitarian debates suggested. This, I should emphasize, is not so much because the terms of that debate are flawed but because the huge potential in Walzer's work has never been recognized. In both cases the 'trigger' for a move towards globalism is increased 'interdependence' and 'globalization'. These terms are certainly problematic and hotly contested, but any adequate description of the current state of international society would have to focus on the increasingly porous nature of political, social and cultural boundaries. As the peoples of the world struggle to re-conceptualize their multiple identities, the terms of any moral and political debates have to change also. Walzer, far from being a statist who has converted to cosmopolitanism, is a key part of a theoretical tradition that has the tools to help here.

Unpacking this last comment forms the final argument of this chapter. It is perhaps startling enough to claim that Walzer shares political ground with the cosmopolitans. However, the purpose of demonstrating this is to suggest that the way in which Walzer reaches his conclusions, the way he is able to deal with the changing circumstances of international politics, offers more to current debates than does cosmopolitanism. Walzer's theory has been called many things. Of the most usual epithets, neither statism nor communitarianism is, I have argued, appropriate. Despite the fact that the main burden of my argument has been to show that Walzer shares ground with Pogge, it is not my intention to suggest that we re-classify him as a cosmopolitan. There are still differences between Pogge and Walzer. For example, Pogge defends an absolute commitment to global economic justice, whereas Walzer does not.[56] It is not that Walzer cannot defend such a position or that he has no desire to. Indeed, following my interpretation of Walzer, it is even possible to go as far as making theoretical sense of one of his more astonishing claims (that Australia, should its people not wish to admit refugees from South-East Asia to full citizenship, has an obligation to cede part of its territory to them[57]). However, what stands between Pogge and Walzer is the way in which they argue for universal principles. Pogge's commitment to a strong Kantian notion of autonomy means that increasing interdependence activates a pre-existing obligation to global justice. Moral universalism of a specific type is a precondition of Pogge's cosmopolitanism. This feature of his work has two weaknesses that Walzer does not share. First, a foundational commitment to the basic principles of Kantian ethics is extremely hard to justify (within western political theory let alone globally). Second, Pogge's universalism takes the form of 'covering-law universalism' (to use Walzer's term), and at the outset of an inquiry this seems to prejudge the moral and political solution to our problems. We are progressively moving towards a complete expression of human autonomy. The major problem here is that the best (morally speaking) mode of human life is given in advance. The political conditions that foster this may vary but it is this conception of what it means to be a human agent that sets our sights for us. One way of looking at this is to say that for Pogge the different ethnocultural and social groups that exist are empirically signifi-cant but not (as is the case for Walzer) morally significant. I am not convinced that this has the ability to speak to a multicultural world. Miller, when exploring the difference between covering-law and reiterative universalism, reaches the same conclusion.

> '[C]overing-law universalism' ... affirms the rightness of a particular way of life, and sees one nation as the bearer of that way of life ... 'reiterative universalism' ... recognises that, subject to certain minimal constraints imposed on all, there are a number of radically different and valuable forms of life which flourish in different places.[58]

Walzer, however, can argue to politically universal principles without this starting point. It is not the case that we can have either globalism or cultural and political diversity. With Walzer we can have both. His 'reiterative univer-salism' is one of the most promising theories within a more adaptive tradition of moral and political philosophy. As he puts it, 'why should we value human agency if we are unwilling to give it any room for maneuver and invention?'[59] In a world characterized by a multiplicity of ethnocultural traditions that are expressed in a wide variety of social contexts, we are much better placed to understand what has happened and what should happen in international poli-tics if we think about universalism in reiterative terms.

This is not the place to embark upon a comparative analysis of the work of these two important thinkers. In any case, I have probably made enough controversial arguments for one chapter. In summary, however, I give a few words about the wider tradition in which I think it useful to situate Walzer. Walzer's reiterative theory is a specific type of constitutive theory. This tradi-tion does appear to be particularly useful when we are considering a political arena in flux or transition. Indeed, in this volume both Martin and Boucher work within this tradition to shed light on aspects of our current global situa-tion as it has been dramatically effected by claims concerning multiculturalism, identity and rights. Building an account of human rights and group rights from an account of the ways in which we lead intersecting and divergent lives gives us the opportunity to think afresh about vital political concepts (such as rights or universality) without the cultural baggage that the cosmopolitan tradi-tion draws from the Enlightenment.

Notes

1 B. Orend, *Michael Walzer on War and Justice*, Cardiff: University of Wales Press, 2000, p. 153. Here Orend is outlining the views of Walzer's critics rather than levelling the charges himself.
2 M. Walzer, 'Response', in D. Miller and M. Walzer, eds, *Pluralism, Justice and Equality*, Oxford: Oxford University Press, 1995, p. 293.
3 M. Walzer, *Just and Unjust Wars: A Moral Argument with Historical Illustrations*, New York: Basic Books, 1977, part 2.
4 M. Walzer, 'Governing the Globe: What Is the Best We Can Do?', *Dissent*, vol. 47, pt 4, Fall 2000, pp. 44–52, p. 47. An earlier version of the paper is available as 'International Society: What is the Best that We Can Do?' Paper number 8 (*www.sss.ias.edu/home/papers.html*), June 2000 (accessed 8 June 2002). This paper (an earlier draft) was also published in the journal of the European Ethics Network, *Ethical Perspectives*, December 1999. All references will be to the latest (*Dissent*) version.
5 Orend, *Walzer on War and Justice*, p. 176.
6 Walzer, 'Governing the Globe', p. 50.
7 Ibid., p. 51.
8 M. Walzer, 'Nation and Universe', *The Tanner Lectures on Human Values XI*, 1989, ed. G. Peterson, Salt Lake City: University of Utah Press, 1990, p. 509.
9 For Walzer's principal defence of non-intervention, see Walzer, *Just and Unjust Wars*. For a representative sample of criticisms of this stance, see articles by C. Beitz, D. Luban and G. Doppelt in *Philosophy and Public Affairs*, 8–9, 1980.
10 See, for example, C. Beitz, 'Bounded Morality, Justice and the State in World Politics', *International Organization*, 33, 3, 1979, p. 410.
11 See, for example, T. Pogge, 'Cosmopolitanism and Sovereignty', *Ethics*, 103, October 1992, pp. 48–75.
12 J. Rawls, *The Law of Peoples*, Cambridge, Mass.: Harvard University Press, 1999.
13 The important thing to note here is that Walzer reaches this position by starting at the opposite end of the theoretical continuum and still regards the position occupied by the cosmopolitans to be very dangerous.
14 M. Walzer, *Thick and Thin: Moral Arguments at Home and Abroad*, Indianapolis and London: University of Notre Dame Press, 1994; M. Walzer, *The Company of Critics: Social Criticism and Social Commitment in the Twentieth Century*, London: Peter Halibran, 1989. For *Just and Unjust Wars*, see n. 3 above.
15 M. Walzer, *On Toleration*, New Haven, Conn.: Yale University Press, 1997, p. 87.
16 Orend, *Walzer on War and Justice*, pp. 178–9.
17 I. Kant, *Perpetual Peace and Other Essays in Politics, History and Morals*, trans. T. Humphrey, Indianapolis: Hackett, 1983.
18 See, for example, Pogge's vertical dispersment of sovereignty in 'Cosmopolitanism and Sovereignty'.
19 See my discussion of the cosmopolitanism of Beitz and Pogge in P. Sutch, *Ethics, Justice and International Relations: Constructing an International Community*, London and New York: Routledge, 2001, ch. 2.
20 Walzer, 'Governing the Globe', p. 49.
21 Walzer, *Thick and Thin*, p. 10.
22 Walzer, 'Nation and Universe', pp. 514–15.
23 M. Walzer, 'The Politics of Difference: Statehood and Toleration in a Multicultural World', *Ratio Juris*, 10, 2, 1997, p. 168. First published in R. McKim and J. McMahan, eds, *The Morality of Nationalism*, Oxford: Oxford University Press, 1997.
24 Walzer, *On Toleration*, pp. 19–20.
25 Walzer, 'Nation and Universe', p. 527.
26 Walzer, *Thick and Thin*, p. 17.
27 Ibid.

28 M. Walzer, 'The Moral Standing of States: A Response to Four Critics', *Philosophy and Public Affairs*, 9, 18, 1980, p. 222.
29 Walzer, *Thick and Thin*, pp. 18–19.
30 M. Walzer, 'Response to Veit Bader', *Political Theory*, 23, 2, 1995, p. 249. Here Walzer is responding to Bader's demand for large-scale economic redistribution and open borders.
31 Walzer, 'The Politics of Difference', p. 168.
32 Walzer, *On Toleration*, p. 21.
33 Walzer, 'Governing the Globe', p. 49.
34 See, for example, W. Kymlica and M. Opalski, eds, *Can Liberal Pluralism be Exported? Western Political Theory and Ethnic Relations in Eastern Europe*, Oxford: Oxford University Press, 2001, ch. 1.
35 See Walzer, *Just and Unjust Wars*, chs 3 and 4.
36 Walzer, *Thick and Thin*, p. 6.
37 Walzer, *The Company of Critics*, p. 229.
38 Walzer, *Thick and Thin*, p. 101.
39 Walzer, *On Toleration*, pp. 24–30.
40 Walzer, 'The Politics of Difference', p. 175.
41 M. Walzer, 'Nation-States and Immigrant Societies', in Kymlica and Opalski, eds, *Can Liberal Pluralism be Exported?*, pp. 150–3.
42 Walzer, 'The Politics of Difference', p. 175.
43 Walzer, 'Governing the Globe', p. 48.
44 Ibid., p. 47.
45 Walzer, 'The Politics of Difference', p. 175.
46 Ibid., p. 176.
47 Walzer, 'Governing the Globe', p. 51.
48 Ibid.
49 Ibid., p. 50.
50 Pogge, 'Cosmopolitanism and Sovereignty', p. 52.
51 Ibid., p. 59.
52 Ibid., p. 58.
53 Ibid., p. 63.
54 Ibid., p. 64.
55 See, for a clear expression of this line of argument, Walzer, 'Nation and Universe', p. 522.
56 See Pogge, 'Moral Universalism and Global Justice', *Politics, Philosophy and Economics*, 1, 1, 2002, pp. 29–58.
57 M. Walzer, *Spheres of Justice: A Defence of Pluralism and Equality*, Oxford: Blackwell, 1983, pp. 44–62.
58 D. Miller, *On Nationality*, Oxford: Clarendon Press, 1995, p. 10.
59 Walzer, 'Nation and Universe', p. 523.

Index

operative public values and terms of inclusion 102–3; Parekh Report 102–3

Orend, B. 214, 216

Paine, T. 197

Parekh, B. -6, 20–1, 34, 98–102, 117, 121, 143, 146–7, 152; and the multiculturalists 95–8

Parekh Report 94–110

particles of difference 49–52; agentic fragmentation 50; difference blind 50–1; emancipation 50; gender 52; groups 51; identity 50; individuality 49–50; meaning of politics 52; nationality 50–1; postmodernism 52; psychological multiplicity 50; racial difference 52

Phillips, A. 42, 45, 55

philosophical difference 47–9; alterity 49; dissonance 49; monadology 47; postmodernism 48; poststructuralism 48

Plato 182, 195

pluralism 2, 42–3, 100–1; global 216–23; principled 155

Pogge, T. 215, 217, 226–7

Poland: Solidarity 201

political participation 132–8

political philosophy 10–24, 98–102

political pluralism 44

political rights 175–94

political theory 1

politics of difference 4, 78–80, 112

politics of recognition 78–82, 112; minority groups 80–1, 166

polity 9

Pope John Paul II 201

postmodernism 48, 52

poststructuralism 48

Potts, G. 137

practical reason and identity 10–24; co-operation 10; coercion 15; communication 10; communitarianism 16; comprehensive doctrines 15; conflicts of value 13–14; constructivist position 18–19; dialogue 21; intelligibility 22; Italian unification 16; mobility 14; model of deliberation 11; multicultural politics 21; public space 15–16; social co-operation 15; Soviet implosion 17

Price, R. 197–8

Priestley, J. 197–8

Priestley, J. B. 201

psychological multiplicity 50

public decency 37

public goods 4

public order 37–8

public space 15–16

publics 46

Pueblo Indians 113

Pufendorf, S. von. 198

Quebec 126–8, 164, 168, 170

Quebec Hydro 129

Rabbossi, E. 196

racial difference 52

Rastafarians 80, 160

Rawls, J. 13–14, 95–6, 99–101, 103, 144–5, 149–52, 180, 187, 196, 204–5, 207–8, 215;

A Theory of Justice 61–2

Raz, J. 25, 53, 62, 100–1, 108, 117, 143, 181

recognition 5, 179–83; narrow 78–80; narrow and democracy 89–92; politics 80–2; wide 82–9, *see also* theorizing recognition

reflective equilibrium 149–50

refugees 213

Reid, Bill 131

relational difference 53

rights: international society in transition 213–30; global pluralism 221–3; statehood and toleration in multicultural world 223–8; Walzer on global pluralism 216–21; Walzer on international justice 214–16

rights 213; discourse 129–32; human 7–8; minority 3–4; natural 8, *see also* civil rights

rights and human rights 175–94; civil rights 175–6; civil rights and democratic institutions 176–9; government role in human rights 183–5; human rights: summary and application 186–8; human rights: two main camps 179–83; international human rights 190; UN Universal Declaration of Human Rights 188–90

Ritchie, D. 199

ritual animal slaughter 29–30

An environmentally friendly book printed and bound in England by www.printondemand-worldwide.com

#0282 - 170615 - C0 - 234/156/14 - PB - 9780415860000